Exemptions

Exemptions

NECESSARY, JUSTIFIED,
OR MISGUIDED?

Kent Greenawalt

Harvard University Press

Cambridge, Massachusetts
London, England
2016

Printed in the United States of America

First printing

Library of Congress Cataloging-in-Publication Data

Greenawalt, Kent, 1936– author.
Exemptions : necessary, justified, or misguided? / Kent Greenawalt.
pages cm
Includes bibliographical references and index.
ISBN 978-0-674-65987-2
1. Liberty of conscience—United States. I. Title.
KF4783.G739 2016
342.7308'5—dc23
2015031199

Dedicated to the memory of my late wife Sanja, who taught me so much about caring for others, to our sons, who have meant so much to both of us, and to our grandchildren

Contents

1 Introduction 1

2 Exemptions for Military Service 23

3 Tax Exemptions and Deductions 47

4 Forbidden Substances 64

5 Receiving and Participating in Medical Procedures 76

6 Contraceptives and the *Hobby Lobby* Case 112

7 Prisons and Land Use 130

8 Same-Sex Marriage and Sexual Relations 154

9 Religious Bodies and the Role of Common Law 185

10 Conclusion 211

Notes 227

Acknowledgments 257

Index 259

Exemptions

1

Introduction

IN OUR ERA, the granting of exemptions from otherwise applicable legal requirements has become an increasingly intense, controversial issue. Most obviously, its connection to the extension of marriage rights to same-sex couples and to the required insurance provision of contraceptives has raised the sharp question of how exemptions based on religious and moral convictions fit with basic values of equality and liberty. From the more straightforward perspective, one may see the liberty of individuals to do what they believe in as competing with the rights of others to be treated equally without discrimination. But, as we shall examine in a number of contexts, affording exemptions to some people can actually interfere with the liberty of those disfavored to accomplish objectives they seek, such as obtaining abortions, and various claims of conscience can include an assertion of equality. Most obviously, persons with strong minority convictions may urge that they should be respected as are those whose views coincide with the outlooks that are now dominant.

Generally speaking, as the laws of societies reach more broadly into what individuals and organizations may and may not do, controversies are bound to arise over what requirements are warranted, and, if they are, whether everyone should be required to comply or whether some individuals and organizations should be excused. This broad concern about government regulation of the lives of citizens raises a narrower question about what counts as an "exemption" and how much this matters. If the government should obviously not interfere with free choices, such as whom to marry or invite to one's home, we have no general rule of duty and no occasion for an exemption. Similarly, if an "accommodation" to widespread religious practice is that no one is required to work on Sunday, that is not an "exemption." By contrast, if a legal duty is formulated in broad terms and the question is whether some people should be relieved, that possible accommodation does concern an "exemption." The intermediate situation is one in which the duty itself is formulated to cover only some people. Thus, if various kinds of counselors must reveal certain kinds of damaging information but no such requirement is formulated for ministers, they are not receiving an actual "exemption," but they are effectively being treated differently from others. My focus is not on the precise dimension of "exemptions," but when special treatment is or is not warranted. In considering that broad question, people need to avoid falling into the rhetorical mistake that limited requirements are often warranted but exemptions are not.

Although at certain points the book does treat issues of constitutional and statutory interpretation, primary attention is focused upon what considerations legislators and interested outsiders should give to proposed exemptions. I mention the role of political factors and how prevailing cultural norms in different localities can matter for the exact range of certain exemptions. But for the most part I concentrate on the general culture of the country, and ask what elements should carry weight when we consider when exemptions should be granted.

The purpose of this book is to highlight just what is at stake, to explore competing considerations, and to show how they apply in a number of particular contexts. Although expressing views about how a range of circumstances may best be treated, that is not the book's major objective. Rather, it strives to counter the idea that resolving all these issues is simple.

Regrettably, oversimplification is the common character of political rhetoric bearing on controversial subjects. Why those advocating particular outcomes put forward their arguments as powerful and obviously determinative is certainly understandable, but we also have a tendency not only to advance our contentions in that way but also to convince ourselves that matters are really highly one-sided. This tendency may well be enhanced by the attraction for media and broader electronic communication of forceful arguments for one side or the other over disputed subjects.

The aim here is to explore the complexity of many concerns about exemptions and implicitly encourage those on opposite sides of particular controversies to recognize, and perhaps even acknowledge, that competing considerations do carry some weight. Not infrequently those who favor general compliance and those who support exemptions both have sound arguments based on autonomy, equality, and concern for others.

To be clear, I am not asserting that people just need to pay attention to competing positions. We have in our present society a deep division of opinion about what is true and morally correct. This is most evident in respect to abortions, certain contraceptives, and same-sex marriage. Some religious people believe life begins at conception and that God has ordained that marriage be between men and women. Others believe equally sincerely that these views are silly, and some proponents of gay marriage favor a rejection of the notion of religious exemptions more generally. We now have a genuine and fundamental dispute over what should be seen as the basic values and their relative priority in our liberal society. What I want strongly to urge is that even when one sees a belief as badly misguided, that itself does not determine what respect should be given to those who maintain that conviction. Someone who is persuaded that all religious convictions are completely irrational should still see reasons for society not simply to tramp down on those convictions. As Chapter 8 analyzes, a person convinced that any opposition to same-sex marriage is foolish can still have a reason for not requiring opponents to participate in it. Similarly, one who does not believe in same-sex marriage should understand why people with that inclination differ and wish to be respected by others in our culture.

People thinking about possible exemptions also need to recognize that the law's capacity to reflect what are fundamentally the most just resolutions is not unlimited. Basic enforcement of certain legal duties can itself be very difficult; and when the best outcomes call for assessments of sincerity or a balancing of competing considerations, judges and other officials may find that too hard to do. This can strongly affect just how legal standards should be cast—not only what general legal duties should be imposed but also whether any exemptions should be granted and how they should be formulated. "Law" is a practical feature of human life, and the appropriate formulation of legal standards often must vary from the lines one might ideally draw between what should be allowed and forbidden. If those on both sides of many exemption controversies consider these obstacles to what might be seen as "perfect law," that could assist the making of desirable legislative choices, and perhaps it can also reduce to a degree the intensity of conflict between those with contrasting views.

In our society, caring about our fellow citizens and encouraging their concern for each other should lead both to treating people with dignity and respecting what individuals' consciences tell them to do. When these competing considerations are genuinely in play, our discussion of issues would benefit from becoming less antagonistic, more tolerant, and perhaps even wiser. Since my aim is not to "put down" those who, engaged in strong advocacy of one side or another, make oversimplified arguments that are hostile to their opponents, I do not offer many specific illustrations but instead rely on readers' perception of the commonness of such advocacy and why countering it may be helpful. I should also note that, in contrast to much academic writing, including my own, this book does not seek to explore in depth the range of views developed by others. Instead, it concentrates on what I see as genuine competing claims and how they may be resolved, with only some references to defended alternatives.

We are now living in an era in which by far the most intense and publicized issues about exemptions concern religious convictions and same-sex marriage. Beyond the effort to develop understandings of why and when exemptions of various kinds may be warranted, part of the book's purpose is to put the present controversy, which may well be the most striking of this sort we have ever had, into a broader context, one that will help readers to step back and make a careful assessment that recognizes some important, if less than obvious, distinctions. The ordering of the book's chapters, which may initially seem a bit odd, is partly a consequence of this aspiration. I initially treat the subjects of draft and tax exemptions, which have long existed but have also been controversial in their scope. I also treat issues about abortion, other medical treatment, and contraceptives before reaching the liveliest controversy of our time: how far, once same-sex marriage is established, individuals and groups who do not believe in it should be required to treat those couples like all other married partners. Readers who do not wish to engage with what are now the less contentious topics of the early chapters can go directly to those that deal with the subjects about which they care most. But my hope is that some reflection on what is now less disputed can assist careful reflection on what is presently the subject of intense disagreement.

Important Categories of Exemptions and Their Effects

For the objective of careful reflection of what may best be justified, I will note here certain crucial variations concerning the character of exemptions from ordinary legal requirements and the effects they may have on others. Those effects can be absolutely central to whether any exemption is warranted and, if it is, how far it should extend.

Among three rough categories, the first is exemptions that do not directly harm others. Permitting the Native American Church to use peyote in its religious services, giving tax exemptions for charitable organizations, granting prisoners the right to wear beards longer than general regulations allow, and excusing pacifists from military service all share this feature. Of course, reasons to oppose such exemptions may still rest on concerns about public welfare, such as financial needs of government, prison discipline, an effective draft, and worries about fraud; but other citizens do not as individuals suffer harms.

A second category involves circumstances in which the primary competing concern is others who may be practically harmed. If doctors and nurses are given a right to refuse to participate in abortions, women seeking them may suffer. A similar worry can exist if companies are freed from providing insurance for contraceptives. If religious bodies violate zoning laws, their neighbors may be less well off. Sometimes it may be simple to identify the individuals who suffer practical harms, but this category also includes circumstances in which the fact of harm is highly likely, though identifying specific sufferers is difficult.

The third category, which includes discrimination against gay couples and individuals, is the most troubling. The people seeking an exemption want a right to treat these people less favorably than they must treat others. This carries a symbolic message of inequality. A rare situation that involves an outright form of rejection of those harmed involves religious groups that decide to shun fallen-astray members by behavior that would constitute a tort of inflicting emotional distress if imposed in other circumstances.

When we turn to the present controversy regarding religious freedom versus equal treatment for gay people, we need to recognize that what an exemption allowing unequal treatment of others itself involves can vary in obvious ways not commonly acknowledged.

People may want to treat others negatively based on basic personal characteristics, such as race, gender, age, national or religious heritage, and disability. Sexual orientation standing by itself fits into this category. Discrimination based simply on personal characteristics is the most directly at odds with the basic values of equality and personal respect that are at the core of our society.

A somewhat different basis for unequal treatment involves a person's status, based on his or her present or past actions and decisions. Suppose one holds the religious conviction that adultery is fundamentally wrong and that married couples should never divorce. He *might* wish not to afford equal treatment to anyone who has committed adultery or chosen to get divorced. A person might take a similar view toward those who choose to be members of a particular religion or who are known to have had abortions. A general right to treat negatively married or unmarried gay couples arguably fits in this category. However, given the strong tendency of most people to seek sexual involvements, and the intrinsic attraction some experience toward others of the same gender, treating same-sex relations in a negative way comes very close to acting on people's basic personal characteristics, not their independent actions.

Not wishing to participate in an act one believes is deeply wrong is the third basis for an exemption claim to afford unequal treatment to others, and it is fundamentally different. Modest reflection on one's own personal and professional life can illustrate this. We all have extensive contact with others whose broader life is unknown to us, and in many professions, including teaching in schools and universities, no one refuses to interact in their jobs with those whose broader lives may not fit their convictions. But suppose, to take the university example, a student asks for assistance to do what the professor regards as seriously immoral. At least in most circumstances, she will say "no." This is what is involved for some in respect to performing abortions and same-sex marriages. Whatever we conclude about specific claims, we need to recognize that direct participation has more to do with normal moral and religious convictions than unrelated treatment of those who happen to have acted in a way not consistent with one's own views.

The significance of not insisting on participation in what a person believes is immoral can also be illustrated by how people typically react if they ask a friend or associate for help in a task, and she responds, "I'm sorry, but doing that would really be against my deep convictions." Unless they thought that position itself was indefensibly immoral and irrational, most would say something like, "Okay, I don't agree with your perspective, but I won't insist. I'll look for someone else to help me."

When one thinks about exemptions in respect to legal requirements that one believes reflect basic moral norms, such as equal treatment of people who belong to different races or genders or have different sexual orientations, it is important to focus on some other important distinctions. If one believes a particular outlook is morally incorrect, is a competing view at least defensible in principle? Most people who think military force is sometimes needed may see pacifism in just this way. Even if one sees perceptions as badly misguided, are they at least grounded in acceptable values, not outright hatred? Certainly pacifism fits here. Whatever one believes about the correctness or supportability of a position, what are common perceptions? Finally, how flexible have attitudes about a subject been over the course of history? If one believes broad movement toward the "correct" view is possible, or even highly likely, is what makes most sense in the near future some accommodation to the opposing view or insistence on conformance by everyone? In terms of what works best at present, what are the comparative values of insisting on unqualified conformance and allowing exceptions? All these questions bear on whether, when the law has reached, or should reach, a status of equality—as has happened for same-sex marriage—what, if any, concessions should be made to private individuals and enterprises with contrary convictions?

The basic distinction between actual participation and other connections is central to reflections on both abortion and same-sex marriage exemptions. As Chapters 5 and 8 explore, it raises the far from simple question of what degree of involvement should suffice for an exemption. As noted, the book's ordering of chapters is designed to put our present intense controversy over same-sex marriage in a broader context; but readers who are dominantly concerned with that, or the subjects of other chapters, may choose to go directly to those. Each of these chapters can be understood on its own. What follows in this introductory chapter is an outline of the various sources of exemptions, a number of the central issues about exemptions, how I mean to distinguish "necessary," "justified," and "misguided," and also the under-recognized value in certain contexts of "alternatives."

Sources of Exemptions

The primary legal sources of exemptions within the United States are statutory provisions. This has long been the case not only for exemptions from taxes designed to promote public welfare and economic growth but also for military drafts that have exempted pacifists (or at least some pacifists) from participation in the armed forces. Although during the Warren Court era, the Supreme Court developed a fairly strict Free Exercise Clause approach that certain exemptions were constitutionally required, the 1990 Supreme Court shut the door on that approach in *Employment Division v. Smith*,[1] holding that if a law is cast generally, no one has a constitutional right based on religious belief to be treated differently. With a notable exception, to which I shall return, that left the granting of federal law exemptions up to Congress. Also, with a few significant qualifications discussed below, it left determinations about exemptions from state law requirements up to state and local legislators and judges.

Since some state courts have interpreted the free exercise protections in their own constitutions to impose greater restrictions than Justice

Scalia's majority opinion in *Employment Division v. Smith* discerned in the federal document, constitutional doctrine within those states continues to play a more active role for possible exemptions.

Exemption statutes come in two basic varieties. They can be highly specific, indicating exactly the particular laws for which they are created and how far they extend. Although differing from each other in important respects, three notable examples of this in federal law have been exemptions from a military draft, from taxes, and from requirements to participate in or refrain from performing abortions.

The other kind of law is cast in a broad and general form. This is exemplified by the federal Religious Freedom Restoration Act (RFRA), whose coverage is now controversial after the decision in the *Hobby Lobby* case, which ruled that it applies to claims of closely held for-profit corporations.[2] The statute provides that the "government shall not substantially burden a person's exercise of religion even if the burden results from a rule of general applicability . . . unless the government shows that imposing the burden furthers a compelling interest" and is the "least restrictive means" to do so.[3] Originally seen as reintroducing the pre-*Smith* free exercise approach and adopted to apply to state as well as federal laws, RFRA's application is now limited to the national domain, since the Supreme Court ruled that Congress could not dictate to the states here because it lacked the authority to override the constitutional conclusions the Court reached in *Employment Division v. Smith*.[4] Given the role of Congress in enacting and repealing federal laws, it *can* create exemptions from their application.[5]

Under the Religious Freedom Restoration Act, courts must make determinations about whether a burden is substantial and whether the government either lacks a compelling interest or has failed to use the least restrictive means. Of course, in many situations executive branch officials initially must make such assessments before judges resolve controversies. The statute's language obviously reaches novel situations, and it neither provides a clear answer to just when an exemption must be granted nor says exactly how far one must extend. This level of uncertainty in application provides an important basis for more specific provisions when that is feasible, although, if one believes that the scope of an exemption should change significantly over time, that could constitute a reason for leaving things up to a vague statutory standard applied by administrators and judges in light of changing values.

In a subsequent law, the Religious Land Use and Institutionalized Persons Act (RLUIPA),[6] Congress relied on its authority to regulate interstate commerce, to control the terms of federal spending, and to counter not infrequent constitutional violations, as bases to reach state laws and practices in two particular domains. The standards for when these statutory exemptions apply are closely similar to those set by RFRA.

If statutes can provide exemptions, so also can administrative regulations that set out the scope of their own applications. Beyond this, particular officials may use their discretion not to require persons they supervise to perform particular tasks within their general duties. A personal illustration occurred during a year in which I was the deputy solicitor general reviewing government briefs in criminal cases going before the Supreme Court. I told the solicitor general that, based partly on prior academic work, I did not feel comfortable engaging myself in defending extensive secret government surveillance of organizations opposed to the Vietnam War. Erwin Griswold accommodated my sentiment by assigning the case to another deputy. Others have told me that a not uncommon practice in states with capital punishment is not to insist that government lawyers with strong objections to that practice participate in briefs and oral arguments that urge its taking place. For those, like myself, relieved of a duty based on moral convictions, one might say they are "exempted" from performing that duty; but there has been no legally set exemption. For this reason, I am here distinguishing discretionary choices as a kind of alternative to exemptions. An interesting intermediate situation is one in which the head of a government office provides a notice of intentions that falls short of a legal restraint: "I do not intend to require anyone to work on a capital punishment case." Here there is a set standard on which a job applicant might rely, even if it falls short of a legal guarantee. What is important to keep in mind is that for some kinds of specific duties, a failure to grant a definite legal exemption does not necessarily mean that a person with a strong objection or reservation about performance will inevitably have to disregard that or take the consequences of a failure to do his duty. His boss may decide to excuse him.

A constitution can provide a basis for certain required exceptions from general duties, which may be seen as effective exemptions. As already indicated, the federal Constitution's Free Exercise Clause since 1990 has been interpreted fairly narrowly in this respect. However, in *Hosanna-Tabor Evangelical Lutheran Church and School v. Equal Employment Opportunity Commission,*[7] every justice on the Supreme Court resolved a few years ago that the religion clauses do guarantee a ministerial exception, which allows churches and some other religious bodies to choose and dismiss "ministers," who include some teachers in religious schools, without complying with laws that forbid discrimination and without even showing that their claimed religious reasons are genuine. One might characterize this as a basic right, not an exemption, but it does involve required non-coverage of a general duty not to discriminate. We will subsequently look at the coverage of that decision, but it clearly represents an important qualification to *Employment Division v. Smith.*

Two other constitutional limits concerning religion involve coverage and purposes. If an exemption is granted for certain kinds of claims, it cannot be denied for others. Most obviously, an exemption cannot be afforded to members of one religious denomination and denied to members of another who have essentially similar views and practices. To so favor one religion could be seen as violating both religion clauses, definitely "establishing" the favored group and arguably inhibiting the "free exercise" of the other. In an opinion by Judge (now Justice) Alito, the Third Circuit Court of Appeals held further that if an exemption is granted for certain nonreligious reasons, it cannot be denied for religious ones.[8] In the particular case, given that police officers were allowed to wear beards if shaving would hurt them medically, Newark had to accord a similar exemption from the general rule that police had to be clean-shaven for those with the religious belief that they must wear beards.

A similar constitutional concern about categorization involves freedom of expression. If individuals and groups are engaged in communicating ideas to others, government cannot discriminate in choosing who to relieve from general obligations. One important Supreme Court case used this basis to strike down tax relief limited to religious publications.[9] In certain other circumstances, those advocating political positions cannot be subjected to restrictions that apply to those pursuing financial or other personal objectives.

A different ground for finding unconstitutional categorization, likely to lead to invalidation of the law itself rather than an extended exemption, applies even to laws whose actual specification of what is forbidden is cast in general terms. If the law's coverage is evidently underinclusive and the process of its adoption strongly indicates that it was directed to counter a specific religious practice, its restriction of that practice is unacceptable. The Supreme Court case holding invalid this kind of law involved a city's ordinance that failed to protect animals from being killed and harmed for all sorts of reasons but did forbid animal sacrifice, which was practiced by a relatively small, unpopular religious group.[10] When the legislators' aim to discourage a religious practice while not touching nonreligious acts that cause similar harm is evident from the law's boundaries, it violates the Free Exercise Clause.

A basis for claims of special treatment that differs from statutes and constitutional provisions is the common law, as it can develop. Notably in respect to civil liability for tortious acts, some standards involve a kind of balancing of harm done against the reasons for behavior. As Chapter 9 explores in some detail, even if not required directly by a constitution or statute, judges may give weight to the values of religious exercise and free expression in formulating applicable common law standards and resolving particular cases, such as when an infliction of emotional distress may not actually constitute a tort.

Issues About Exemptions

Many questions about exemptions are not straightforward "either-or" situations, answerable by "yes" or "no." The resolution of whether *any* exemption should exist for otherwise required duties can itself be complex, partly dependent on how various concerns are addressed. These can also bear crucially on the scope of an exemption if one is to be granted. When one thinks about the range of an exemption, who should actually qualify? Should an exemption be given to individuals or organizations or both, and, if so, to exactly whom? In *Hobby Lobby*, whether RFRA should be understood to reach closely held for-profit corporations was a central question. As Chapter 6 explains, the Court's majority opinion treats the case as a fairly simple application of statutory terms, but I urge that the more appropriate approach to a vague statute takes into account context and wisdom.

Another issue is whether the exact content of a person's objection to what he would otherwise be legally required to do should matter. Should the source need to be religious? And is the substance of the objection crucial? In respect to the latter, a leading example is whether an exemption from a military draft should reach only pacifists or also those who believe that involvement in a particular war would violate their conscience. The competing answers to this particular question, hardly simple, are explored in the following chapter.

A third problem about the range of exemptions is who should be required to comply with them. For the military draft, tax exemptions, and many other examples, what is involved is a privilege not to perform a duty owed to the government. It is, thus, up to the government to observe that right. But certain statutory exemptions reach beyond this. They require that private enterprises exempt some individuals from duties placed on other workers or forbid those enterprises from subjecting any of their workers to certain duties. A notable example of a law doing both these things is the federal statute that requires private hospitals and other organizations to allow objecting employees not to participate in abortions and also bars such entities who themselves object to abortions from penalizing any members of their staffs who choose to engage in them off their premises.[11]

In addition to what kinds of individuals and groups shall qualify, the appropriate range of some exemptions concerns how far they should extend to claimants whose connection to involvement in a practice is somewhat or highly indirect. To take the example of abortions, an exemption obviously must reach doctors and nurses who would otherwise be participating in actual performance; should it also reach workers who prepare rooms for operations, nurses who would take care of women before and after they receive their abortions, and registrars who supervise the filling out of forms of patients entering the hospital? If pharmacies need not supply particular drugs to which they strongly object, should a similar privilege be accorded individual pharmacists who work in stores providing those drugs, to personnel who hand the drugs to customers, and to cashiers who receive the payments for the drugs? A somewhat similar issue about peripheral involvement arose in *Hobby Lobby* over whether the provision of insurance was or was not too remote from the actual purchase and use of contraceptives to which the company owners objected. One illustration of the indirectness issue is whether people and organizations should ever receive exemptions from paying taxes, all or part of which may finance practices they find objectionable.

When one evaluates the reasons for and against exemptions, needless to say it matters hugely what reasons can outweigh those favoring a grant. The most obvious reasons in this domain concern impairment of practical objectives. When governments and private enterprises impose duties, they believe performance will serve desired consequences. If individuals or organizations who would otherwise have to perform the duties receive exemptions, perhaps that will undermine what needs to be accomplished, and it may do so in a way that strikes many as an injustice for those who lose out. To take three obvious examples, if too many people decline to help with abortions, that could impair a woman's right to receive one; if exemptions from taxes are broad, that will reduce needed revenues; if exemptions from military service are extensive, and successfully claimed, that *could* reduce a country's ability to succeed in wartime. Exactly when such concerns are realistic is a question about likely effects; often the genuine answers are clear even when rhetoric may suggest the contrary.

A particular kind of practical impairment involves just distribution rather than overall consequences. If some men are drafted because others get exemptions, is this unfair? If some organizations pay taxes that others avoid, is this unjust? Just when unfairness is genuinely involved is not itself an empirical question and is often less than straightforward. This can produce in people honestly held, different, and defensible opinions. When governments engage in very limited restraints on what individuals and organizations may do, they may obviously engage in behavior that gives some people advantages over others. And even in our era of much more extensive regulation, those in the private sector retain many rights that may be exercised in a way that works to the disadvantage of others. But some may believe that any exemption with that direct consequence is harder to defend than one that simply imposes a cost on the general society. And, at least in certain instances, the unequal treatment that results should plausibly be seen as a violation of the constitutional right to equal protection of the law.

For certain exemptions, the grant itself may produce concerns about justice and fairness that reach beyond substantial practical impairments. Suppose a gay couple arrives at the bureau for a civil marriage; they are told by the officer who would otherwise perform the ceremony that he objects to such marriages and will go get someone else. Within a minute another official arrives, ready to perform the ceremony. The amount of delay for the couple is insignificant, but they may feel rejected and perhaps even humiliated. No one likes to feel such sentiments, especially if he or she is about to engage in the joyous ceremony of marriage.

Beyond the offense to their dignity that individuals may experience on the occasions when an exemption has some direct effect on how they are treated lies the general message that its granting may send. Although it may seem convenient to allow some exemptions for beliefs that are not really defensible, when claims are made that people warrant an exemption, part of the basis often is that their outlooks are understandable and not totally objectionable. The granting of an exemption may seem to reduce the power of the government's message that certain behavior is out of line with the basic values of the society. This is perceived by some as the government's failing to acknowledge the equal dignity of those whom others are allowed to treat unequally.

Both senses of dignity harm are offered as reasons no exemption, beyond the privilege of religious bodies to decide whom they will marry, has been granted for those who object to what is typically called "interracial marriage." (I put the term in quotes because in southern states that used to ban such marriages, a person who was three-fourths white and one-fourth black counted as "negro" and could marry someone who was all black but not someone who was all white. As I develop in Chapter 8, this was not truly a bar on interracial marriage, viewed by any standard other than a prejudicial cultural categorization of races.) Those who object to exemptions regarding same-sex marriages frequently offer a similar argument about dignity and equality and draw on the analogy to interracial marriage to support their position.

Two crucial questions about exemptions that are interrelated involve tests of sincerity and administrability. As later chapters develop, this does not present a genuine worry *if* the claim for an exemption is one we can hardly imagine a person raising for purely self-interested reasons. If a drugstore sells contraceptives that sometimes operate after fertilization, would an employee refuse to participate on some ground unrelated to conscience? That is *conceivable;* perhaps the worker is dating a devout Roman Catholic and wants to persuade her that he is "on board." But here the likelihood is highly remote that someone will offer a false claim of what their conscience tells them to do. This is not true of military service, and of many other granted and possible exemptions. When the concern about genuine conviction becomes substantial, whether and how to assess sincerity becomes a critical concern. Draft boards and reviewing administrative agencies did undertake to assess whether asserted pacifist convictions were sincere, but one may worry about whether government officials are capable of doing this fairly and whether it is even appropriate for them to try. This is a central problem about *some* exemptions; subsequent chapters will focus on which ones.

Tied to the problem of sincerity is administrability. Apart from what one might conclude basic principles would suggest for a possible exemption, is it one that officials will be able to administer, or will it too often raise unanswerable questions and generate claims that are simply fraudulent or are more weakly based than the basic criteria call for?

This brings us to two fundamental and controversial issues about how the qualifications for exemptions should be set. The right answer definitely depends on exactly what exemptions are involved. A pervasive question is whether, and when, it is appropriate to limit claims to ones of religious conviction and practice. Some believe that this categorization is always acceptable, others that it is never so, still others, including myself, that it is sometimes appropriate and sometimes not. The following chapters explore this question in various contexts.

A more subtle question, especially relevant when nonreligious claims are included, is exactly what kind and degree of conviction should be needed. When the surveillance case came to the solicitor general's office, I did not want to be involved, and I objected strongly to the government's actual position; but as a lawyer with particular duties that did not necessarily accord with what I saw as the best outcome of a case, I did not genuinely feel I would be doing something deeply immoral if I reviewed and offered edits for the government's brief. That is, I had a kind of objection to participation but not one that amounted to a genuine claim of conscience. Once we realize that there is such a threshold, and that crossing it may properly be needed as the ground for many claims for exemptions, we can recognize that others can sometimes find it hard to determine not only if a claimant is being outright honest or dishonest but, even if not dishonest, whether his convictions rise to the level on which an exemption should depend. This obstacle greatly intensifies the problems of administrability and can raise doubts whether any exemptions should actually depend on such assessments. The alternatives are to grant the exemption for anyone who requests it, to require a statement about underlying convictions and to accept it on its face, to require an ascertainable religious connection, or simply to refuse to grant any exemption. Chapters to follow explore these alternatives in particular settings.

Necessary, Justified, or Misguided?

Although the evaluative terms of the book's title and this section are hardly precise, they do help to capture estimations about the appropriateness of particular exemptions, the standards for qualification, and the extent of their coverage. Because "necessary" and "misguided" are at opposite ends of the spectrum, I address those first before the key category, "justified."

The claim that an exemption is "necessary" can be taken in what are three fundamentally different ways, ones that the book tries to consistently distinguish. The first is that the exemption from an otherwise general duty is constitutionally required. Even in this respect, it is important not to confuse various assertions. One is that the decisions of the Supreme Court establish a constitutional right to an exemption. This can now be said about the ministerial exception supported by a unanimous court. Before the 1990 case *Employment Division v. Smith,* free exercise doctrine covered a broader variety of claimed exemptions, notably barring the denial of unemployment compensation for someone who refused to perform a task that offended her religious convictions. In accord with a standard practice in constitutional interpretation, the *Smith* Court tried to reconcile its ruling with prior cases; and, given its attempt to square its decision with preceding unemployment compensation cases, there *may* still be a limited constitutional requirement for the particular circumstances of those cases.

A different kind of assertion can be that the Supreme Court, contrary to what it has actually indicated in recent cases, or how it would now most probably resolve a novel issue, *should* find that an exemption is constitutionally required, if that is needed for the exemption to exist. Of course, if a statute already provides the exemption, judges do not have to determine whether it is constitutionally required, only that it is constitutionally permissible. Yet another sense of "constitutional requirement" could be that legislators and other officials should view an exemption as mandated by the Constitution, even if no such demand should actually be enforced by judges, who might be following a doctrine such as "political question" that leaves resolution to other branches of government.

A claim of "necessity" need not rest on constitutional doctrine but may instead rest on the assertion that an exemption is required to avoid grave practical difficulties or to accord with the fundamental principles of one's culture or those of political morality, as properly understood. Suppose strong empirical evidence showed that in the absence of an exemption, many, many pacifists would submit to a draft, accept assignments as combat troops, but refuse in actual conflicts to fire weapons at enemies. An exemption might then be necessary to protect the lives of other soldiers and the effectiveness of military endeavors. If one asks about tax exemptions for hospitals, universities, and churches, and deductions for those who give them contributions, one might conclude that they are necessary to promote public welfare and religious freedom.

Yet a third sense of "necessity" is that an exemption is required if the aim is to adopt a law that generally requires or forbids behavior that many oppose. As Robin Wilson has shown in great detail, at least at the early stages, the granting of exemptions proved absolutely necessary within many states to accomplish the extending of marriage rights to same-sex couples.[12] Whether an exemption is "necessary" in this pragmatic political sense can, of course, shift significantly over a period of time. Once a right is established, as with respect to abortion or more recently same-sex marriage, the more subtle and longer-term pragmatic issue is what approach will be most likely to reduce conflict and promote general approval over time. Many people may be much more accepting of a legal guarantee of equality if that does not require them and others to do what they actually believe is morally wrong. As noted earlier, on an issue such as same-sex marriage exemptions, in different parts of the United States, as well as in different countries, cultural considerations and pragmatic realities can vary, but this book does not attempt to explore those differences in depth.

If a person claims that an exemption is necessary in any of these senses, that by itself does not determine either the criteria for qualification or the extent of coverage. And apart from whether "necessity" requires *any* exemption from a legal duty, if some people are to receive one, it may *then* be necessary to provide it for others, since certain ways in which qualifications are restricted may themselves be unconstitutional, basically unjust, or impractical.

By "misguided," I mean that on balance a proposed exemption is unwise or unjust. That claim, like the one of necessity, can focus on the qualifications for an exemption or its scope, as well as its general desirability. Arguments that existing and proposed exemptions are misguided, which have increased greatly in recent years, can rest on claims about basic values—including unfair impositions on others—on certain constitutional standards, or on concerns about fraud raised by the reality that the grounds offered for the exemptions would not be effectively administrable and would thus invite dishonest claims. A different contention would be that in contrast to being politically necessary, proposed exemptions would invite unacceptable political divisiveness or could not generate enough political support now to be worth seriously advocating.

The term "justified" in this context is employed here to cover situations in which an exemption may not be "necessary" in the various senses mentioned but is, nonetheless on balance warranted. For many purposes, whether an exemption is believed to be necessary or only justified will not be of major importance. Instead, the fundamental disagreements will come down to whether it is justified or misguided. As with the other terms, "justified" concerns not only an exemption's existence but also its range of coverage and those who qualify. To take RFRA and the issues in *Hobby Lobby*, one might believe that leaders of some organizations should receive an exemption from having to provide or pay specifically for a use of contraceptives that they believe sometimes amounts to abortion but that the exemption should not reach "for-profit" companies or the providing of insurance, which falls short of actual payment. Although RFRA does not directly settle these questions by its terms, and the justices were in theory interpreting the statute's application, not deciding exactly what coverage would be wise, legislatures may best directly resolve such issues when considering many specific forms of exemption.

An Important Alternative

Roughly speaking, we may distinguish exemptions as falling into the following categories. (1) Benefits that others would like to have, that do not do direct harm to anyone, that serve broad social purposes, and for which it does not make sense to impose any alternative burden on those who benefit. Typical tax exemptions fall into this category. (2) Privileges that others would have no significant self-interested reason to wish be granted and that do not disadvantage other people. The desire of Orthodox Jewish groups to kill animals in ways that may be generally forbidden fits basically in this category. (3) Benefits that people not influenced by conscience would not wish to have but whose granting may impose hardships on others. Being free not to participate in the performing of abortions could amount to this, if women find it harder to obtain abortions. (4) Benefits that others would like to have that do not themselves impose direct harms on others. Excusing pacifists from military service falls into this category (so long as one assumes that many pacifists would go to jail rather than serve and that even if someone else happens to be drafted because a pacifist is not, that does not count as a direct hardship). (5) Benefits that some others without any genuine objection in conscience might like to have, whose exercise does impose hardships on others. Privileges to discriminate or not to provide benefits to employees fit here.

For these last two categories, there can be serious questions about who should qualify; for example, should selective objectors to military service be included, and what amounts to a genuine claim of conscience? Here the problems of categorization, judging sincerity, and administrability are especially significant. One might conclude that an exemption granted only for those who satisfy a certain qualification is both justified *and* misguided. How can it be both?

The answer is that an alternative is to provide everyone with the option of choosing what may be granted to the objectors. This, of course, can most simply be done by never imposing or eliminating any duty whatsoever, leaving all individuals the choice whether to do something. Thus, one response to religious claims to use a forbidden drug or to grow a beard in prison is to simply repeal any general prohibition. This form of alternative is troublesome if actions do cause harms to others or if the government's interest in a general duty is otherwise strong.

A different alternative is to require anyone who chooses to abstain from a general duty to, instead, undertake something most people would not prefer over the duty being avoided. For example, the law could permit any potential draftee to agree to an alternative civilian service that would last three years, as compared with two for military duty. If, unlike the draft, requiring performance of the general duty is done to avoid harms to others, this alternative makes good sense only if the government has another way to prevent or minimize the harm.

Critics of this approach for military service have sometimes responded that such treatment is unfair to those whose conscience does not allow them to satisfy the general duty. The answer is that those individuals have chosen not to perform a duty that others *must* and that this modest extra burden they are required to undertake is a way to assure that *all* those who really are against performing the general duty are accorded that right. This slight extra burden alternative is not nearly as bad as being sent to jail and is one that has existed in some other countries. It warrants much more general attention and wider use in the United States for certain classes of exemptions.

Conclusion

The primary aim of this introductory chapter has been to clarify what sorts of questions are at stake over exemptions and how one should understand evaluative claims. The chapter also suggests how what is often contested is not only whether some exemption in principle may be warranted but what kind of claimants should qualify and how far the exemption should extend. All this has shown that often the particular controversies involved are far from simple, that competing arguments for and against can both have substance, and that this can be so even for those who believe that the views of those on the other side are badly misguided.[13] In the chapters that follow dealing with various exemptions granted in the United States, with occasional reference to other liberal democracies, I aim to demonstrate these realities in more detail in different contexts. Were advocates of various positions to acknowledge that things are not always grossly one-sided and that their opponents are not necessarily evil, our country's discussion of existing and proposed exemptions could be more civil and less divisive.

2

Exemptions for Military Service

Introduction

IN U.S. HISTORY, and that of other Western democracies, the quintessential exception for individuals from general duties imposed on others has involved pacifists not being required to perform as military personnel, which can be understood as the most demanding of the obligations governments place on citizens. In this day and age, given voluntary military service and technologically advanced weapons that render it extremely unlikely that this country will require the vast number of troops on the ground for which a draft is necessary, these exemptions may seem far removed from the highly controversial issues of our time. In fact, a limited version of the exemption does still exist, and its boundaries remain significant, since someone already in the armed forces can be relieved of his obligation to perform the remainder of his term if he has become a pacifist. In other, smaller, countries that regard themselves as potentially subject to invasion or another military threat, the question of how a draft should be formulated remains a significant question.

Even more important for our purposes here, the draft example provides a sense both of how possible exemptions have been viewed over time and of certain issues that arise across a wide range of other actual and possible modern exceptions from legal duties. The range of an exemption has been difficult and controversial and has changed over time. Once limited only to members of pacifist religions, it was explicitly extended to religious claims more broadly and then implicitly to what were really nonreligious convictions. Selective objectors, however, have been consistently denied similar treatment.

Here are a few of the central issues that bear heavily on other exemptions. How should the idea of individual autonomy be squared with the sense that citizens should perform general duties? If substantial reasons do favor an exemption, how should competing interests be assessed? Does the basic concept of human equality play a role here, and, if so, how? To what extent should possible exemptions be seen as an accommodation of religious liberty; and if that is significant, can it justify drawing a line between religious and nonreligious claimants? If so, what counts as "religious"? Who exactly should qualify for an exemption, what convictions do those people claiming one need to have, and should membership in particular organizations matter? Should an exemption based on a statute be cast in specific or general terms? How is the government to determine whether those who claim to qualify really do so? Can some alternative satisfy the reasons for an exemption and avoid its difficulties?

The History of Underlying Rules and Actual Treatment of Pacifists

The basic idea of pacifism can be traced back at least to early Christianity, as Roland Bainton explains in a book that explores changing attitudes toward wars of Christian groups over the centuries.[1] As a rough generalization, the belief in the United States, and the other Western liberal democracies, that pacifists should be relieved from military service can be seen as largely based on the Protestant Reformation and the Enlightenment. Both of these, though in different forms, emphasized individual convictions as contrasted with what the dominant church and prevailing political order told people they should do. In a number of the American colonies, settlers were partly those whose religious beliefs and practices failed to conform with what the Anglican Church or English government dictated. Notably in respect to pacifism, the Society of Friends, Quakers, settled in what is now Pennsylvania.

In the period leading up to the Revolution and formation of the United States, the most influential Enlightenment author in American thought was John Locke, who wrote a 1689 Letter Concerning Toleration. He urged that churches should be treated as voluntary associations, with people being free to worship God in the way they choose. Locke himself did not contend that people's religious convictions should confer immunity from general laws, and he regarded it as entirely appropriate for a government ban on the killing of cattle to apply to religious sacrifices of cows.[2]

In early American history, some important concessions were made to religious convictions.[3] Many colonies did not require dissenters to pay tax assessments that supported dominant churches and did not force those who objected on religious grounds to take oaths before testifying. In several colonies, members of the Quakers and other groups were exempted from bearing arms. The Continental Congress, at the time of the American Revolution, referred to "some people, who, from religious principles, cannot bear arms in any case," and assured them that it intended "no violence to their consciences."[4]

The history of exemptions from military service, having begun before the founding of the United States, developed from then until modern times. Most early states, either by legislation or constitutional right, did exempt conscientious opponents to military force from bearing arms. In some of those states, only members of particular sects qualified; in some, men relieved of duty had to produce a substitute or pay a fee. Interestingly, Madison's original proposal for the Bill of Rights contained a clause providing that "no person religiously scrupulous of bearing arms shall be compelled to render military service in person." That clause was dropped in part because most of the Bill of Rights was going to apply only to the federal government, and states were the bodies that then engaged in conscription.[5] The Civil War Draft Act of 1864, which instituted national conscription, excused conscientious objectors whose denominations' articles of faith forbade the bearing of arms.[6] In World War I, the Draft Act of 1917 by its language limited its exemption to combatant service and granted that only to members of "any well-recognized sect" or organization that forbid members from participating "in war in any form."[7] During that war, the War Department actually ameliorated the membership requirement by ordering that men with "personal scruples against war" be treated as conscientious objectors; it also relieved some objectors from noncombatant military service by furloughing them for civilian service.[8]

The 1940 Selective Service Act, whose basic provisions remain intact, broadened statutory coverage, partly due to the legislative efforts of "peace" churches. A person did not have to belong to a pacifist sect so long as he "by religious training and belief, is conscientiously opposed to participation in war in any form." As this language makes clear, to qualify for an exemption, a man still needed a religious basis and could not be accepting of some wars but be opposed to participation in a particular war because it was unjust. Courts of appeal divided on what counted as "religious training and belief." The Second Circuit ruled that an individual's response "to an inward mentor, call it conscience or God" qualified as a religious impulse.[9] The Ninth Circuit disagreed; an individual had to believe "in his responsibility to an authority higher and beyond any worldly one."[10]

Congress responded in 1948, setting the stage for the major Supreme Court decisions on the subject and sharply raising the basic questions about appropriate coverage. Its amendment to the statute provided that "Religious training and belief in this connection mean an individual's beliefs in a Supreme Being involving duties superior to those arising from any human relation, but do not include essentially political, sociological, or philosophical views or a merely personal moral code."[11] Clearly Congress had agreed with the approach of the Ninth Circuit, not the Second Circuit's broad construction of religion.

Before we look briefly at the three important cases, it helps to draw two fundamental distinctions. The first is between what the language of a statute covers and what the Constitution requires. If one reading of a statute is likely unconstitutional, judges will often choose to construe it differently.[12] The second distinction is between what the Constitution *might* require about a direct claim to be afforded an exemption not otherwise granted and what lines are constitutionally acceptable when Congress chooses to grant exemptions only to some individuals or groups. As various state constitutions had provided and Madison's early draft of the Bill of Rights specified, the government could be constitutionally required to grant religious pacifists an exemption. For such an argument about our actual federal Constitution, the relevant provision now would be the Free Exercise Clause. That *could* be read to prevent the government from requiring people to do what their religious conscience tells them is deeply wrong, *unless* it has a very strong reason not to grant this concession.

The Supreme Court has never actually declared that free exercise rights cover such claims in respect to military service. In the 1920s and 1930s, it clearly indicated in dicta that this was left to legislative judgment.[13] When in the 1960s through the 1980s the Court rendered a generous interpretation of free exercise protections, for example, deciding that Amish parents cannot be required to send their children to school after the age of fourteen,[14] one might well have concluded that religious pacifists did have a constitutional right to an exemption. But in 1990 the Supreme Court declared in *Employment Division v. Smith* that general laws need not create religious exceptions. According to the basic standard of this case, the granting of a federal exemption is left up to Congress.

A different constitutional issue concerns how a statutory exemption is drawn. Suppose only members of one sect are covered, despite the existence of other pacifist religions. That would definitely violate the Establishment Clause, which precludes government favoring of particular religions, and could also be seen as impairing free exercise by encouraging some members to leave their group and join another. Less obvious is whether in this context the government can limit an exemption to *members* of pacifist religious groups and whether it can favor religious pacifists as compared with nonreligious ones. The 1940 act eliminated the first question by making the exemption depend on individual convictions, not membership, but whether membership can ever be required for an exemption still carries importance in other contexts, explored in subsequent chapters. Congress's 1948 endorsement of the "Supreme Being" language sharply raised the question about favoring religious bases over nonreligious ones. Under the Establishment Clause, does a grant limited to religious claimants unacceptably "establish" religion in general as compared with other outlooks?

Given that this book's aim is to evaluate the basic appropriateness of exemptions and how they may best be formulated, it does not explore in depth just how the constitutional Free Exercise Clause and Establishment Clause have been, and might best be, interpreted.[15] But since the religious clauses do reflect basic values of our society, and to a large extent those of other liberal democracies, reflection on unquestionable and debatable constitutional limits on what the government may do often carries broader significance. A relatively brief account of some key draft cases can contribute to a fuller understanding of possibilities and disputes over the acceptability of certain key distinctions.

During the Vietnam War, which over time developed intense opposition within this country, the Supreme Court decided three important controversies, addressing the Supreme Being requirement, the coverage of "religious training and belief," and the limitation of "war in any form." The first case was *United States v. Seeger,*[16] which actually involved review of three appellate decisions involving objectors whose claims did not fit neatly into the language Congress had chosen. The three court of appeals panels being reviewed by the Supreme Court justices had reached various conclusions about the statutory and constitutional standards. Two panels determined that the claimants were not covered by the statute itself because they did not believe in a Supreme Being. These two divided on the constitutional issue, one concluding that Congress was free to require that belief, the other that such believers could not be favored over other religious objectors. The third panel avoided the constitutional issue by reading the statute in a broad way. A unanimous Supreme Court chose that alternative.

The applicant in one of the decisions being reviewed, Seeger, had characterized his opposition as based on "religious" belief but referred to a "skepticism or disbelief in the existence of God," articulating his "belief in and devotion to goodness and virtue for their own sakes, and a religious faith in a purely ethical creed."[17] Contrary to what any ordinary reading of the statute would convey, the Supreme Court concluded that "Supreme Being" language did not designate "God" but merely clarified "religious training and belief." A belief qualified so long as it "occupies a place in the life of its possessor parallel to that filled by the orthodox belief in God. . . ."[18] This construction effectively eliminated the legal significance of the statutory requirement of belief in a Supreme Being.

Five years later the Court reversed a decision denying the exemption for Elliot Welsh, who had struck the word "religious" from his application and referred to "reading in the fields of history and sociology." He based his objection on his sense that "the military complex wastes both human and material resources" and "fosters disregard for . . . human needs and ends. . . ."[19] Four of the eight sitting justices read the statute as not including Welsh, which is what its language clearly indicates. Another four justices read the language very broadly to cover all registrants whose beliefs "play the role of a religion and function as a religion" in their lives. This could include deeply held "beliefs which are purely ethical or moral in source and content . . ."[20] This approach effectively eliminated any requirement of what counts as a religious conviction in the normal sense, and it sharply reduced any significance for Congress's specific exclusion from coverage of what are "essentially political, sociological, or philosophical views or a merely personal moral code."

Among the four justices who read the statute's language as not reaching Welsh, three of these accepted Congress's power to give special treatment here to religious convictions.[21] Justice Harlan did not believe Congress had such constitutional authority; he rendered the fifth vote necessary for the Court's sustaining of Welsh's claim. He urged that in this context, it was unconstitutional to favor religious pacifists over equally sincere pacifists who were not religious.[22] Given that Congress's primary aim was to afford the exemption for the great majority of pacifists, Harlan concluded that extending coverage to those like Welsh fitted its purpose better than striking down all exemptions. By joining the actual result reached by the highly strained statutory reading of four other justices, Harlan made theirs a plurality opinion.[23] The Supreme Court had, thus, effectively eliminated the need for a genuine "religious" conviction. Given the judicial practice of interpreting statutes to avoid constitutional invalidity or doubt, many, including myself, have assumed that some or all of the four justices in the plurality shared the constitutional concerns developed by Justice Harlan, even though they did not explicitly rely on them.

The third important draft case was *Gillette v. United States*,[24] which involved a "selective objector" who was conscientiously opposed to participating in the Vietnam War but not all wars. Because the language of "war in any form" definitely referred to all wars, the statutory limit here was straightforward. The serious issue was whether Congress could constitutionally exclude those who objected to participation in particular wars. Surveying a number of considerations, to which we shall return, the Court, 8–1, held that limiting the exemption to those who are complete pacifists was acceptable. This, of course, does not resolve whether doing so is, or is not, the wisest policy.

An element of the history of draft exemptions different from basic coverage is how they were to be implemented. According to the law of 1940, all applicants had to register. A pacifist who claimed he could not even register had violated the law and was subject to time in jail. The issue about registration has, as Chapter 6 describes, arisen in respect to insurance for contraceptives, with some organizations refusing to formally register their objection to the general duty.

Claims by conscientious objectors who did register were initially considered by draft boards. A young man whose assertions would otherwise qualify could be refused on the ground that he was insincere. Review of local draft board decisions took place in appeal boards, a presidential appeal board, and courts.[25] The general judicial approach to decisions by administrative bodies is to overturn a decision only if it lacks a "basis in fact" or suffers from an error in law or procedural defect. This approach was somewhat ameliorated in review of draft cases but still if a draft board's determination of insincerity was accepted by an appeal board, that could defeat a claim.[26] By the latter stages of the Vietnam War, judicial review had become much stricter, and courts would sustain rejection of a claimant as insincere only if there was objective evidence, such as blatant contradictions or false claims of church membership, that pointed in that direction.[27] This is a standard that is hard to satisfy if the main source of evidence is a person's own statements of belief.

A final aspect of the practice of exempting conscientious objectors is what the consequences were of an exemption being granted. If a man objected only to active combatant military duty, he could be assigned a noncombatant role within the military. If he was opposed to any military service, he was assigned alternative civilian service. After World War II, those subject to a draft had to spend two years within the military or alternative civilian service of the same length. If a pacifist refused even to do the alternative service, he was violating the law and could be jailed.[28]

BASIC ISSUES ABOUT DRAFTS AND PACIFISTS, AND THEIR BROADER IMPLICATIONS FOR EXEMPTIONS

Although a military draft may seem far removed from our present reality in the United States, it *could* conceivably recur someday, and its nature raises a wide range of broader issues. A major theme of this book is that these issues need to be considered in context, and determining the most just and desirable resolutions depends on that.

Does an Exemption Make Sense, and for What Reasons?

A military draft has effectively covered young men within a certain age group, such as eighteen to twenty-six.[29] Were such a law to be reintroduced, it might now well include women as well as men of that age, as is already true in some countries.[30] A draft necessarily does not reach those who are physically or mentally disabled from effective military service; "exemptions" for these individuals are obviously needed.[31] Drafts sometimes also do not reach those who are engaged in work vital to a country's welfare.[32] Whether an exemption should be granted to persons with convictions that participating in the military is deeply wrong raises many questions. Among those are how human autonomy should figure in relation to democratic judgment, the place of religious liberty and liberty of conscience, the force of concepts of equality, what message is conveyed, and practical considerations about uses of resources and effective armed forces.

Let us start with practical considerations, some of which are straightforward. So long as the government does not really need virtually all healthy young men in its armed forces, granting exemptions to pacifists will not interfere with the effectiveness of its service members. Indeed, the opposite may well be true. Suppose a young man is a genuine religious pacifist but is terrified by the prospect of spending years in jail and believes God will forgive even very serious sins. He might submit to the draft, be engaged in armed combat, but find himself unable to shoot to kill enemy troops. This could actually endanger his fellow soldiers and undermine the effectiveness of a military endeavor. And what of the pacifists who do refuse to serve despite being legally required to do so? They will spend time in jail. This is strikingly less valuable for the society than if they perform alternative civilian service in occupations that help others; and prison is extremely unlikely to promote their beneficial development over time, given that their only crime involves caring too much about other human beings, not too little.[33] Indeed, both incarceration and the denial of exemption could embitter and alienate many pacifists, making them less valuable as citizens. Concerns about an effective military and the wastefulness of the jail time are strong reasons to grant exemptions to genuine pacifists. And, as Paul Horwitz has urged, this general concern about alienating those forced to act against their convictions or suffer criminal punishment applies to many other existing and possible exemptions.[34]

Other practical concerns are less simple. They involve the dangers of fraudulent avoidance and the message an exemption may send, the latter being a dominant issue about various other possible exemptions. Since concern about what an exemption communicates depends largely on considerations of fairness and equality, I shall address those subjects before developing their tie to practical worries about fraud and administrability.

What is the prevailing American view about our liberal democracy, and what *should* such a view involve? Clearly, we believe both that individuals warrant substantial autonomy in how they live their lives and that the democratic process, subject to some constitutional constraints, determines what actions the law requires of citizens. Excusing only some from duties imposed on others may seem unjust, especially if performing those duties can involve great sacrifice and risk. Faithful citizens comply with legal requirements, at least if it is expected that they will do so (something not true about many formal speed limits that are set). Among the aspects of valued autonomy, with deep historical roots, is freedom of religious exercise. How is the value of autonomy to be squared with the notion that representatives of the majority are to decide what people must legally do or refrain from doing?

We can easily identify three possible positions about this, one of which is obviously misguided. The two extreme positions are that exemptions based on religious conscience, or conscience more generally, should always or never be granted. The plainly foolish position is the first. If a person's conscience tells him he should commit acts of terror and kill ordinary citizens, or if he believes God has told him to kill members of his own family, he cannot be granted an exemption from legal prohibitions;

however, if judged insane, he *might* be excused from criminal guilt and subjected to civil commitment. The second position is that sketched by John Locke. Although people must be left free to believe what persuades them and to engage in acts of worship that have no negative consequences, they should never be afforded a right to perform acts contrary to ordinary legal standards that are not directed against religious practices. Thus, if the drinking of alcohol is forbidden, that should cover wine for church services. In a notable case in the late nineteenth century, the Supreme Court, reviewing polygamy, took just this position about Free Exercise Clause protection. It drew a sharp distinction between belief and action, saying that "Congress was deprived of all legislative power over mere opinion but was left free to reach actions which were in violation of social duties or subversive of good order."[35]

One theme in this book is that, however one sees the constitutional limits, the intermediate position about what the government should do is definitely right. Usually it should require that all comply with general laws; *sometimes* it should make exceptions. The force of competing considerations varies hugely, depending on the particular legal requirement; and often people can reasonably disagree strongly about the balance, but no sensible person can suggest that all claims of exemption should be granted or refused. Given the history of the country, including settlement by the Quakers and the consistent practice of allowing at least some pacifists not to serve in the military, the argument for an exemption from military service is very strong *if* the alternative is a compulsory draft that allows no exceptions.

Tied to the tension between autonomy and democratic mandates is how in this context to view human equality—now a basic premise of all liberal democracies, though far from a feature of our original Constitution. Equality is a decidedly slippery concept because people can disagree sharply over exactly what kind of equality should count. Should the government treat all people equally under its requirements, or should it accord equal recognition to strong claims of conscience? The latter would lead to an exemption, the former to the opposite conclusion. What we need to acknowledge is that both kinds of equality do and should matter in respect to military service. Attempting to force a pacifist to join in killing enemy forces does not respect one of the most basic premises of his life; on the other hand, excusing him grants a benefit that others, whose lives may be lost or endangered, do not receive.

The draft situation differs from those in which an exemption for one group of persons directly and obviously imposes a burden on others. If a pacifist gets an exemption, one might conclude that another man who is drafted would not otherwise have been. But given all the other exceptions as to who is actually drafted, it would be nearly impossible to say that any one individual is drafted *because* of this exemption. Moreover, if a pacifist were faithful to his convictions and chose jail over military service, he would not have been successfully drafted in any event. Thus, it becomes impossible to know how many military slots would otherwise have been filled had an exemption not been granted. Despite all this, some may believe that if anyone is drafted because a pacifist is not, this is a kind of unfair burden. Needless to say, the alternative civilian service, which imposes a required length of time in work to benefit the public and which has not been freely chosen, goes a substantial distance to meet equality concerns about favoring pacifists. In respect to uncontested exemptions that do not involve any alternative burden, such as the ones here for medical conditions, their scope can bear on whether other exemptions should also be afforded, a consideration that comes into play in respect to various kinds of legal duties considered in chapters that follow

What message does a pacifist exemption send to others? Given the small minority of pacifists and the clear consistent assertion by the government that military force is often justified and sometimes vitally important for the country's well-being, the exemption does not itself convey genuine doubts about whether we need armed forces that should sometimes fight. Rather, it communicates a respect for strong convictions and perhaps seems to acknowledge implicitly that killing in war, though needed, is genuinely unfortunate. Although some draftees may have felt they were being unfairly disfavored in comparison with exempted pacifists, and certain religious groups have at times been resented in part for their pacifism, I do not believe either of these has ever become a major concern, and the worry about such groups being favored is substantially countered by alternative civilian service.

Both the equality concerns and the message sent depend partly on other features of how the draft system is working. If those subject to a draft initially are placed in a lottery and only some are actually drafted, that reduces the concern that only the objectors are ending up better off. Indeed, if they must perform alternative civilian service without going through a lottery, they actually end up bearing more of a burden than those who are simply never picked by the draft lottery. During the Vietnam War, a more troubling kind of inequality was a delay for those pursuing college or graduate studies. If, in fact, a teenager enrolled in college after high school and then pursued graduate work up to the age of twenty-six, he was nearly certain not to be drafted at any time. This inequality in terms of intellectual involvement was itself commonly related to the social class of young men's families. Perhaps all this could be justified in terms of a sensible use of resources, given that only some young men needed to be drafted, but it raised a much more substantial concern about unfair inequality than did an exemption for pacifists.

How to Classify: The Respective Places of Religious Conviction and Conscience

A crucial question about many exemptions is exactly how to cast them. Given the history of exemptions from military service in this country, it was definitely desirable for Congress to address the question of who qualified for an exemption, what officials would determine eligibility, and what alternative obligation those exempted would have to fulfill. Whatever one concludes about a possible constitutional right to an exemption, this was clearly not a subject desirably left within the scope of a generally worded statute, such as the Religious Freedom Restoration Act.

Do religious organizations or religious convictions properly play a key role in who should receive an exemption? Despite a possible contention that religious convictions should never be of special importance, religious involvement has been an important element in the lives of many citizens in this country's history, and religious liberty has been a prevailing principle guiding our governments. Saying that accommodation to religious conviction has *nothing* to do with the granting of exemptions is mistaken; but that alone does not settle whether those convictions should be treated specially. We can look at that problem both as a matter of principle and of effective administration.

If one asks about comparative convictions, are there nonreligious pacifists, and are their beliefs about the wrongness of killing in war held as intensely as those of religious pacifists? No one can now reasonably doubt that nonreligious pacifists like Welsh do exist. Some writers, however, have contended that the convictions of religious pacifists more strongly forbid engaging in wartime killing.[36] Unfortunately, no one is in a position to assess precisely the range of intensity of convictions held by various groups of people; but any claim that genuine belief in a divine prohibition is inevitably especially powerful is subject to an important qualification. Perhaps a person who believes that God forbids certain behavior and will send us eternally to hell if we engage in it will typically have a more powerful sense that he cannot commit particular acts than will a nonbeliever who is sure our whole life ends with death on this earth. But this country is still mainly Christian; many Christians believe that all of us are sinning frequently and that what counts most for our status is not whether we sin but whether we ask God for forgiveness. Suppose a person is sure he is committing multiple sins and regards potential wartime killing as only one kind, which, like others, God will forgive. He *may* still feel that following God's will carries more power than a nonbeliever ascribes to avoiding a deep moral wrong, but concluding that a religious pacifist will almost certainly find military participation more repulsive than a genuine nonreligious one is unwarranted. This conclusion strongly supports granting exemptions to genuine pacifists, whatever their religious beliefs.

Matters may seem less straightforward if one moves to problems of admissibility. How can draft and appeal boards determine whether someone is a genuine pacifist? Initially, it might seem that this concern could be a reason to require membership in a pacifist religious organization. For certain possible exemptions, organization membership should be important, but in this context, at least in modern times, that definitely would be misguided for draft exemptions. One reason, grounded in Establishment Clause values, is that such a rule would encourage individuals to join particular religious organizations, thus promoting those religious groups over others and over nonreligious organizations.

If virtually every member of a group maintained certain convictions, and if the group's demands on its members were such that few people would join it in order to avoid being drafted, one could believe that an organization requirement would constitute a genuine protection against fraud. It is difficult to imagine, for example, that many young men would become Amish, with all the special and stringent requirements of Amish life, to avoid being drafted. But various larger religious groups with a strong pacifist tradition are very different. Many Quakers are not pacifists, and one can join the Society of Friends without undertaking arduous practices. Any feasible group membership requirement would, standing alone, include many non-pacifists who joined for religious reasons and would not preclude fraudulent joining by non-pacifists who seek to avoid service.

Does "religious training and belief," in its ordinary sense, do a better job of separating the sincere from the insincere? Even if that does not categorically genuinely test intensity of pacifist convictions, does it at least help prevent fraud? The clear answer is "no." Draft boards and even appeal boards may be much more likely to believe someone who offers traditional pacifist religious convictions than men like Seeger and Welsh. Especially if religious membership is not a requirement, it is simple enough for a young man to formulate convictions related to God's word. The manner in which Seeger and Welsh both stated their beliefs is actually a nearly certain indication that they were telling the truth, not lying, since they clearly recognized they were putting themselves in a doubtful position. Of course, once their right to the exemption was established, others with similar views were less vulnerable, but many local draft board members may still have found it easier to accept stated convictions referring to God. In short, neither does a requirement of group membership nor a conviction that is "religious" in any typical understanding make sense in modern times for draft exemptions. The same is true for present relief from military service for those personnel who have become pacifists. An added reason not to draw the line at religious belief is that, as both the *Seeger* and *Welsh* cases indicate, deciding just what counts as "religious" and what does not is itself far from simple.

This brings us to the really troubling question of what kind of belief about war should be required. No one supposes that an exemption from compliance with a general law should be granted to everyone who thinks it would be somewhat morally better not to perform the act. A person should not avoid the draft just because he honestly believes he can do more good by being a social worker than a soldier. In the ensuing section on selective objection and subsequent chapters, we look in more detail at the difficulty of drawing appropriate lines related to who should qualify. The particular question about strength of conviction is not a serious concern for those who honestly believe that actual participation in war "in any form," and also military service that might lead to such participation, are wrong. Consider first a pacifist who believes it is never acceptable to kill another human being. It follows that, however he would actually behave, he thinks he should not kill a robber or terrorist who is setting out to murder his entire family. Even if a pacifist does not rule out all killing, he thinks it is wrong to kill in wartime. This means he believes that citizens of a country being invaded by a horrible foreign power that itself has exterminated millions, such as Nazi Germany, should not offer resistance. If someone honestly holds such a view, it is hard to dismiss his convictions as not sufficiently serious, *even* if it is likely that had that person lived in England during World War II, he would probably not have arrived at the same conviction. Given the rejection by a person of all the competing reasons wartime killing might be needed, the assessment of whether he qualifies for a draft exemption comes down not so much to the strength of an honestly stated conviction but primarily to sincerity. This, of course, is not to suggest that sincerity will always be simple to determine, especially when those who claim to be pacifists may not themselves be certain exactly what they believe.

Selective Objectors: Should They Be Treated Similarly?

Should those who are conscientiously opposed to a particular war be treated similarly to general pacifists? As we have seen, the Supreme Court ruled that selective objectors had no constitutional right to equal treatment, but that conclusion, even if sound, does not settle what a desirable legislative approach would be.

Many religious faiths subscribe to some version of a "just war" doctrine, according to which a country's cause must be just and waged by means that are neither prohibited nor disproportionate to the good likely to be achieved.[37] Roman Catholicism, for example, has a developed doctrine of numerous requisites for a just war.[38] We also have a very important secular legal analogue, namely, the standards of international law that set out when a military engagement does or does not comply with that law.[39] In accordance with that law, individual countries and collectives such as the European Union also have legal criteria for when and how use of force is permitted.[40] Although courts in the United States are unlikely to declare that a basic military engagement undertaken by the executive branch fails to comply with international or domestic law,[41] judges may determine that an unwarranted killing of civilians or instances of outright torture are forbidden. Actual military personnel, or potential draftees, may refuse participation on the basis that a particular war or the tactics being used are actually illegal. This could be one nonreligious basis for a claim of conscience.

Given that conscientious objections to a particular war may well be based on religious convictions, should we regard a limitation of exemptions to general pacifists as favoring the religions that adopt that position? If this is seen as a "yes" or "no" question, the answer is "no." So long as sound reasons apart from religious premises support limiting the class of those eligible for an exemption, and the standard is not directly tied to one's membership in a religious organization or to his adherence to the doctrines of a particular religion, the fact that many more members of one religion than another will qualify is not itself a religious classification. But the unequal impact in respect to members of different groups does present one reason for extending the exemption to selective objectors, especially since the requirement of opposition to involvement in all wars may entice some individuals to join pacifist groups.

The most fundamental arguments for this extended exemption are more straightforward. If someone is genuinely conscientiously opposed to participation in the military because of how our armed forces are being used, should he not be treated similarly to those who would object no matter the war in which the country is engaged? The concern about a possible undercutting of the military forces themselves also has relevance here. If a selective objector submits to the draft to avoid jail, perhaps he will be a less-than-effective soldier. When push comes to shove, he may be more likely to shoot at an enemy than an outright pacifist, but he may also be even more likely to undermine the morale of his fellows by complaining to them that the country is risking and sacrificing their lives and physical well-being for illegitimate objectives.

A review of the reasons for exempting selective objectors raises the further issue of who should count as one. If a draftee's conscience tells him he cannot fight because a particular war is unjust or illegal, he definitely qualifies. But what of a young man who simply cannot bring himself to engage in a war against a country from which he originated, and where many of his relatives still live, or a young man, such as a Scottish nationalist, who believes that the formal boundaries of his country, Great Britain, are grossly unjust? Neither of these is really a moral objection to either war in general or to a particular war, but each could be seen as a feeling of conscience about how one should behave.

The genuine grounds for not covering selective objectors are more complex. For the United States, at least, we can initially put aside the possibility that doing so would simply leave too few individuals available for military service. At no time since World War II has the country needed the great majority of able young men in the armed forces; and, in any event, if a selective objector actually refused to serve, he would not add to the number available. In respect to needed persons for the military, it is relevant that during World War II Great Britain, much more threatened than the United States, required for its privilege not to serve only conscientious objection to participation in combatant duty or military service. And, after some conflicting views, most British tribunals even exempted those whose opposition was grounded in Scottish and Welsh nationalism or an unwillingness to participate in a war against his country of origin.[42] Other countries have resolved these issues in various ways. In Romania only clerics are exempt from military service.[43] In the Ukraine, only members of ten minority religious groups qualify.[44] In Israel the Supreme Court in 2002 accepted a rejection of selective objectors;[45] and in 2014 the Israeli Defense Force formally refused to accept objections to participate in action that would "harm the Palestinian population in the West Bank," although it did later reassign those objectors to alternate duties.[46] If one can generalize, the more a country regards itself as seriously threatened, and the more it needs extensive military personnel, the narrower the scope of exemptions is likely to be.

Deeper concerns about an exemption involve the way selective objection to unjust wars develops and the problem of drawing the line of its coverage. Notably, its relation to factual data differs from pacifism. One *might* see pacifism as based largely on some premise about social facts, such as what would happen to society if many individuals or some countries, or both, adopted a refusal to kill in war. However, we have no decisive empirical data that shows that pacifism is from the standpoint of human history a healthier approach than fighting just wars. By contrast, selective objection is typically based on what is believed to be true about a particular war. An individual selective objector may rely largely on a factual premise that itself is demonstrably false or an assessment of the government's reasons for involvement that differ significantly from those the government offers and on which it may actually have relied. Whether mistaken or not, the typical selective objector disagrees clearly with the country's particular policy in a way that is not true about pacifists. A concession to selective objectors *may seem* to send the message that the propriety of government action is genuinely in doubt, something not really a problem with exempting pacifists.

The concerns about what constitutes a genuine claim of conscience and how others can assess that are much greater here than with pacifists.[47] Suppose that many young men are persuaded that a military involvement of the country is seriously misguided. Absent an exemption, a substantial percentage of them will nonetheless believe that, given the obligations of a citizen and their desire not to be convicted of a crime and sent to jail, their submitting to the draft is preferable to refusing to serve. But suppose an exemption is extended to selective objectors. This could easily encourage numbers of those men who believe it would be far preferable for them to do something other than fighting in this unjust war to ask themselves whether they actually have an objection that rises to one of conscience. And how is a draft board or an appeal board to discern whether once it believes the claimant's statement that he regards the war as unjust, his objection to participating in it rises to a genuine conscientious objection? Both for completely honest individuals themselves and for outsiders making assessments, this concern about whether a conviction not to perform a general duty reaches the level warranting an exemption can present a very difficult issue—one that extends to many other actual and possible exemptions.

Tied to this concern is one about honesty. If someone really believes a war is unjust and would strongly prefer not to participate, he can have a strong incentive to overstate the force of his objection if it actually falls short of a sense that participation would be deeply immoral. He need not tell an outright lie about what he thinks is right or wrong; he may merely express his conviction in a way that is not completely accurate. Given the tendency of virtually all people to overstate or understate the force of their objections in various circumstances, and the difficulty they themselves have in thinking about just what expression exceeds the boundaries of honesty, we can understand how it could be hard both for possible claimants and those reviewing what they say to determine if they really cross the lines both of being candid in their assertion to be selective objectors and of having the needed intensity of conviction about not serving in the military.

A different concern about selective objectors is what they should be relieved of. During the Vietnam War, many American troops were stationed in Europe, in order to discourage aggression by the Soviet Union. If an objection is to one use of armed forces, why should it lead to a total exemption from military service? Of course, it is conceivable that a person who strongly objects to a limited war will believe he should not then perform military duties of a totally different kind. Moreover, setting things up so that certain draftees can only be sent to some places and not to others could be inconvenient for the military, although, interestingly, in the summer of 1971, the army assured those men who actually enlisted that their first sixteen months of service would be in the United States and Europe. Providing an exception from all military service is much less obvious for selective objectors than for pacifists. A general exemption from a draft would seem particularly doubtful if the involvement to which a person objects is relatively minor and involves few military personnel. And, of course, unlike with pacifism, the grounds for selective objection can change over time. It can be created by a new use of armed forces or of a particular tactic that strikes someone as offensive, or it can be eliminated by the end of a war or tactic.[48]

When someone considers all these reasons for and against including selective objectors in the provision of an exemption, she could reasonably reach either conclusion. My own view is that given the importance of not forcing people to participate in killing others against their conscience, their inclusion would be preferable,[49] and this is indeed the position taken by the United Nations Commission on Human Rights[50] and the Council of Europe.[51] Among the reasons for this conclusion is the reality that if an exemption is limited to pacifists, those who do have strong objections to a particular war may be inclined either to state falsely that they are actually pacifists or to actually persuade themselves that pacifism is really the right approach to all wars. Although hardly outright proof of this assumption, the percentages of conscientious objectors was substantially higher during the Vietnam War than during World War II,[52] which was fought when most of those in the country strongly felt after the Japanese attack on Pearl Harbor that we were fighting against genuinely evil and powerful forces that threatened much of the world. As with many aspects of our lives, we all tend to develop general theories of right and wrong partly in response to the specific circumstances that face us.

IS AN ALTERNATIVE PREFERABLE?

This chapter has thus far suggested that when a military draft exists, offering an exemption for pacifists is strongly desirable so long as they are required to perform some form of alternative service. The exemption should not be limited to members of particular organizations or to those whose basis for pacifism is religious. Despite the actual statutory language, this was essentially the coverage of exemptions as interpreted by the Supreme Court, until the draft was effectively dropped after the Vietnam War. Although fairly powerful reasons exist for not extending an exemption to selective objectors, the chapter has also concluded that, on balance, that would be desirable.

All the difficulties and complexities that have been discussed, however, raise the basic question of whether an alternative to this scheme is actually preferable.[53] Chapter 1 explains why this issue takes on special importance when noncompliance with the general standard of behavior does not directly harm others *and* many who are not conscientious objectors would prefer not to be forced to comply with the general requirement. The military draft strikingly fits these criteria. The non-conscription of a small percentage of young men does not really harm other individuals or the broader society, and a significant number of young men would prefer to avoid military service.

Of course, the most obvious alternative is to make military service voluntary. This is effectively our present system, although once a person is committed to service for a number of years, he or she cannot simply resign whenever he or she wants. If an adequate number of men and women decide to serve in the military, receiving enough compensation, training, and benefits to make this a rational choice, that definitely seems preferable to mandatory service. After all, all other forms of work, including government jobs, are chosen, not mandated—even if economic circumstances leave disadvantaged individuals a very limited range of options.

There are some counterarguments. One might think it is healthy for a society to require young persons to spend a part of their lives devoting themselves to serving the public. That *could* help them to perceive that a commitment to their fellow citizens should be an aspect of their lives. More subtly, a draft could help restrain the government from engaging in unwise, unjust military endeavors.

If young persons are subject to draft, the opposition to an unpopular war is likely to be more intense than if service is voluntary. Evidence of this is that, although the military involvement of the United States over time in Iraq and Afghanistan has been subject to criticism, we have seen nothing like the powerful demonstrations that reflected intense opposition to the Vietnam War, a war in which many young men who regarded it as misguided feared that they might be drafted to fight. It is at least possible that the existence of a draft might make the government a bit more hesitant to undertake military missions involving many troops. Depending on her overall political sense, a person might conceive such hesitancy as desirable or undesirable.

A different alternative to exemption standards is to have a general draft, or other legal requirement, but to relieve anyone who chooses, so long as he or she performs an alternative service. To make this work, one needs another task that would not be broadly preferred and that does not reflect a genuine injustice. On the latter point, if anyone could avoid both the military and any alternative service by paying $500,000, that would constitute an unacceptable favoring of the wealthy, given that most people would not possess enough money to make the choice. A much more appropriate alternative would be to allow anyone to choose three years of civilian service instead of two years of military duty.[54] The longer period of civilian service would discourage that choice by those without objection to military duty. Germany at one point effectively had such a scheme, requiring ten months of military service or thirteen months of civilian service.[55] Although one had to apply for a kind of conscientious objector status, there was no review based on whether one really qualified, and in 1995, more men chose the civilian service than military duty.

If the alternative, in contrast to that in Germany, is one that would not be chosen by most young men, or young men and women, it can be objected, as Chapter 1 suggests, that this is unfair for the genuine conscientious objectors. Why should they have to suffer for following their deep convictions of conscience? The unsimple answer to this objection depends substantially on concerns about administrability.

It should first be noted that this option is far from as harsh for the pacifists and other objectors as having no exemption at all, which has been the situation in the United States for selective objectors. And given that military service often involves serious risks of death, physical injuries that can last for life, and psychological trauma, it is not clear that a longer period of civilian service is seriously unfair.

But the main concerns here are with the difficulties of classifying who should qualify for an exemption and administering that classification. We have seen both how hard it is to decide if it is better to include selective objectors and to define the intensity of conviction needed to qualify for an exemption. We have also noted both the worry about fraud, which allows some of those not genuinely eligible to succeed, and the danger that some genuine objectors may fail to convince officials and be granted the exemption. Providing an alternative service anyone can choose guarantees that no genuine objector will be put in jail for refusing military duty, and it also eliminates worries about fraud. Given the serious difficulty of defining the eligible class of those who can get an exemption and of discerning fairly who then actually qualifies, the voluntary alternative actually adds a strong element of fairness to the whole system. That benefit can well outweigh the concern that the alternative possibly imposes on the genuine objectors a burden that is modestly greater than would seem ideal.

Not only in this domain but some others as well, our country has given inadequate attention to the strategy of voluntary alternatives, a subject taken up again in some other chapters of the book.

Conclusion

Apart from the few of those who already within military service may become pacifists or selective objectors, the specific subjects of this chapter are not of pressing concern in our country's present life. The exemptions for pacifists are not only a vital aspect of understanding the history of such privileges but also illustrate a number of basic principles and competing considerations that do carry over to the more intense controversies of our era treated in chapters that follow.

3

Tax Exemptions and Deductions

Introduction

THIS CHAPTER DISCUSSES the most historically grounded exemptions from ordinary legal requirements, ones that almost certainly have the greatest overall social consequences and are by far the most detailed and complex in their actual coverage. Going back in English history and consistently in this century, churches and other religious bodies have not been treated for purposes of taxation like for-profit businesses and various other kinds of organizations. In the United States today, this favored treatment extends to broadly defined charitable organizations and a variety of other nonprofit endeavors. In different respects, the treatment is determined by federal, state, and local law, often with somewhat vague categorizations but with highly specific provisions of exactly what the degree of privilege amounts to.

In contrast with most other subjects addressed in this book, no attempt is made here to suggest exactly what degrees of coverage are the most just and desirable, about which a vast literature exists among tax scholars. Any reasonably full account on this score would require not a single chapter but at least one book and likely more than one. Perhaps even more relevant, this is not an area in which I possess competence, and it is one in which such competence is not easily acquired, especially if one does not specialize in tax law and has not mastered the kind of economic analysis that here counts heavily. Nonetheless, rather than simply leave this topic entirely out of the book's coverage, I believe providing at least a summary of some of its major aspects is important.

The most significant consideration is how far the tax benefits are grounded in reasons quite different from those for most exemptions and how far these do touch certain other areas of special privileges. A fundamental variation with draft exemptions, and many others, is the weight of individual conscience. Although one can see the history of allowing nonservice in the military as partly related to the status of religious groups like the Quakers, that exemption was always seen mainly as not requiring people to do what they felt was deeply wrong. In the modern United States, individual conscience has been *the* basic criterion to qualify. Tax exemptions are quite different. For those, what is socially desirable generally, including the relative independence of nongovernmental bodies, is key. Ties do exist to what behavior is healthy for individuals in a liberal democracy, but in this respect, the aim is encouraging people to do what is good for them and their fellow citizens rather than permitting them to refrain from violating their consciences. The elimination of existing tax exemptions would not compel people to act against conscience any further than present tax requirements now do.

Much of this chapter focuses, although briefly, on a range of claims about the proper bases for such exemptions, whether these should result in extending or curbing who qualifies and what the extent of various privileges should be.

Are these considerations really only about tax benefits, or do they extend further? As we shall see in Chapter 7, the Religious Land Use and Institutionalized Persons Act (RLUIPA) restricts the application of zoning laws and some other legal interferences with uses of property, including perhaps historical preservation requirements and outright condemnation. Although the basis for the land use part of the act was mainly to counter instances of discrimination against some or all religious groups, the act's application often requires a balancing of the public need to interfere with religious practice. This bears some similarity to the kind of balancing that legislatures and agencies often need to do in determining the range of appropriate tax exemptions. An aspect of balancing that is crucial for many exemption claims but not tax exemptions is whether they will hurt people seeking needed treatment and avoiding discrimination based on their sexual orientation or other quality. Tax exemptions do raise a rather dissimilar issue about discrimination, namely, in ways I shall note, that they may favor the wealthy over the poor. But typically, the primary competing concern is the public's need for tax revenue to provide important services and maintain their needed amount of financing.

This chapter discusses three different forms of favored tax treatment within the United States. The first is an exemption afforded many nonprofit organizations that prevents them from having to pay income taxes, primarily at the federal level. The second is relief from property taxes, a subject of state and local regulation. The third, not formally an "exemption," is the deductions from taxes allowed to individuals for donations they make to churches, charities, and a number of other organizations. The reasons for these individual benefits connect closely to those for not requiring the organizations themselves to pay income taxes, but some of the claimed justifications differ in force.

Having read a range of accounts of why these privileges are warranted, I came away with a general observation that has a much wider application. No single theory covers everything; multiple reasons typically support a practice and carry varying weights in different contexts. This reality applies to many particular issues about government concessions not to perform general duties. Once this is recognized, people should not expect matters to reduce to a single justification that clearly warrants some exemptions and does not warrant others, even if with many exemptions, the competing considerations are more straightforward and easier to discern than those related to taxes.

Exemptions from Income Taxes for Nonprofit Organizations:

WHICH ORGANIZATIONS ARE COVERED

Exemptions from having to pay federal income taxes apply to a wide variety of nonprofit organizations. The history of such exemptions can be traced back to the 1601 British Statute of Charitable Uses, practices in colonial America, and early state constitutions in the United States.[1] The federal Revenue Act of 1894[2] contained most of the kinds of exemptions that were enacted into later statutes and that we now have.

Exemptions extend to a wide variety of nonprofit organizations, and the appropriateness of some are more debatable than the appropriateness of others. The key provision of the Internal Revenue Code §501(c)(3) covers entities that are organized "for religious, charitable, scientific, testing for public safety, literary, or educational purposes"; it also reaches those that foster "national or international sports competition" and aim to prevent "cruelty to children or animals."[3] Subsections of the code grant exemptions to particular organizations such as professional football leagues. To qualify under §501(c)(3), an organization's net earnings may not go to private shareholders or individuals. This means an organization can count as nonprofit even if it pays its leaders high salaries, but it cannot grant them a percentage of its net earnings. Given the diversity of organizations covered, it is hardly surprising that "[t]he list of potentially exempt purposes has developed over time without any overall guiding principle."[4]

BASIC JUSTIFICATIONS

In addressing various justifications for these exemptions, we can distinguish fairly straightforward policy bases from reasons grounded in economic analysis and the difficulties of determining what would properly count as relevant income for certain kinds of organizations. For this purpose, I shall initially concentrate on typical charitable organizations and then turn to other institutions such as museums and colleges, for whom the reasons are a bit different and whose favorable treatment may be more debatable. It is worth reiterating at the outset that many of the reasons for these exemptions also reach tax deductions for individual contributions to the same organizations.

Saving the Government Money

Most charities serve those who, in one way or another, live at a substantial disadvantage. Giving food to the poor is an obvious illustration. If charities such as Feeding America did not provide these services, the government would need to do so. Since these charities are thus saving the government money, their income, which helps them to be effective, should not be taxed. This has been cast as a public benefit subsidy theory.[5]

It is clarifying here to draw a distinction in terms of just what may be claimed. One possibility is that the granting of the exemption itself enhances the ability of an organization to provide its services and actually saves the government from having to spend a comparable amount of money. If this is true, the exemption is not really costing the government on balance. A more modest version that does not depend on this causal connection is that because it provides services that the government would otherwise have to pay for, the charity *deserves* the exemption, even if a failure to grant one would not significantly reduce its contribution to social life. In this event, eliminating the exemption would actually benefit the government financially.

A rather different distinction is also worth mentioning. What of benefits that go to nonresidents? Many charitable organizations, such as CARE and Oxfam, mainly provide help for those in the poorest countries of the world. Of course, the U.S. government also gives such assistance, but if these charities did not exist, our government would likely not provide the same amount of aid.

MORE EFFECTIVE PROVISION

Nonprofit charities may in some ways be better suited to provide certain services than either the government or for-profit enterprises. With its workers devoted to helping the disadvantaged and typically being paid lower salaries than they could earn in the private sector, the charities may simply be more effective and efficient than we can generally expect government agencies to be. If the services were provided by for-profit enterprises based largely on donations from outsiders, the primary concern would be whether those who stand to profit would effectively diminish the amount of effective service in order to increase their own income.[6] Since those donating money do not directly benefit from either increased profits or the organization's services, they may have less incentive and ability to discern this kind of manipulation than they would with a typical business.

ORGANIZATIONAL AUTONOMY

Apart from effective services and the government's saving money lies the basic value of organizational autonomy. In a liberal democracy, institutions outside government are very important,[7] helping to protect independence and diversity of outlooks. For the government to dominate all forms of life would be deeply unfortunate. The tax exemptions given to the great variety of nonprofit organizations help to serve this value, one that extends to many other possible exemptions.

ENCOURAGING CARING

Closely tied to this last value is the desirability of encouraging caring among citizens.[8] Although a main source of the importance of concern for one's fellows comes from religious traditions, that concern is widely valued by those who are nonreligious as well. Help to the poor can, of course, come not only from assistance that individuals choose to give on their own but from government provision. However, the deep involvement of religious groups and other charities helps to connect their members, who make donations and assist in other ways, more strongly to those in need than does their payment of taxes to the government. Thus, this tax benefit to these nonprofit private organizations can enhance the development of caring among members directly or indirectly involved.

THE LACK OF RELEVANT INCOME AND DISCERNIBLE TAX STANDARD

Among the four justifications we have just examined, the latter two are primarily normative evaluations of what is healthy for individuals and for the kind of society for which believers in liberal democracy aspire. By this I do not mean to suggest that factual estimates are completely absent. One may well believe that individuals are generally happier and feel better about their lives if they help others instead of always pursuing self-interest, and one may also be convinced that if nongovernmental organizations decline too far, officials are more likely to become dictatorial and arbitrary, even if what exists is still a form of democracy. But these "empirical" judgments are not easily confirmed. The notions that nonprofit charities are overall more effective in what they do than similar for-profit enterprises and government providers of services is more fact based, and it may be shown to be true or false for particular instances; but again, it is not easily confirmed in some general way. The assertion that, in one sense, charities save the government some money is undeniably true, but what the effect on the charities would be if these exemptions were eliminated is really unanswerable, depending heavily, as it does, on how those who support those charities would react to the rising cost.

In contrast to these largely evaluative justifications, the nature of which is at the center of the vast majority of exemptions claims, Boris I. Bittker and George K. Rahdert offered in 1976 a basic rationale that does not depend on premises about what is really good for individuals and society and of how promoters of charities would react if exemptions were eliminated.[9] In a substantial article that explores many details, they argued that genuine nonprofit charities do not really acquire an income that could justify taxation. As they put it, "we will argue that nonprofit organizations engaged in 'public service' activities, broadly conceived, should be wholly exempted from income taxation, because they do not realize 'income' in the ordinary sense of that term and because, even if they did, there is no satisfactory way to fix the tax rate to the ability of beneficiaries to pay."[10] Under this theory, we would not need to think of the exemption as a "subsidy" that needs to be justified as socially desirable.

The first problem the authors raise concerns relevant income. Given that gifts and bequests to other individuals are not taxable, should these gifts and bequests given to charitable organizations—as well as membership dues and income from endowments rooted in such gifts to public service organizations—be treated differently?[11] And should the organizations not be seen basically as conduits of gifts from donors to ultimate recipients, rather than having an "income" and life of their own?[12] Another problem is what would count as "gross income," if that income is to be taxed? Should all that the organization spends in providing its services, including its salaries, count as "ordinary business expenses"? Given that individuals who take the time and energy on their own to provide such help receive no tax benefits, should not paying others from donations received at least count as a business expense?[13] If these are treated as business expenses, and the money that eventually goes to the disadvantaged is regarded as ordinary gifts, no relevant income to be taxed would remain.

If somehow one could discern a relevant income, Professor Bittker and Rahdert urged that the tax rate should presumably depend on the rate set for beneficiaries. Since most of these are poor, that would be very low or nonexistent, and it would be impossible to determine with accuracy.[14] An interesting aspect of the Bittker and Rahdert account is that it shows how the underlying complexity of a system of taxation or regulation can support an argument that an exemption is appropriate or even that it should not really be seen as a true "exemption" but merely an implementation of the basic criteria.

Given all their reasons, the central idea of Bittker and Rahdert is that the exemption simply fits the logic of why for-profit organizations pay taxes. Notably, their basic theory, as they clearly state, does not cover "mutual benefit" organizations, such as labor unions and social clubs, as contrasted with public service endeavors.[15] They conclude that the mutual benefit organizations should not escape income taxes altogether.[16]

One might regard the theory of Bittker and Rahdert as *the* basic explanation for why tax exemptions for organizations should or should not be accorded, or as *a* ground that could by itself totally or partly justify some such exemptions. I shall not explore these options in depth, but as critics have pointed out, their theory does not cover all nonprofit organizations that provide needed services. Some of these, notably nonprofit hospitals and universities, do acquire a great deal of their assets by charging for their services. Those charges could be taken as relevant income.[17] And the basic idea of no genuine income plainly does not touch either whether individual donors should get tax deductions or whether nonprofit charities should be relieved of property taxes. In a subsequent section, I suggest that evaluating the value of property of these organizations could often be less than simple, but that property is definitely worth something—and frequently it is worth a great deal.

However, none of these reservations show that the grounds these authors provided are not one significant basis for granting certain exemptions.[18] Whether these reasons are ever sufficient by themselves can depend on whether one accepts their various claims about how income should be calculated and rates appropriately set. Even if one recognizes, as Bittker and Rahdert do, that their account does not warrant some present exemptions, it does not follow that those are necessarily unjustified, only that one must look for other rationales.

CONSTRAINTS ON CAPITAL FORMATION

A different rationale was advanced five years after that of Bittker and Rahdert by Henry Hansmann.[19] Discerning that the nonprofit sector is a "growing share of the national economy"[20] and that nonprofit firms often now compete with profit-seeking firms and resemble their organization and operation, Hansmann identified difficulties in the theories previously advanced. Relying partly on the basis that nonprofit firms are in many areas likely to serve consumers better than profit-seeking firms, he emphasized their disadvantage in raising capital in comparison with typical for-profit counterparts.[21] Granting them a tax exemption compensates for this obstacle.[22] As I have already remarked in respect to Bittker and Rahdert's theory, this cannot really stand as *the* fundamental justification for all these exemptions, but it can provide one basis for granting them.

Concerns About the Scope of Coverage

The various justifications as well as the present extent of coverage of nonprofit endeavors raise some fundamental questions about what is really appropriate. What should be done if an otherwise eligible organization is actually violating an important public policy? Should nonprofits really be categorized in these areas differently from for-profit enterprises that are providing similar services? What should be done about organizations that are built to provide benefits to their own members? Do present exemptions undesirably favor the wealthy? How should educational institutions be treated? This last question provides an example both of concerns about the well-to-do and comparison with other organizations providing similar services. It also carries over to the topics of private deductions and property tax exemptions explored in subsequent sections.

VIOLATIONS OF PUBLIC POLICY

Clearly, if an organization otherwise entitled to an exemption is doing something deeply at odds with fundamental justice or crucial public concerns, its exemptions should be removed. The notable case involving this kind of question was *Bob Jones University v. United States,* which after *Brown v. Board of Education* and the 1964 federal statute barring much racial discrimination, maintained a policy against interracial dating among its students. The Supreme Court accepted the Internal Revenue Service's interpretation of the tax exemption statute as not covering an educational institution engaged in racial discrimination.[23] Although the agency's reading of the statute may have involved a degree of stretch, and the Supreme Court's approval may have been justified partly on grounds of basic constitutional principles, without doubt, legislatures or courts properly preclude exemptions for organizations that deeply offend central public values. Just how far this should reach institutions like Bob Jones University, which perform important public services but in their internal life follow religious convictions that are at odds with public policy, is debatable; but no doubt the deep worry about continuing racial segregation played a role in that decision.

Obviously, the argument *against* an exemption for those violating public values has a much wider potential coverage. Opponents of an exemption from laws barring sexual orientation discrimination often rely on the racial analogue. In Chapter 8 on same-sex marriage and sexual orientation, I address the question of how convincing the comparison with racial discrimination is for what individuals and institutions should now be allowed to do. Of course, between the granting of a complete exemption and the outright barring of divergences in treatment lies the intermediate possibility of the *Bob Jones University* case: removing a tax exemption but not directly forbidding the behavior itself.

THE FOR-PROFIT COMPARISON

No one asserts that ordinary for-profit businesses engaged in providing valuable services for which people are ready and willing to pay full value should get tax exemptions. These are the obvious entities to be taxed if the income of organizations should ever be taxed. However, Anup Malani and Eric A. Posner have urged that when for-profit corporations are providing services similar to those of nonprofit charities and are relying at least partly on donations, they may be just as effective as the nonprofits and should also receive exemptions.[24] Recognizing that this proposal will strike many as unacceptably bold,[25] the authors also suggest a more modest change that would allow those operating nonprofit organizations to receive a "fixed fraction of profits" as an incentive to increase the efficiency of operations.[26]

MEMBER BENEFITS

Whether organizations set up to benefit the members themselves should receive exemptions is a genuine question,[27] one that can be analyzed at two different levels. At the relatively simple level, we can assume that the organization provides ordinary facilities and services to its members. A nonprofit tennis club would be a good example. One issue is whether this provides a genuine public benefit. If the members are simply satisfying their own desires, why should their organization get favored treatment from the government? On the other hand, if a few people in a neighborhood got together and built a tennis court, kept it in good condition, and shared its use, their expenditures would not count as income to their own informal grouping. (Of course, insofar as they paid outsiders to keep the courts in shape, that would count as income for the workers.) If rather than the informal grouping, the interested players chose to establish a formal organization to which they pay dues that are used to keep the tennis courts operating, why should that count as income for the organization? Considering these straightforward, competing reasons, one might reasonably conclude that an exemption is or is not warranted.

This brings us to the deeper value of organizational autonomy, and more narrowly to church–state relations. The creation of private organizations is usually healthy, even if their overarching objective is to serve their members. Such organizations, even sports clubs, can give individuals a sense of belonging and of community with some or all fellow members. That may itself be desirable enough to support an exemption strategy that encourages such associations.

Within this broader category lie many churches and other religious bodies for which community worship is a central element. Spending money to build beautiful churches and support the worshiping of God is a kind of benefit for members, but in human history it is a special one. That the government should largely keep its hands off the functioning of churches is widely accepted as a core value in American history, embodied in both the Free Exercise and Establishment Clauses of the First Amendment. Most religious bodies also provide needed services to the poor and until relatively recently were the main source of such help. One *might* see such help as the primary reason to treat churches like secular charities and urge that drawing any line depending on how much of this help a church provides is too difficult for the government to administer. But most citizens of this country would not believe that is the overriding justification for a church exemption. They would take the core function of providing worship of God as, by itself, a basis for similar treatment. This conclusion about religious groups can itself provide a ground not to treat differently nonreligious, nonprofit organizations that are built to provide benefits to members.

FAVORING THE WEALTHY?

Both for many organizations that provide member benefits, especially those not primarily engaged in religious worship, and for many charities that provide public services, the primary financial support comes from those whose financial status is well above average. Whether one is focusing on taxing organizations' income, on individual contributions, or on property taxes, does it make sense to afford this financial advantage to the wealthy?

If the tax exemptions actually enhance the quality and costs of services provided to those who are much less well off, the fact that they reduce costs to wealthy contributors is hardly a concern. And even if one doubts that the government is basically saving money, it is, after all, not the wealthy in general who are benefitting, it is only those who have voluntarily chosen to contribute to the welfare of others in the society. They do not actually save or make money by contributing to the Red Cross or some other charity. If one is genuinely concerned about inequality of wealth, a more general raising of taxes on those with high income may well make more sense than an elimination of tax exemptions for the charitable organizations to which only some of the more wealthy contribute.

The concern about favoring the wealthy becomes greater if the organization receiving the exemption primarily benefits members of that class. This would be true both about organizations that are formally "for members" and others, like art museums and opera houses, which are mainly attended by the well-to-do. One may still defend exemptions here as preserving important cultural values that warrant this indirect degree of government subsidy.

EDUCATIONAL AND OTHER INSTITUTIONS

The concerns about member benefits, favoring the wealthy, and for-profit comparison noted in the last three sections apply to private universities[28] and some other kinds of institutions, such as hospitals. Both universities and hospitals depend heavily on receiving payments from most of those (or their parents or insurers) who receive the services they provide. And insofar as they also receive donations, these come from those who are financially secure. When it comes to private universities, many of them, especially prestigious ones, provide services that mainly go to those whose parents have higher education and above-average financial status. Of course, the education these institutions provide may not only help the graduating individuals but a broader public that benefits from the abilities they acquire, many of which contribute to the technological skills and advances in the United States that make possible its key role in the world's economy. But this aspect raises the question whether nonprofit universities should get benefits not available to for-profit universities.

Historically, much of education was provided by organizations connected to religious bodies, and such organizations have not disappeared. Although that historical explanation for special treatment is not in itself an actual modern justification for a broad set of exemptions, the value of universities and their organizational autonomy still remain vital factors. In some American states, the dominant universities are connected to the government, but in many, private universities continue to have great importance. These typically do receive substantial government assistance, so they are not completely independent, but one may reasonably conclude that preserving the degree of independence they now have is valuable[29] and that the tax exemption helps to promote that. Finally, if one regards exemptions as appropriate not only for charities but for member-benefiting organizations, it would be hard to defend that and also propose eliminating exemptions for universities, given that one might see the students and their parents who pay tuition as kinds of "members" in a broad sense who benefit from what they pay and how they participate. Whether exemptions should be denied to for-profit educational institutions presents a hard question.

Income Tax Deductions for Individuals

Another form of tax benefit—not technically an exemption but operating with a similar effect—is a reduction of a person's income tax based on contributions to charitable organizations, government entities, veterans organizations, and cemetery companies.[30] Charitable deductions were first made part of federal law by the War Revenue Act of 1917.[31] The way a deduction operates is that one can reduce from one's to-be-taxed income the amount one has contributed. This deductibility can be up to 50 percent of a person's adjusted gross income for contributions to public charities and 30 percent for most private foundations. One then pays according to the tax rate for the income that remains.[32] Thus, if a woman in a 30 percent tax bracket has donated $10,000 to her church or to the Red Cross, she will actually save $3,000 in taxes.

The basic reasons for the deductions overlap with those supporting tax exemptions for the organizations: they will encourage gifts to organizations that effectively contribute to public goods and may save the government from having to supply various services; they help produce organizational autonomy and individual involvement in organizations; and they contribute to people understanding that caring for others is an important part of their lives. Of course, concerns about what counts as income in an ordinary sense do not apply here, although it can be argued that we could fairly characterize the donating of a part of one's salary as a reduction in one's effective sense of income if that giving is not a means to pursue self-advantage or to help those to whom one is personally attached. That logic, of course, has no application for dues paid to an organization that benefits its own members. Indeed, such an organization does not in fact qualify for a deduction, even if the organization itself is free from paying income taxes.[33]

Concerns both about actual effects and wealth distribution apply here, as well as for organizational exemptions. Would people really donate less if they did not receive a tax exemption? In general, that is very hard to say. My own guess would be, based partly on personal experience in the second category, that this may depend for some on whether they are extremely wealthy or not. Perhaps for a person with hundreds of millions of dollars, the yearly income tax is not a major consideration. But if one has sufficient income to contribute something but also is careful not to spend excessively, the tax benefit may likely play a role in how much one donates. It is worth noting in this respect that of the roughly $300 billion of total 2011 charitable contributions, nearly one-third went to religious organizations;[34] these typically have many contributing members who are not wealthy.

The distribution concern here is substantial. Roughly two-thirds of taxpayers choose to take a standard deduction instead of itemizing.[35] It follows that only the remaining one-third can take advantage of deductions for charitable contributions.[36] Of course, this alone does not disadvantage individuals who choose to make substantial contributions because, if they do so, they will have a strong incentive to itemize.

Inequality of tax rates is more worrisome. Suppose two people each donate $10,000. Jean is fairly well off and, both before and after the deduction, has a rate of 30 percent. Michael, much less wealthy, has donated a high percentage of his income for which, before and after, his rate is 10 percent. Michael saves only $1,000 as compared with $3,000 for Jean. One might defend this as encouraging the wealthy to contribute and as being responsive to their respective tax rates, but a fairer form of subsidy might be to give a set tax credit that depends on how much one donates and is not based on one's tax rate.[37]

A quite different issue about federal tax deductions is whether people should continue to get them for the state and local taxes they pay. Such deductions may help nonfederal parts of the government to feel free to charge taxes. Living in New York City, I may be in the location where the deduction matters most. When the taxes are withheld from one's salary, they hardly feel like available income, so the deduction strikes one as appropriate. On the other hand, if a person chooses to live in a city where the government is providing substantial benefits, such as cleaning paths in parks from snow, why should he be paying less to the federal government than someone with a similar salary who resides in an area where such services are lacking? Whether the deduction seems a kind of unfair advantage depends a great deal on how far the collected state and local taxes are largely used to benefit those who provide them or to help those unable to pay.

PROPERTY TAX EXEMPTIONS

Another very important tax benefit is freedom from local property taxes for churches, hospitals, and other charitable organizations.[38] These exemptions derive from the historical practice of not imposing such taxes on churches. The monetary savings for the nonpaying organizations varies hugely. In remote domains, the value of property is fairly low; in the center of major cities, it is extremely high. The main Columbia University campus, not including the medical school and new facilities being constructed, is roughly 36 acres. In Manhattan, that amount of property is worth a lot, and New York University enjoys a yet more central location. Among concerns about these property tax exemptions are that in some areas, they may substantially reduce tax income, that they unfairly benefit excessively facilities located in major cities, and that many elite universities, in contrast to hospitals and churches, are actually largely helping those who come from outside the area and will leave the area once they graduate.[39] One thinks here of institutions such as Harvard, Yale, and Princeton. Why should local taxpayers be effectively subsidizing these benefits that do not go to themselves?

In favor of these exemptions is the idea that having these nonprofit organizations in all communities is important and that calculating the appropriate property value could be troublesome, especially for worship facilities. It would be regrettable if churches and hospitals were discouraged from remaining in the central part of large cities because property taxes were too high. And if one thinks of a famous church like St. Patrick's

Cathedral, how would its property be valued? Should the calculation be based on what a nonreligious enterprise would pay to take over the land and construct a large office building, or should it be based on what another religious group might pay for it? An added concern here would be about administrative neutrality: would those assessing value be affected by whether they were dealing with a religion they favored or disliked? Yet another complication was one St. Bartholomew's faced when it wanted to sell its community building adjacent to its church. It could not do so because the facility was covered by a historic preservation law. If no one could build a different construction on the spot, that would of course radically affect the market value of a property.

In relation to the benefits afforded outsiders, it is also true that the universities I mentioned are important contributors in various ways to the economies of the towns in which they are located. The property of Princeton University, for example, is a large part of the town of Princeton; the fact that the university is there has meant a great deal to the growth of the township.

Although in some areas the relief from property taxes may actually impose a substantial burden on the community, that can be partly relieved if the organizations make some payments in lieu of taxes (PILOTS) or services in lieu of taxes (SILOTS).[40] As with the other tax benefits, multiple factors bear on the justification for property tax exemptions and their desirable scope, which itself is genuinely contestable in some instances.

Conclusion

Without trying to arrive at precise recommendations, this chapter has explored various bases for central tax exemptions and deductions. Here, what is in the public interest, including the desirability of autonomous organizations helping citizens, is the central basis for a privilege, not what violates an individual's conscience. And the primary grounds for disfavoring privileges are not discrimination or the denial to particular individuals of required services but the necessity for government revenues. Although tax benefits are in those ways fundamentally different from most other existing and proposed exemptions, subsequent chapters nonetheless reveal certain overlaps in what relevant considerations should count.

4

Forbidden Substances

Introduction

THIS CHAPTER CONSIDERS whether when the national or a state government decides to ban the use of various substances, it should ever grant exemptions, and if so, what these should look like. The main thesis of the chapter is simple: exemptions are sometimes warranted, but their appropriate scope is radically different than with respect both to draft exemptions and tax privileges. The lines between unconnected individuals and organizational members and between the religious and nonreligious are here much more defensible than for pacifists. However, as with draft exemptions, initial legislative choices that are specific are highly desirable, although some coverage under generally worded statutes, such as the Religious Freedom Restoration Act, and under broad constitutional provisions, should also be granted. Here, as in other chapters, the great importance of context is illustrated. With even modest reflection, one can see why sensible approaches to proposed exemptions differ so greatly depending on what is involved.

Forbidden Substances and Why Exemptions May Make Sense

Governments forbid their citizens from eating, drinking, or smoking substances primarily because their ingestion is seen as harmful or dangerous. Moral judgments can also be involved here, but these are based on the physical and psychological effects the substances create. I am assuming in what follows that at least in the United States and most other countries the basis for such a prohibition is itself grounded on natural human appraisals of harm, not the idea that ingestion of a particular kind of food, such as pork or beef, that has no apparent negative effects violates a religious premise about God's commandments. The basic reasons for prohibiting people from ingesting a substance is that their doing so directly creates a serious risk of harm to themselves or is likely to generate their engaging in dangerous behavior, or may encourage others to use, who will then be subject to those risks. In the case of alcohol, for example, those who drink both heavily and persistently risk their physical well-being and their ability to function positively in family relations and vocations. Even moderate use can lead to impaired automobile driving that causes fatal accidents. With heroin, the risk that death will be caused by an individual overdose or a dose that includes an unexpected dangerous ingredient is significant.

In addition to straightforward risks of physical impairment, one may believe that ingestion of certain substances can have psychological effects that lead to undesirable perceptions, attitudes, and behavior. Again, alcohol provides a familiar illustration. Apart from physical risks, people who become "high" or "drunk" may sometimes act irresponsibly or inconsiderately toward others.

A reader may be puzzled by my use of alcohol as an example. After all, although some American counties remain "dry," and restrictions on the sale and use of alcohol are still common, an outright prohibition on drinking is far removed from present political possibilities in most parts of the country. Nonetheless, in our history, that use was once widely forbidden and still is not allowed for minors. More importantly, the effects of use of alcohol are the most obvious for members of a modern society.

Another point that reflection on alcohol clearly illustrates is that whether a prohibition of substance use is practically feasible depends significantly on how far use of that substance is already entrenched within a culture. A viable prohibition is extremely difficult if drinking or smoking is too pervasive to allow effective enforcement. Of course, a legal ban may still discourage some people from using, and it can send a kind of symbolic message, but the costs of having obviously frequent violations and of generating the criminal behaviors of those supplying the substance are significant. These are among the reasons prohibitions on the sale and ingestion of alcohol have been repealed. They are also the reasons an outright ban on smoking tobacco, which is clearly bad for the health of many users,[1] is not seen as a genuine option at this time.

An effective ban on the sale and use of substances must involve substances that are not taken pervasively throughout a society. In the United States, such prohibitions have been adopted for drugs like heroin, cocaine, marijuana, peyote, and methamphetamine. Of course, a fundamental initial question is whether any prohibition of a particular drug is itself justified. That has become a key issue for marijuana, and four states and the District of Columbia have repealed prohibitions, except regarding use by minors.[2] One argument against forbidding use is that if ingestion by most people is either actually desirable or harmless, that offsets the fact that a few users may suffer. Additional reasons can be the costs or ineffectiveness of enforcement and that treating users as criminals may itself be undesirable. Keeping people in jail is expensive, and few marijuana users are likely to develop positively as persons because of harsh prison conditions.[3] Perhaps it is better to use resources to help those who have suffered from overuse. Nevertheless, the risk of harm from some substances *can* be great enough to warrant outright prohibition. And the competing considerations about legalizing or not are actually less than simple in crucial respects. The concern about unproductive jail time could be countered by setting up a system of administrative courts that requires users of illegal drugs to be subject to various constraints, such as frequent testing (with brief confinement if use has continued) rather than ordinary criminal sentencing.[4] And, if in the absence of prohibition, high taxation is employed to discourage widespread use, an extensive black market of illegal sales is virtually certain to continue and still require substantial enforcement efforts and expenses.[5] People can reasonably reach different conclusions about whether the ingestion of particular substances should be forbidden, but most assume that a prohibition remains desirable in respect to heroin and cocaine.

Can it be both that a general prohibition *and* an exemption are warranted? For those who believe that absent an extremely high risk of danger—for example, that one out of every fifty times a substance is ingested, the user dies—no prohibitions are called for, it may follow that desirable prohibitions should never carry exemptions. But for people who think general prohibitions need not rest on such extreme dangers, certain exemptions can make sense. And even those who believe a prohibition itself is unsound may conclude that if one is nevertheless adopted, certain special circumstances call for exemptions. Similar questions can arise if prohibitions are limited to minors; should any exceptions allow minors to ingest a particular substance in some circumstances?

One obvious basis for an exemption is a medical need. Perhaps a drug, such as marijuana, can help persons subject to certain illnesses. Any medical exemption creates risks of fraudulent claims and the possible broader availability of a substance, but these worries would not usually be sufficient to defeat allowing a use authorized by doctors as highly beneficial for medical patients.[6] In the remainder of the chapter, I put aside this ground for an exemption and also disregard more complicated laws about various substances that preclude general use but permit some uses beyond medical needs and experimentation. I concentrate on claims of people in normal conditions whose physical reaction to a drug is not unusual. Can there nonetheless be reasons to afford an exemption, and, if so, what should such an exemption look like?

Peyote and Exemptions, and a Comparison with Alcohol

For various reasons, people can believe that use of a substance is so positive for them that they should be allowed to ingest it even if a general prohibition may be warranted. The most important legal cases involving such claims have concerned peyote being employed as a crucial element of religious services.

The Native American Church, whose membership was estimated at 250,000 in 1996, uses peyote as the center its ceremonies and practices.

This use is long-standing, reported by sixteenth-century Spanish sources in Mexico, and well established by the latter part of the nineteenth century in the United States. Members of the Native American Church, many of whom accept certain Christian teachings, believe that peyote embodies the Holy Spirit and allows its partakers to have direct contact with God. According to the California Supreme Court in 1964,[7] the sacramental use of peyote, taken "in quantities sufficient to produce an hallucinatory state," is "the cornerstone of the peyote religion." Use for nonreligious purposes is taken by members to be sacrilegious.[8]

This use of peyote shares a fundamental similarity with the Roman Catholic consumption of wine in communion but also differs in two important ways. For Roman Catholics, and some other Christian religions, wine as an aspect of communion is either necessary or highly desirable because of the belief that at the Last Supper, Jesus asked his apostles to eat bread and drink wine as a representation of his body and blood before his being crucified. For Roman Catholics who, unlike most Protestants, believe that a transubstantiation actually takes place of consecrated wine at the time of communion, substitution of grape juice or another liquid is not acceptable. The sacramental use of wine at communion has consistently been permitted when other uses of alcohol have been legally prohibited, and even now it is allowed for minors, who are otherwise not supposed to drink it.

One way in which the sacramental use of peyote differs from wine at communion is obvious: the amount and effects are radically different. Except for priests who after services subsume leftover consecrated wine, the amount drunk is very small; it neither gives one the feeling of being "high," which is the major appeal of alcohol for many people, nor does it create the negative effects of drunkenness. In these respects, its only risk of danger is that a small sip of wine in a religious service *may* lead some to seek more to drink when the service is over. By contrast, the use of peyote within the Native American Church does produce a hallucinogenic state not radically different from what an individual user may experience.

This point is related to a second variation. Virtually no one has a strong interest in taking a tiny sip of wine in ordinary life, whereas individuals may believe their personal use of peyote benefits them in ways not so different from those claimed by members of the Native American Church in their services. Their experiences may themselves be seen as religious. In defending against a prosecution for importation of marijuana, the once well-known Timothy Leary asserted that he belonged to a branch of Hinduism that encouraged its use as a way to enhance meditation.[9] When the effect claimed as a basis for an exemption resembles ordinary consumption in important ways, that can constitute an argument against granting any special privilege to use. It can also render more difficult the question of how exactly to draw the line if such an exemption is to be granted.

Despite these difficulties, the argument in favor of according an exemption that allows members of the Native American Church to use peyote in their services is very powerful. The California Supreme Court ruled in 1964 that indeed the federal Free Exercise Clause conferred such a right.[10] The U.S. Supreme Court's later sharp restriction on what that clause directly protects dealt with a similar case. The two claimants then had not actually been prosecuted; in fact, the state was not trying to enforce its criminal prohibition against those who used peyote in Native American services. But given that the two members had lost their jobs because they had violated the criminal statute, the validity of that prohibition became the key issue in *Employment Division v. Smith*.[11] The majority in an opinion by Justice Scalia held that no Free Exercise right exists to violate a law that has general coverage and is not directed against religion.

The Scalia opinion unpersuasively suggests that things may be different if a free exercise claim is joined in a hybrid with another constitutional argument. Drawing such a distinction between hybrid claims and those based exclusively on free exercise does not make sense for three reasons. (1) The approach requires a difficult judgment of just when another clause is also genuinely involved. (2) It is wildly implausible that a free exercise argument could consistently carry weight in hybrid situations and *never* be sufficient by itself. (3) The evaluation in a hybrid context of free exercise would require exactly the kind of difficult contextual assessment that is Scalia's whole basis for rejecting the then dominant Free Exercise Clause approach.

Justice Scalia's opinion is clear that a legislature can, if it chooses, make accommodations to free exercise concerns, even though it does not have to do so. Scalia's concern that courts should not be required to determine whether exemption claims succeed under vague legal criteria, like those in the previous free exercise doctrine, could be taken to imply that specific legislative determinations are far preferable to inconclusive general standards; however, the opinion does not rule out even the latter approach so long as a legislature adopts it.

Congress with virtual unanimity did just that shortly after *Employment Division v. Smith*. It passed the Religious Freedom Restoration Act (RFRA), which effectively reinstated the constitutional doctrine that preceded the Supreme Court's sharp curtailment.[12] Intended to apply against both the federal and state governments, the act stated that "Governments may not substantially burden a person's exercise of religion even if the burden results from a rule of general applicability . . . [unless] it demonstrates that application of the burden to the person (1) is in furtherance of a compelling governmental interest; and (2) is the least restrictive means of furthering that . . . interest." The Supreme Court subsequently held that RFRA was invalid as it applied to state governments because Congress has no power to reject the Supreme Court's ruling about what the federal constitution requires, and it lacks any other basis to undercut the application of state laws in this way.[13] However, given the authority of Congress over federal statutes and federal executive actions, the Court later ruled that the act could apply to federal laws. On this basis, it sustained a claimed right, holding that the Controlled Substance Act could not bar the importation of an otherwise covered hallucinogenic tea used by a small group in religious ceremonies.[14]

Bases for Exemptions Allowing Use of Forbidden Substances and the Issues Needing Resolution

When it comes to drug use or other possible exemptions, we can conceive of four possible legal bases to do what an otherwise valid law forbids. The first is that a claimant has a direct constitutional right under a general free exercise standard. Although this approach has been rejected for the federal clause, some states have continued to interpret their own constitutions to provide such a right. The second basis is that a federal or state statute grants a specific right to engage in that behavior. Third, a claim may rely on a more general statutory standard that can be construed to confer the right. Thus, under RFRA, people can claim that a law imposes a substantial burden on their exercise of religion and that the government either lacks a compelling interest in enforcement or could achieve that objective by an alternative means. (A word of caution is needed about "compelling interest" in this context. For claims of exemption from otherwise valid laws, the courts never have insisted on interests as compelling as are needed to justify categorizations that impair racial minorities or interfere with freedom of speech. Although recent cases leave it a bit unclear just how strict the Supreme Court's majority will now be, what has been involved is a kind of "intermediate" scrutiny, less severe than "strict scrutiny" but more rigorous than "rational basis."[15]) The fourth possible argument for exemption is a different constitutional claim, namely that if an exemption is given to one group of persons, it cannot be denied to another similar group. Most simply, one religion cannot be favored over another that does not radically vary from it in some crucial and relevant respect.

Without engaging in just how far constitutional principles rather than statutory standards should determine exemptions, we can turn to what lines make sense if an exemption is being considered for the Native American Church and possibly other users of peyote. Should an exemption cover individual use or only use within group meetings? Should the only eligible group meetings be religious ceremonies for which ingesting peyote is very important? Is it acceptable to single out the Native American Church or to distinguish in some other way between eligible and ineligible religious associations? Is it desirable for a legislature to focus specifically on all or some of these issues or to leave their resolution to judges applying a general standard like that of RFRA?

We can quickly see that if an exemption were extended to individual use beyond prescribed medical needs, any general prohibition could be seriously undermined, although this effect would be reduced if ingestion of the drug is unpleasant, as may be true for peyote. One problem would be ascertaining who genuinely qualifies. Whether or not a claim to use relied on a religious basis, such as that made by Timothy Leary, how could officials decide if the claim was genuine? For every individual who claimed a right to ingest a forbidden drug, government officials would hardly be in a position to undertake a close investigation about sincerity and intensity of conviction. And with a hallucinogenic drug as it applies to individual users, saying what counts as religious is itself extremely difficult. If a woman claims that the drug allows her to achieve a deeper insight into universal reality and its fundamental governing spirit, is that by itself religious? Another difficulty is that if individuals are given the right to use peyote by themselves in their own locations, what is to prevent others, with or without their consent, from taking part of their supply and using it? In short, when it comes to forbidden substances, creating exemptions for individual users does not ordinarily make sense.

One might see an exception to this if to qualify one needs to be a member of a particular group that regards use as religiously important, and it is not easy for outsiders to join or claim to be members. Something like this is involved in the proposal that members of Rastafari be able to use cannabis (of which marijuana is one category) in Great Britain.[16] Generally, however, if one comes to believe that the benefits of the drug are substantial and its dangers not very great, the wise course is to allow its general use, at least by adults; and this is the movement that is taking place in parts of the United States for marijuana.

Allowing general use is, of course, an alternative to exemptions; if one believes some use is definitely warranted, deciding which approach makes better sense depends on multiple factors, including the harm of ordinary use and the costs of enforcement. If any exemptions are to be granted for substances whose use is otherwise prohibited, they should be limited to ingestion within group meetings, at which time the amount for each individual is under control, as exists most obviously with wine during Christian communion.

Is it acceptable here to restrict use to religious ceremonies? As earlier chapters have suggested, religious freedom is an important value in this society and in other liberal democracies. A central element for virtually all religions is worship services. It does not follow that groups should be able in those services to do anything in which they sincerely believe; they cannot be allowed to sacrifice human beings, even if those sacrificed somehow consent. But the government should need a strong interest to interfere with the fundamental practices of worship. If it cannot be shown that those who subsume a drug within services are inclined to abusive use outside of that context, if actual use within the services never or rarely causes demonstrable harm, and if evidence is lacking that the presence of the drug within religious services somehow spreads to broader availability in other contexts, then the argument to permit use is very strong. It is just such an analysis that led the 1964 California Supreme Court to determine a free exercise right in favor of the Native American Church. And when the Supreme Court applied RFRA to the importation by the small religious group using a hallucinogenic tea, it similarly discerned a lack of evidence of any substantial harm.[17]

That sufficient reasons exist to protect religious ceremonies does not itself tell us whether nonreligious use within groups should be treated similarly or differently. If the amount ingested is limited and the drug is taken to enrich the understanding and experience of life for the participants, and use does not spread outside, an argument certainly exists for the same treatment. The difficulty is this: if nonreligious groups can use a drug, individuals who wish personally to do so will have an incentive to get together and form a group and to schedule meetings at a convenient time so that what really happens is that the individuals can take the substance for whatever purposes move them. These concerns are fairly powerful reasons not to extend this exemption to nonreligious groups.

That leaves us with two problems, however. One is how to draw the line between religious and nonreligious groups. I have indicated that with respect to individuals, that line is especially hard to draw when it comes down simply to convictions about why taking a drug is valuable. At the edges, the categorization of what counts as religion is never simple,[18] but at least when one asks about what a group is doing when meeting together, certain practices and affirmations are characteristic of most religious bodies. These could be used as an important basis to determine whether a group using peyote or another substance is genuinely religious.

However, there is a second problem. If individuals wanting to use a drug could be tempted to create a nonreligious group, could they not also be tempted to create one that at least on the surface is religious? The California Supreme Court failed to find evidence that use of peyote within the Native American Church had led to broader use and fraudulent claims.[19] If this concern about fraud could not be avoided so simply, it might be addressed in at least one of three ways. Officials could consider how and in what circumstances a group was formed and what its practices consist of in determining if it is genuinely religious. In a case in which that seemed seriously in doubt, a court denied drug use to a Massachusetts group, without explicitly relying on that basis.[20]

A second possibility is to limit the exemption to one or more specific groups, as was done by statutory exemptions for the Native American Church. The problem with this approach is that it, potentially at least, favors some religious groups over others, even when certain groups in the latter category may seem to have as strong reasons to use peyote as those granted the right. A special feature of the Native American Church is that it is made up of a group that suffered severe oppression in the past and that has also been conceded to have a semi-independent culture. Since this possible rationale based on distinctive status has no application for most claims for exemptions, I shall not pursue it here; but it would seem to have less force for Native Americans living within the general society than for those on reservations in which they constitute all or nearly all the residents. As a general principle, we can say that exemptions specifically limited to single religious or nonreligious groups are misguided. But the fundamental idea that closely knit religions and other groups should have a degree of autonomy within a broader society has significance in respect to many exemptions.

A third alternative would be to define necessary conditions for qualifications, such as that the religious group must have existed for at least 50 years, or be spread over a fairly broad area, or have a minimum number of members. None of these requisites seems entirely fair in principle, but they could discourage phony attempts to form ostensibly religious groups in order to use drugs.

This brings us to the question of specificity versus generality. Given that legislatures determine what uses of substances are forbidden, it is sensible for them to address which substances are genuinely part of religious services and whose use therein does not create too great a danger of direct harm or of leading to wider use outside the services. This is one among many areas in which specific legislative focus is desirable. However, both generally worded statutes and constitutional notions of religious equality should also play a role. One cannot expect Congress or state legislatures to focus on every persuasive religious claim to use a substance in worship. If the group is very small, and its members have recently immigrated to the United States, it will almost certainly not have engaged legislative attention here. Also, as far as federal law is concerned, it will be harder to seek a specific concession than within individual states where a group is fairly substantial. These limitations were obviously true for the small group that successfully sought to use RFRA to protect its importation of hallucinogenic tea. It follows that statutes like RFRA, or similar state applications of constitutional free exercise provisions, do play an appropriate role in exemptions for uses of forbidden substances. And standing in the background is also that basic principle of religious equality, which forbids the favoring of one or more religious groups over others that are essentially similar in ways that count.

Conclusion

In many respects, exemptions from use of drugs are special because they allow noncompliance with laws that are basically designed mainly to protect the very people who wish to ingest those substances. As our culture has seen historically with alcohol and more recently with marijuana, exactly what uses should be prohibited and allowed can be highly controversial, but at least for drugs that are not highly dangerous, the argument for exemptions of services of religious worship can be strong. For reasons of overall enforcement and prevention of fraud, it makes sense here to limit exemptions, at least those apart from medical procedures, to use within groups that are actually religious. This is in stark contrast with draft exemptions, which properly depend on individual convictions and, despite actual statutory language, do not require that these convictions be religious in any ordinary sense.

Comparing these illustrations shows why gross generalizations about whether religion and group membership are called for in respect to exemptions are misguided. One needs to focus on exactly what kind of exemption is involved and what is workable for effective administration. As with most major exceptions from statutory requirements, specific legislative focus on the scope of possible exemptions is desirable; but more general formulations such as those in RFRA laws are also important here.

5

Receiving and Participating in Medical Procedures

Introduction

IN MANY RESPECTS, various actual and possible exemptions from medical procedures present issues more diverse and complicated than those concerning the military draft and drug use. For those the questions are whether some persons or groups should be exempt from general government requirements that ordinarily treat disobedience as making one subject to criminal punishment. Although I have noted that what works politically can matter, the chapters' overarching focus has been on what is just and desirable. When we turn to medical procedures, a greater variety of problems present themselves, and many of those carry over to the related following chapter on contraceptive provision.

Because of religious convictions or other reasons, persons may refuse medical treatment, such as a blood transfusion, that would be accepted by nearly everyone else and perhaps be necessary to save their lives. If a woman refuses such treatment, she is the one who directly suffers. For this reason, the key concern here is not about possible punishment but whether she should be compelled to undergo the medical procedure. There are, however, three different ways in which failures to accept medical procedures can affect others. If someone, or her parent, refuses her receiving a vaccination, and later she acquires the illness the vaccination would have prevented, she may communicate that disease more broadly. If a parent with young children refuses lifesaving treatment for himself, he may be indirectly inflicting on others hardships more severe than accompany most deaths severing human relationships. Finally, and most obviously, if children are the ones who will or will not receive medical treatment, and their parents make the decision to decline, the children are the ones who directly suffer physically. In this last context, the questions of both criminal punishments and exemptions are significant.

A relatively minor issue about medical procedures is whether people should be able to claim a right to have them extended, or not extended, beyond what would be normal. This arises mainly in the context of the end of life. If the general practice is to consider someone dead if his brain no longer functions, should family members be able to insist on continued support for a man's body if they believe, for religious or other reasons, that his life has not yet ended? An interesting twist of this question is whether the state may appropriately require that a woman who is both pregnant and brain-dead *must* be kept breathing even if her family believes she should be considered to have died. A statute in Texas that seemed to require this, and was initially applied in that way, was interpreted by a state district court not to do so.[1]

The most pressing issues about medical procedures do not involve rights to refuse treatment or to have it continue beyond its normal course but whether entities or individual professionals should broadly be *required* to provide or assist certain treatment itself, or to finance it directly or indirectly, and, if so, whether exemptions should be granted. This has been a central concern about abortions and particular contraceptives, which, along with same-sex marriage, present the most intensely disputed exemptions issues of our time. Although this reality could be seen as a reason to begin this chapter with abortions, my idea, as with the book in general, is that reflecting on other circumstances can help one's assessment of what is now most controversial and sharply debated.

Beyond what it directly requires, what should the government do about the relations between individuals who provide services and the hospitals or other medical enterprises for whom they work? How far should it restrain the enterprises from reacting in certain ways to the choices of those who work for them? That has almost certainly been the most important feature of legislation regarding abortions. It is a slight stretch to characterize all such provisions as "exemptions" in the ordinary sense. Putting aside professionals, such as doctors, with legal duties, and government workers who can be seen as required by law to perform their tasks, provisions according rights of conscience to employees reach beyond their nonconformance with legal responsibilities; rather, they impose a legal constraint on when private organizations may discipline or dismiss individuals who do not carry out tasks set by the organizations. In effect, the law then requires private enterprises to provide exemptions from their own duties.

When providing medical services is at stake, possible harms for others constitute a much more direct concern than occurs with draft exemptions. These risks sharply raise the question of whether any exemption is warranted, and if so, whether it should be absolute or qualified in terms of how much a person's involvement in a service is needed. Although the primary concern here about the harm others may suffer is physical well-being, one may also worry whether granting various exemptions will convey an undesirable symbolic message. This question involves the relative status of autonomy of choice, respect for the dignity and welfare of others, and equality. Within our society, people can strongly disagree about the respective force of these considerations in particular settings, a reality that is part of the reason why exemptions in respect to same-sex marriage are so sharply disputed.

Somewhat related to possible exemptions for certain medical procedures is how far government funding should be granted or restricted to perform them. This has been an important feature of Congress's response to abortion rights.

This chapter explores in some depth the comparative advantages and disadvantages of preset specific legislative standards versus general provisions implemented by courts; it also notes the possibility of intermediate formulations. Specific rules can have the advantage of not seeming to allow actions contrary to existing legal requirements; and they provide clearer information about what is permitted. They may also sometimes encourage, rather than defeat, what is seen as social progress.[2] On the other hand, general standards can allow protections for circumstances not easily foreseen, and they may help to protect unpopular minorities for which legislators would be disinclined to provide specific protection. Standards cast in general terms may also make it somewhat easier for the content of exemptions to shift with appraisals by judges and other officials responsive to basic developments in dominant cultural values. Although my focus is on what approaches are best, given the values of our liberal democracy, what will work politically at any point in time can also matter greatly for what is proposed and supported, a reality that has strongly influenced legislation about both abortion and same-sex marriage.

Basic Decisions to Refuse Medical Treatment

A basic and general right to make a decision for oneself or one's children is not, of course, an "exemption." Nor would a fundamental privilege of doctors to determine medical treatment constitute one. If sometimes treatment depends on a patient's choice and sometimes the doctor's decision, we might see either as an exception, or exemption, from ordinary standards of whose judgment controls. In this way, we can understand the granting of an across-the-board right to make a decision as essentially like what previous chapters have characterized as alternatives to exemptions. In any event, in considering whether people should be able to determine what medical procedures to accept, it is crucial to ask whether all who are mentally competent should have that right.

ADULTS

Whether people should in principle have an absolute right to refuse medical treatment for themselves raises fundamental questions of morality and political philosophy, but the sensible practical answer is not difficult. I put aside here what should be done about those incapable of making ordinary choices because they are physically severely incapacitated or mentally ill. Should ordinary men and women ever be required to accept medical procedures they choose to decline? Of course, in various circumstances, an individual doctor or hospital may tell a patient that if he refuses an aspect of needed treatment they provide, he should look elsewhere, but should he be *forced* to take a procedure he rejects?

The basic arguments for individual choices are clear. If the benefits and risks are uncertain, the person who stands to gain or lose should have the autonomy to choose. Respect for this autonomy is indeed how medical practice has developed over the past half century, as doctors have provided more complete information to patients. What if the degrees of impairment and risk are actually well established? A woman in an automobile accident has suffered a severe infection in her left leg; she is told that if the leg is not amputated, she will have a 50 percent chance of dying. Although she cannot foresee all the consequences of living without a leg, the decision is rightly hers whether assuring longer life is worth that disadvantage. Yet another aspect of choice concerns pain. Suppose a man suffers from terminal illness; he may either undergo a treatment that will cause severe pain and likely help him to live for about three more years, or he will probably die within six months. Again, this choice is rightly left to the individual.

In principle, serious doubts can be raised if a person's reason for refusing treatment is an actual wish to die or rests on an obviously unreasonable appraisal of likely consequences. Although not criminally punishable for attempting to kill themselves, people generally do not have a right to commit suicide. If a man takes a huge overdose of drugs with that objective, and others become aware of that, efforts will be made to extract them from his system, whatever his actual and perceived wishes. Whether persons with severe and painful terminal illness should be able to take their own lives, and even get help from others in doing so, is now controversial; a few people may even believe in a broader moral right to commit suicide, so long as the choice is not a consequence of serious mental illness. In terms of actual capacity, most people are capable of taking their lives, regardless of the law; but if the general premise in our society is that people should be prevented from suicide when possible, does it not follow that they should lack a right to refuse medical treatment when motivated by the same objective?

This is a place where practical considerations come in. If patients who are not mentally ill have the right to refuse treatment based on their assessment of risks and their wishes to avoid severe pain or other unpleasant reactions, how are doctors and others to single out those whose negative response is based on an actual desire to die? If a patient were aware that such a line would be drawn, he could just say, "I don't want to suffer all that pain" or "I think for me the risks of treatment are much greater than you've indicated." Even if he first says, "Forget about it, I want to die as soon as possible," and the doctor rejects that choice, he may respond, "Well, anyway, I don't want to suffer the physical pain that goes with this." In brief, whatever efforts doctors should make to persuade, a legal rule that allows refusal of treatment on every other ground but a wish to die is not viable.

The concern about irrational choice is subject to similar analysis. If people cling to definite misconceptions about risks and benefits, we can see an argument for overriding their choices. But determining just when a choice crosses the border of irrationality is very difficult, especially considering that the person *may* have a more accurate sense about how pain affects her and of what her future life is likely to be if she does or does not undergo an operation. Relevant to all this is the powerful capability of doctors to actually persuade patients in dire conditions about what will be best for them.

These realities lead to the conclusion that, at least for people of ordinary competence, the choice to receive medical procedures is properly theirs. And that is the present law. *If* one reached the contrary conclusion, the question of religious exemption would raise itself. For example, if irrational by ordinary standards, should a Jehovah's Witness refusal to receive a blood transfusion based on biblical sources, or a Christian Scientist's declining of physical medicine, be accepted because of their religious convictions? This becomes a serious and genuine issue when those needing procedures are minors.

Before addressing treatment of minors, I shall note that one might believe that parents of small children should not have rights to refuse medical procedures for themselves as absolute as those possessed by others. A society might take the view that having engaged in acts that yield developing persons who are heavily dependent on them, parents should be obligated to act reasonably to preserve their own lives and maintain their physical health. There are two reasons to reject limiting the right to choose for these parents. One is the difficulty of determining when a choice is irrational. The other is that given other ways parents can avoid responsibilities to their children, such as putting them up for adoption, or divorcing and leaving care to one's former spouse, forcing medical treatment in order to assure care seems out of line with other allowed practices. Even if one agrees with this conclusion, one might think that pregnant women, who have reached beyond the stage at which they can have an abortion, should not be able to refuse treatment if the consequence will be that they will not give birth to the child.

MINORS

The concerns about choice become much more significant when minors may need a medical procedure. These situations involve the basic question about how far the actual range of wishes of parents to refuse treatment, or to not seek medical help, should control when others are in a position to override their choice. Also important, and much more controversial, is how far standards of criminal liability should reach for decisions that are reckless or negligent according to ordinary legal standards and that do result in death or serious physical harm. Especially in respect to criminal liability, whether religious exceptions should be afforded is far from simple. A different problem is when minors should be considered to have reached an age when they can make all or some choices about medical procedures for themselves, with or without parental agreement.

Let us start with children who are indisputably of an age at which the decisions of their parents would ordinarily determine their medical help. Should hospitals, doctors, or other medical personnel be able to override parental choices, and should it matter whether the parents are resting on religious convictions? When competing choices fall within the range of reasonableness, parents clearly have the right to decide. Reasonableness includes now only an appraisal of the probabilities of particular harms and benefits but how much these matter comparatively. Among other reasons, were parental choices frequently overridden, that might have the unfortunate consequence of leading parents to hesitate to visit doctors or take their children to medical facilities.

However, suppose that by ordinary standards of appraisal, a choice, conscious or not, is really unreasonable. Parents have a duty to afford decent care for their children. If they are generally failing to do so, the state may intervene and supply that care, notably by removing the children from parental custody. If the parents are simply failing to provide obviously required medical care, a state official aware of this can see that it is given.

Does it matter if what the parents are doing, or failing to do, depends on a self-conscious decision that takes into account all relevant factors and is not the result of mere negligence based on casual ignorance or on a recklessness that risks severe harm to a child by giving far too much priority to other things the parents care about? An example of the latter would be parents leaving a small child with a severe and dangerous illness alone because they wish to enjoy themselves at a party. More narrowly, does it matter if the parents' self-conscious decision is grounded in their religious belief about what is right for the child?

We may begin here with how society should see its responsibility for children as relating to that of parents. One might conceive of children as basically members of a broad community, with special responsibilities assigned to parents only because that works well. At the other extreme, one might regard children as fundamentally attached to parents in kinds of small independent communities. This latter view could grant parents absolute authority to make decisions about their offspring so long as these do not impair the interests of others outside their families. In modern liberal democracies, obviously neither of these extremes is socially accepted, although it is at least arguable that the actual view about this of particular parents, or of larger collections of parents within groups, should bear on whether they get an exemption. If parental choices seem plainly harmful for the children, the state is widely regarded as free to intervene; but parents, as others acknowledge, widely feel that they have an intrinsic stake in the lives of their children and an authority to make choices that is not based solely on what works well for society. This intermediate position affords parents considerable latitude to make decisions about their children, but without conferring on them completely unconstrained discretion. Even if parents believe on the basis of ordinary reasons that they should not subject a child to standard medical procedures, that decision can be overridden if the choice is clearly misguided in terms of the child's welfare.

Does it matter if the basis for parental judgment is religious conviction? Two basic reasons present themselves. The first is that, especially with close-knit religious groups, like the Amish and Hasidic Jews, it is much easier to think of those than individual families as basic communities, which do and should enjoy substantial independence from the broader society. The second reason is the evaluation of what is good for the child. A Christian Scientist may well believe that spiritual healing will work much better than ordinary medicine. And imagine a faithful Jehovah's Witness who is convinced that God has forbidden blood transfusions. She may believe not only that it is wrong for her to authorize such a transfusion but also that if a failure to do so results in the child's death on this earth, that consequence will both meet God's wishes and lead to life after death for the child within heaven. Once one brings into play the idea that existence on this earth may be only an early stage of eternal life, saying what is *really* in the child's best interest becomes essentially indeterminable. On both the bases of religious community and this broadened scope of a child's "welfare," some religious parents believe they have special grounds to decide against ordinary reason about what is best for their child. They can further assert that, whatever their exact range for creating legal rights, federal and state constitutional protections of free exercise reflect this value. However, within a liberal democracy, it is an implicit premise that beyond what they decide about their own lives, people are constrained by what is "welfare" in terms of life on this earth.

In one of the most important free exercise cases, *Wisconsin v. Yoder*,[3] the Supreme Court declared that the Amish had the right to remove their fourteen-year-old children from schools after eighth grade, despite a state law that required attendance up to the age of sixteen. Given that most Amish children did stay within that community and that, once leaving school, they were engaged in practices that prepared them for life within it, the Court concluded that an exemption was called for. Whether this decision now stands, despite the determination in *Employment Division v. Smith*[4] that people have no free exercise right to violate general laws, is both tricky and not very important for our purposes. It is tricky because in *Smith,* Justice Scalia distinguished *Yoder* as being based on a hybrid right of free exercise and parental rights. As Chapter 4 indicates, a crucial reliance on whether a claim is hybrid, with necessary weight coming from each of two constitutional provisions, is wholly implausible as a general approach.[5] Not surprisingly, lower court judges have not picked up on that as an effective strategy.

The exact status of *Yoder* at this stage of history is much less significant for this chapter than the values for which it stands. One is that religious claims of this variety should be given much more force than nonreligious ones, both because of the value of free exercise and because of the dangers of fraud if any claim of conscience is treated similarly. The second is that the religious claim should succeed only if it is not outweighed by a contrary general interest. The opinion strongly implies that were a religious group opposed to *all* ordinary education, it could not deny to its children the basic abilities to read and write and to learn about many fundamental aspects of reality.

In our modern times, the extent to which parents should be able to provide home education for their children has been a serious question in many states. The laws that provide this require what is adequate education by ordinary standards. The question raised by *Wisconsin v. Yoder* is how far religious groups should be able to fall short on that. One can see here both issues about religion and group membership. That most youngsters would remain within the group, carrying on lives for which further education was unneeded and could actually be disquieting, was a key factor in *Yoder*. That prospect of lives within the group is a strong reason not to allow individual parents whose children will function in the general society to have a similar privilege, whether their basis to deny education is religious or not. What of a very close-knit nonreligious group with a moral sense that the advanced ways of living are wrong, one that carries on its communal life without the need for much education? We can *conceive* of such a group, but I am unaware of any that has held together over time. If a group with such an outlook did exist, and if it retained most of its youngsters, it would have a fairly strong argument to be treated like the Amish, even if that were not constitutionally required.

How do these general observations about medical and other decisions by parents fit with what is and should be the law? That answer is straightforward in certain respects but quite the opposite in others, partly because the issue of criminal liability is hard to resolve, is treated differently in various states, and is often confusing in certain respects. We can phrase the three concerns about legal rights and liability as follows: (1) When should parental choices about medical care be overridden if an opportunity to do so presents itself? (2) If a parental choice made from religious conviction would be irresponsible by ordinary standards, should the parents be criminally and civilly liable for child neglect if the child suffers harm? (3) If the child actually dies as a consequence, should the parent be guilty of manslaughter or even murder, and should that ever vary from the approach to the crime of neglect?

In respect to the first concern, both the sensible approach and existing law are fairly clear. Although religious association and conviction might possibly lead to a somewhat wider range of choice than that afforded to other parents, they should not extend to decisions that create a serious risk of avoidable death or severe physical impairment. The broader society possesses a legitimate interest in providing basic care for children determined by standards of ordinary reason, even when that care may fall afoul of a parental religious conviction that includes a sense of the child's welfare beyond this life.

Although the Supreme Court has held at various times that parents may make "decisions concerning the care, custody and control of their children,"[6] all states embrace the limit of a *parens patriae* doctrine, which derives from English common law.[7] If parental decisions mean that they fail to care for a child's well-being,[8] jeopardizing the child's health or safety,[9] the state may intervene to see that necessary care is provided. For Christian Scientists and other religious groups that do not believe in all or some particular form of medical treatment, even this degree of interference may be troubling,[10] but the idea that "prohibiting this form of treatment is the functional equivalent of outlawing the religion"[11] is decidedly exaggerated. A minor point here is that efforts at spiritual healing are not forbidden, but these groups are instead not given the right to replace what are broadly seen as needed medical procedures. Of more fundamental importance is a vast number of respects in which, if practices of a particular religion are generally seen as threatening the welfare of others, they can be curtailed. Members of any religion need to understand that this is an aspect of liberal democracy that is not seen as violating basic rights of free exercise. Protecting children is an important aspect of ensuring a society's general welfare.

When we turn to possible civil and criminal liability for failure to get needed medical treatment, matters become much more complicated. One underlying concern is that some children die because they do not receive treatment they need. For example, a seven-year-old Christian Scientist died from diabetes after his parents had removed him from effective medical care and relied on spiritual practices;[12] as another example, a two-year-old died, in what became a well-known Massachusetts case, from a treatable bowel obstruction.[13] According to one study, of one hundred and seventy-two reported fatalities of children who did not receive the help of ordinary medical care for religiously based reasons, including fifty-nine who had just been born, approximately one hundred and forty would have survived if parents had relied on standard medical procedures.[14]

In respect to criminal liability, and to a somewhat lesser degree civil liability, a genuine dilemma exists, one that resembles in some ways whether selective conscientious objectors should be subjected to criminal penalties for refusing to serve in the military. The parents involved here have not been neglectful in any ordinary sense; they have done what they believe is right not only for themselves but also for the children to whom they give spiritual healing. On the other hand, what they have failed to do can result in death or serious physical impairment. Are criminal penalties appropriate in that context, and does it matter just how great is the negative consequence for the child?

The present law varies about this and is often actually disturbingly confusing. As a consequence of a federal law,[15] which has since been repealed,[16] nearly all states enacted exemptions for decisions based on religious convictions from statutes that make child abuse and neglect criminal. These laws, which most states retain,[17] do not directly address the status of other crimes; courts in some states have upheld convictions for manslaughter when the child actually died.[18] Apparently the statutory exemptions led some of those in faith healing groups to believe the right to determine medical treatment was basically theirs,[19] but no state actually forbade intervention from officials to provide crucial medical assistance declined by parents. At the other end, it may seem odd to tell parents they cannot be regarded as neglecting their child but can be punished for causing death if their choice works out badly.

This distinction can be defended as principled. The threat of serious punishment may help to assure that even parents with religious convictions against certain forms of medical treatment will either authorize the treatment themselves or in some way inform officials of the medical condition of their children, which will lead the officials to see that the treatment occurs. Given that "neglect" strongly implies a kind of recklessness or negligence in respect to care, it really does not reach parents who make deliberate and careful decisions about what is right to do for their children. Nevertheless, given that manslaughter is a much more serious crime than neglect, it remains a bit incongruous that one can be guilty of the former while protected against liability for the latter.

At the very least, state laws should actually be somewhat explicit about what is the actual range of legally protected parental choice and what is the scope, if any, of the freedom from criminal punishments that fall on others who have failed to provide adequate medical care of their children, or have not at least informed those with official power of the declining condition of a child who is not receiving ordinary treatment.

To think about sensible resolutions, it helps to review the basis for criminal punishment itself. Although community sentiment does not apparently contain sharply different views about parental rights to choose and the absence of criminal penalties,[20] it is far from obvious that all seriously harmful choices should be treated as criminal.

The purposes of criminal punishment include individual and general deterrence, retribution, confinement, and rehabilitation.[21] Whether retribution alone is sufficient to justify punishment is itself controversial, but it is broadly agreed that a penalty should not be radically more severe than the quality of an offense. Loving parents who on religious bases do not seek or accept medical treatment for their children are almost always doing what they sincerely believe is right for those children. Unless one mistakenly sees retribution as relating only to an objective appraisal of an action, having nothing to do with its basis, that is not a ground for criminal punishment here. Similarly, possible needs for rehabilitation in any broad sense and for standard confinement are virtually irrelevant. If one assumes these parents cannot be trusted to care for their other children, taking away custody makes much more sense than a jail sentence. So really the proper objective of any substantial criminal punishment in this setting must be deterrence, trying to discourage individuals faced with similar choices from refusing treatment and, perhaps more generally, making it less likely that individuals will join groups that are antagonistic to forms of needed care.

If one concentrates on individual deterrence, what effect will the threat of criminal penalties have? Some of those asserting affirmative defenses to manslaughter have claimed that they were relying on belief that what they did was not legally prohibited,[22] but especially given legal advice that this may be a helpful defense, one has to wonder if they really would have acted differently if the risk of criminality had been clear. Imagine a parent who thinks spiritual healing will be effective or who even understands that her child will probably die if he does not receive a blood transfusion or an ordinary operation. Parents who love their children are dismayed over their deaths. *Perhaps* believing that one has performed God's will can sometimes reduce that feeling, but a parent must have a really strong conviction if she is ready to deny a child ordinary lifesaving treatment. For certain parents, a clear directive that they must inform someone else may be more effective than a requirement that they directly authorize treatment. Some Jehovah's Witnesses may not mind if someone else authorizes a blood transfusion; and a Christian Scientist who perceives a child's health as steadily worsening despite spiritual assistance may be willing to inform a person in authority of this development.

For many parents believing that treatment violates God's will, the threat of a subsequent criminal penalty may actually add little to the reasons against refusing treatment. In short, even if a parent in this position is aware that criminal penalties *could* follow, it is highly uncertain how many choices would actually be altered and lives saved.

The general deterrence argument is even harder to assess. Simply what is on the books as formal law is not likely to have nearly as much effect in discouraging people from joining faiths that reject basic medicine as is the recognition that these positions are definitely at odds with ordinary reason. However, a highly publicized actual criminal conviction might affect people's emotional feelings about belonging to a religion that encourages such choices.

Yet a different kind of argument that embraces both deterrence and retribution is that criminal penalties are needed to prevent fraud by those who are not genuinely religious from claiming that they are. In contrast to drug use and draft avoidance, it is hard to think people will join a religious group *in order* not to provide medical care for their children. And after the fact, parents who have been simply irresponsible or even cruel will find it difficult to offer a plausible religious basis.

When one puts all this together, what conclusion is best? Although the state should definitely override parental choices that will likely lead to avoidable death, given the harshness of imposing severe criminal penalties on parents who do what they regard as best for their children by not seeking or by declining medical care, the argument that exemptions from serious criminal penalties are warranted is substantial and can even reach circumstances in which the parents' choice results in death.

There are two alternatives. One is a policy of nonprosecution despite formal legal coverage. Another is to establish special courts or procedures that can affect involvement before parents carry out their decisions to deny medical care and that may lead to different kinds of penalties, if a failure is treated as criminal, than the ordinary imprisonment of those convicted.[23] People can reasonably disagree, both about whether such exemptions, consistent nonprosecutions, or an alternative approach, are ever warranted, *and*, if so, whether they should reach the extreme consequence of loss of life.[24]

Resolving the issue of criminal penalties, at least when children suffer serious and predictable harmful consequences, is best made the subject of specific legislative determinations. Even if the standard for when this particular exemption should be granted is formulated in a way that requires estimation of competing considerations, the basic question here cannot wisely be left to judges by a broad and vague statutory standard, as that in the Religious Freedom Restoration Act (RFRA). Among other reasons, judges would rightly be extremely unlikely to determine a privilege here to be free of criminal liability under a very general statutory standard. Clearly a government has a "compelling interest" in protecting individual lives. Although, as I have indicated, the extent to which criminal penalties will accomplish that in this circumstance is far from obvious, the government also lacks any "less restrictive means" to accomplish the objective.

That should be sufficient to defeat any RFRA-like claim, if a state legislature has failed to provide any more specific freedom from criminal penalties for conscientious religious parents.

The issue of civil liability is also debatable. In brief, if a child suffers a serious impairment because of a parent's faith-based decision, it seems appropriate to allow the child to recover actual damages, although punitive damages may well be out of place. A similar conclusion seems sound if the decision of an outsider or one parent has the harmful effect of causing death, and a parent who has lost her child but would definitely not have accepted the decision which caused that sues for her loss. In these respects, the basic standards of ordinary society should be a legitimate basis for recovery.

MATURE TEENAGERS

A particular question about refusing medical treatment is whose choice should control if the person who would be treated is still a minor teenager but has reached a certain age. Here we need to distinguish what might make the most sense as a matter of principle from a feasible legal approach. Against any argument that, even for older teenagers, parents' choices should control, unless overridden by public concern for the life and health of their children, lie two contrary bases. One is the established constitutional right of pregnant teenagers to have abortions, regardless of their parents' views and even whether they have informed those parents.[25] If teenagers are free to make this decision, should they not also be able to make certain other choices that will affect their physical and mental well-being in the future? The second reason for according weight to a teenager's decision is that virtually all religions involve confirmation for members by the age of sixteen. If the religious groups treat these young people as capable of making that fundamental decision, it is a bit hard to say that parental religious convictions should control against ordinary standards of judgment if their child no longer shares them.

Exactly who should count as a mature teenager is itself difficult to say. One could imagine a subtle inquiry into the qualities of particular individuals and their family relations, but that is not a determination we should demand of doctors and judges. A legal approach that treats older teenagers differently from younger children needs to set the border at a certain age. I shall assume here that the age set would be fifteen or sixteen to eighteen, so that minors in this range would be treated a bit differently from both small children and adults.

We first need to recognize that almost always parents and their older children will work out an agreement about what medical treatment is to be received. The instances of direct conflicts before doctors will not be common; disagreements that survive to be heard by judges will be even rarer. Nonetheless, it is worth asking whose decisions should control if a conflict does present itself to a medical practitioner.

It helps first to distinguish choices that violate normal standards of reasonableness from those that are within that range. If an older teenager wants treatment that would obviously be desirable according to normal estimations, she should be able to receive it even if her parents disagree. In particular, a child of sixteen should not be controlled by religious convictions she now rejects. What if parents want a medical procedure definitely called for by ordinary reason, but the child wishes to refuse? If we are talking about the usual right of persons to make medical decisions for themselves, we should not take sixteen-year-olds as mature enough to make medical decisions that are *both* unreasonable and against their parents' wishes. To take just one example, it is not so uncommon for teenagers to go through brief periods when they become extremely discouraged and no longer wish to live, not fully grasping that these periods pass and that a full and satisfying life may lie ahead of them. To allow them at that stage to refuse a lifesaving procedure would be deeply unfortunate. In brief, if one puts aside a mature teenager's possible religious convictions, if either she *or* her parents want her to receive medical treatment clearly called for by ordinary standards of assessment, that choice should control.

Although more debatable, the same conclusion probably should follow even if the teenager's basis for refusing treatment is religious conviction. Especially if her life or physical well-being is likely to be lost by a refusal, she should not be able to override what the medical professionals and her parents are convinced she needs. Part of the reason for this conclusion is that teenagers are with some frequency attracted to religious and other convictions that they later dismiss as they become more mature. It would be unfortunate if at this stage, they were given the right to sacrifice their physical well-being against the judgments of their parents.

A yet more troublesome question is what if the parents and teenager *agree* on refusing treatment called for by ordinary reason. Parents do not have the right to allow small children to die on that basis. Should parents and their older children together have this right? If an older child and his parents are loyal members of a religious community, perhaps they should be able together to adhere to its convictions to the extent that the child could do alone when he reaches eighteen. A practical argument in favor of such a right is that if adults take the same view as their ill or injured teenager, the consequence of saying that even together they cannot refuse certain forms of medical assistance, such as a blood transfusion, might lead them to decide not even to go to a hospital or consult a doctor. As a consequence, a rule that their joint decision about a particular form of treatment will not be followed *could* result in the injured teenager getting less rather than more medical assistance.

On the other hand, it is highly plausible that until one is actually an adult, he should not be able to decline badly needed treatment. This position is supported by the concern that in many families, parents will still heavily influence how teenagers see things or may threaten unpleasant consequences if their children act contrary to their will.

When we turn to decisions that lie within the boundaries of reasonable choice by ordinary standards, saying whose judgment should control becomes even harder. If the question turns on degrees of risk and benefit, the parents' evaluation would generally seem a bit more reliable, but if the crucial question is what someone should endure to receive certain physical benefits, the sense of the person who will be directly affected might carry more weight. If within the reasonable range, the differences in judgment themselves are based on competing religious convictions, the teenager's should take priority. Because these subtle variations in whose judgment should count for more within the range of reasonable choice are regrettably too complicated for an ordinary legal standard, they raise a serious question about a sensible legal approach.

The exact status of teenage choice cannot be left to some general formulation, such as that in the RFRA. One possibility is simply to grant parents the same degree of official authority for all minors concerning medical care, thus leaving it up to the older children to try to persuade and pressure their mothers and fathers when there is a disagreement. A sensible alternative for legislation would be to provide that any treatment whose provision would definitely be desirable by ordinary standards should be given if either the parents or the child over fifteen or sixteen choose it. However, if a decision to receive or to decline are both within the reasonable range, a choice to decline by either the parents or older child should control. If the treatment is one the state would definitely impose for small children against parental wishes, the outcome should be the same even if parents and a sixteen-year-old assert a conviction that such treatment would be wrong. Details of this proposed approach are certainly contestable, but the approach would yield a legal standard that would clarify the extent of change from the individual rights of small children to those of mature teenagers. It would also help guide both doctors and officials when the views of older teenagers and their parents conflict.

INSISTING ON TREATMENT

A relatively minor concern is whether individuals should ever have a right to insist on treatment despite its failing to qualify as reasonably needed. When it comes to personal matters, such as plastic surgery to make one look slightly better, matters are best left to the economic market. If a person can find a doctor willing to perform the surgery and is able to pay for it, he can receive it. But he has no legal right to require anyone to do it and to receive it if unable to pay. For this, it should not make a difference whether a person offers some religious reason why he should be accorded medical treatment not provided for other members of society.

The time of death does raise these concerns. It is now generally assumed that a person whose brain no longer functions has died, even if his physical body continues to breathe. Yet some people do not accept this, either because they doubt what they are told about the brain or they simply believe that life continues until the physical body is no longer capable of doing anything. Family members with such a belief may insist that their relative on the deathbed should still be sustained in respect to breathing and the ingestion of nutrients. A fraudulent claim *is* imaginable; a spouse might want "survival" of her husband until a person designated for inheritance has himself died and will not be able to decide who shall take the money left to him in the husband's will. But the chance of such genuine fraud here is decidedly minimal, especially if family members bear all or part of the cost of further treatment. For this reason, it makes sense to regard all such claims as sincere. Given that many religions treat the moment of death as highly significant, and we have no simple scientific answer to what counts as death, it is wise to allow family members to get "life support" until death has occurred by all accepted criteria, so long as the family's reason is based on what actually constitutes death, not on disbelief about assurances that a person's brain will no longer function. This right should not depend directly on the claim being religious, since no strong reason exists to distinguish religious from nonreligious beliefs in this context, and the concern about phony claims is minimal, at least if one puts aside a false assertion of conscience by people who simply distrust what the doctors say about their loved one's future.[26]

Vaccinations

A special issue about required medical procedures for children is vaccinations. In virtually every state, important vaccinations are required for children who are to be admitted to public schools. The key question is whether any exemptions, apart from a child's medical condition, should be afforded, and if so, whether they should be framed in terms of religion.

A powerful special factor about most or all vaccinations is that they not only reduce the possibility that a person receiving the vaccination will be burdened with the illness but also help to protect others, who might otherwise catch the illness from the unvaccinated person. This is referred to as "herd immunity" and "community immunity."[27] As the outbreak of measles in 2014 and 2015 clearly shows, a reduction in the number of children vaccinated can have a serious harmful consequence.[28] The broader the scope of the vaccinations, the greater the overall protection against certain terrible afflictions, such as polio, and other serious illnesses, such as measles. If a vaccination is not already widely spread, virtually all parents will conclude that it is best for their children to receive one. Although vaccinations themselves may carry some risk of harm, the risk of getting the illness is much more serious. But things can change if virtually everyone else is getting vaccinated. The chance of one individual contracting the illness is then sharply curtailed.

This reduced chance *could* affect a rational parental choice in the following way. A parent, who like many others, gives overwhelming importance to the protection of her own children might conclude that the risk of the vaccination itself outweighs the risk of the children acquiring the illness without it. To illustrate with arbitrary figures, let us suppose that the typical harm of an illness is one thousand and, given widespread vaccinations for others, the chance of acquiring the illness is only one in one thousand; that would multiply to one. The harm the vaccination itself may cause is only one hundred, but one out fifty takers (2 percent) experiences that harm; that risk would multiply to two. A rational parent *might* decide against the vaccination. But the estimation of the overall effect of refusal might well be quite different. Suppose a child acquiring the illness on average infects two other children. The overall total risk of one child's nonvaccination would then rise to three. Thus, the general interest would definitely favor a child's being vaccinated. This possible conflict with a parent's assessment of the best course for her own child is enhanced by misguided actual perceptions about the risks and benefits of various vaccinations, which can increase parental decisions of avoidance.

Of course, that some parents will not make rational choices to benefit their own children in the sense suggested above is itself an obvious public concern. Instead, parents may grossly overestimate the risk of a vaccination itself. Such misassessments may have been substantially responsible for the modern resurgence of opposition to vaccines, influenced in part by a 1998 study by Andrew Wakefield that linked the measles, mumps, and rubella vaccine to childhood autism.[29] That conclusion had not been supported by other studies.[30]

All this bears on whether any exemptions should exist and how they should be formulated. Since the danger of an illness spreading increases as the number of those not vaccinated rises, states have a powerful interest in having them taken by almost everyone. However, avoidance by a very few is likely to have relatively little negative effect. Some persons do believe that vaccinations do not accord with what God has prescribed. In contrast with abortions, it is hard even to conceive a purely secular appraisal that all vaccinations are in principle wrong. If their minor inconvenience and slight risk of harm are sufficient to preclude a substantial likelihood of acquiring a major illness that can result in death or permanent disability, the obvious rational choice is to have a child vaccinated. Parents for nonreligious reasons *might* strongly wish to refuse a vaccination for their children because they are misinformed about likely consequences or seek what is best for their own offspring, even if that is contrary to general welfare. The importance of public welfare should override either of these bases. This is a strong reason to limit any exemption to religious claims, and possibly to ones made by members of religious groups whose convictions are clearly opposed to vaccinations.

Although California has recently eliminated all but medical exceptions, most states still do provide exemptions, and these are divided in how they are cast; most importantly, some are limited to religious convictions and others are not.[31] It turns out that overall those states with more broadly framed exemptions tend to have more children, on average, who do not get vaccinated.[32] Given differences among regions in the country and the fact that some states may adopt the wider scope for exemptions because opposition within them to vaccinations is already greater, one cannot reach a decisive conclusion about the genuine consequence of broader exemptions. However, wider exemptions may well be likely to increase the number of unvaccinated children. It is also troubling that these exemptions make it somewhat easier for parents genuinely concerned only with what is physically best for their own children to announce a kind of opposition in conscience. These reasons support the conclusion that limiting any nonmedical exemption to those with religious convictions may be preferable for the general welfare of children.

Issues About Abortion

When we turn to the medical procedure of abortion, the issues about legal requirements differ greatly from those considered so far in this chapter. In *Roe v. Wade*,[33] the Supreme Court provided women an individual constitutional right to receive an abortion, despite many state law prohibitions. Without being completely explicit, the opinion indicated that women possessed this right, which was more extensive than then existed in the great majority of states, up to the time when a dislodged fetus might actually survive.[34] At the time of the decision, public opinion was sharply divided over whether obtaining an abortion was moral or immoral, and various critics later suggested that it would have been preferable to have left evolving liberalization of the legal right up to legislative development rather than having a dictated judicial rule. The disagreement over the morality of abortions has turned primarily on what the pregnant woman owes to her potential child, an evaluation typically dependent on what a person sees as the beginning of life. Those who believe that life begins at conception or implantation are inclined to conclude that abortion is never morally justified or is so only in exceptional circumstances such as forcible rape, incest, the definite inability of a fetus to survive,[35] or a severe threat to a woman's life if her pregnancy continues.

Actual views about the morality of abortion have not altered hugely since the Court's decision four decades ago,[36] and various state legislatures have passed laws designed to curtail the scope of available abortions. Some people have been surprised by this lack of an overarching shift in public opinion when compared with what transpired after Supreme Court decisions about racial and gender equality under law, which have achieved widespread public acceptance. The answer for this difference almost certainly lies in conceptions about the beginning of life; even someone who grasps that a right to have an abortion does further women's equality may object to being involved in what he or she sees as a practice of destroying an innocent being's life.

I strongly believe that neither the beginning of life nor how much protection should be given to fetuses at different stages of development is subject to a definitive rational answer. These are not scientific questions, although facts of science can play a role here in how people perceive things.[37] Very likely, the frequency with which fetuses will naturally survive to birth makes a difference. Oak trees come from acorns, but given that the vast majority of acorns never mature, we do not see destroying an acorn as essentially like tearing up a young oak. Human pregnancies differ; miscarriages do occur and are usually a cause for deep sadness, but from the time pregnancies are recognized, most fetuses will survive to birth if not destroyed.[38] This can bear on when people perceive actual life as beginning. For the purpose of appropriate legal approaches, much less important than trying to understand the bases for competing positions is the reality that among our population a sharp division still exists over the morality of a standard abortion.

Many people who believe abortion is fundamentally wrong do not actually disagree with the law's allowing them.[39] One reason is that if the law did forbid them, women would still seek abortions, as they did when that constituted a crime, but the abortions would then be more dangerous and more expensive, and an illegal practice would be common. A second, related, reason is a recognition that when the population is sharply divided over whether people should be free to do something, it simply makes sense to allow that choice rather than treat those who are doing what they believe is right as criminals. However, the conclusion that women are properly allowed to have abortions does not tell us whether hospitals and other medical facilities should be compelled to provide them or whether individuals who work for medical facilities should be required to participate. One concern about an exemption here is that it is not always simple to determine the edges between other medical practices and abortions.[40]

Should some exemption be granted, and, if so, how should it be cast? If women possess a constitutional right to have abortions, should those simply be treated like any ordinary medical procedure, or should special privileges be created for noninvolvement? When the line between an abortion and another medical procedure, such as helping a woman in a miscarriage, turns out to be unclear, trying to make the distinction can sometimes interfere with other medical help. This can be seen as one ground for requiring similar treatment.[41] On the other hand, favoring a right of noninvolvement in abortions is the reality that requiring participation could actually reduce the quality of care by driving some organizations out of medical practice.

If various rights of noninvolvement are to be created, the kinds of questions we have considered more broadly—Should standards be general or specific? Who should qualify? Should protection be absolute or qualified? and Should religious convictions matter?—all play important roles.

This is a domain in which Congress adopted highly important federal legislation not long after *Roe v. Wade,* and states have passed laws with various degrees of coverage. The central practical questions are these: How far should medical facilities be required to provide abortions, and should government funding be a basis for such a requirement? Should individual doctors and others have rights vis-à-vis their hospital employers? The individual rights can include both a privilege of doctors and others not to participate in abortions although their hospitals provide them *and* to actually perform abortions when that occurs away from their hospital-employers that oppose them.

INDIVIDUALS AND HEALTH PROVIDERS

Laws protecting the nonprovision of medical services can apply to enterprises and individuals. Ordinary basic requirements to provide services derive partly from federal and state regulations, partly from semipublic bodies such as the Accreditation Council for Graduate Medical Education, and partly from accepted norms of the medical profession. If a created exemption applies to specific circumstances, those refusing involvement cannot be criminally punished or be liable to civil recovery for negligence if they decline to provide an otherwise covered medical treatment. For institutions that engage in medical practices, such as Catholic hospitals, this freedom from potential legal liability is primary.

Although such protections may also apply to doctors and to other individuals who engage in medical assistance, a different kind of right may prove more important for them, one that can support both their nonparticipation and their participation in abortions. Normally employers expect those who work for them to perform their prescribed duties and sometimes not to deviate from the institution's basic values even when they work at another location. By this standard, hospitals committed to providing abortions could dismiss doctors and nurses who refuse to participate. And enterprises strongly committed to not granting abortions might choose to dismiss any of their doctors who are performing them when practicing elsewhere. What a protective law can do is to forbid an employer from disciplining or dismissing a doctor or nurse who chooses to act or not act, in a way that is contrary to institutional policy.

Do such exemptions make sense in respect to abortions? Given both the widespread division in our society about the moral status of abortions and the deep convictions reflected in the positions of some religious groups and felt by some individuals that abortion constitutes a kind of killing of innocent human beings, an argument for such protections is strong. A counterargument is that those who undertake to provide medical services should simply be required to adhere to what is generally understood as appropriate. Standing alone, this is unconvincing. To say that no one should become a doctor or nurse who wants to help people with the vast majority of medical services but has strong reservations of conscience about one or two would both be harsh and preclude some valuable potential medical personnel from that occupation.

A related point, one that bears on certain other exemptions, concerns how things stand when a requirement of a medical service is novel. In many states prior to *Roe v. Wade,* abortion was not a prescribed medical practice; instead, barring exceptional circumstances, it was legally forbidden. Thus, many individuals who, after investing time, energy, and money to qualify, became doctors and nurses before *Roe v. Wade* might have had no problem with all medical assistance then taken for granted. To believe that they should simply resign from their vocations as soon as they feel they cannot perform a particular service that has, largely thanks to a Supreme Court decision, now become accepted as normally required would be both unfair to them and would diminish the overall capacities within their profession. One can think of medical institutions somewhat similarly; if they have had a long history of providing basic services, should they have to go out of business if they feel they cannot engage in one medical procedure? Of course, with institutions, unlike with individuals, a genuine question is whose views should count and why; this bears on how an exemption should be cast.

More particular questions are whether exemptions should be framed broadly or narrowly in terms of grounds of objection, whether religious conviction should matter, what degree of involvement should be relevant, and how far available exemptions should be qualified in terms of competing considerations. Treatment of the latter two questions is reserved for the later section of this chapter on just and wise coverage. The answers to the first two questions are fairly straightforward for individuals. We can imagine someone not wanting to participate in a medical procedure because she is afraid doing so will offend relatives or friends or because she has a kind of relatively weak moral objection, such as wishing not to help with plastic surgery undertaken only to make someone reduce the wrinkles on his face. But when it comes to abortions, virtually all stated objections to participation are likely to be both honest and strong, based on a belief that one is aiding the taking of innocent life. Probably most people with such a belief do connect it to religious convictions, but there are "natural law" arguments that one can rely on ordinary reason to see that fetuses are lives deserving protection,[42] and convictions based on nonreligious reasons and personal feelings are held by some nonbelievers. As a consequence, when the question concerns a privilege for individuals in this context, a limitation based on religious convictions or church membership is unwarranted.

Grounds of objection become more complicated when we turn to institutions. One problem here concerns possible practical reasons not related to actual convictions. An individual who refuses to perform services his hospital is providing is not likely to thus advance his position within the hospital, even if he cannot be dismissed or disciplined. But a hospital in a community where most citizens are strongly opposed to abortions might be inclined to nonperformance in order to satisfy general sentiments or not to offend key donors of money. Another concern is whose views should count. If the small number of individuals who actually own or run a hospital take a particular view of moral right and wrong that is at odds with prevailing medical practice, should they be able to dictate what takes place within the facility when that is at odds with accepted standards? These concerns are much less if the hospital is part of a religious organization, such as the Roman Catholic Church, that has provided medical services throughout most of modern history *and* has, among its many moral stances, consistently and publicly taken positions about abortion that directly conflict with present medical practice. Although many individual Catholics may not subscribe to the Church's position on this and certain other moral issues, the hospitals represent not just the opinions of individual owners but those of a very well-established religious body with broadly stated and understood moral positions.

Yet another consideration, already mentioned, is that if an exemption is denied to such hospitals, a real danger exists that the religious group will remove itself from that enterprise. The same consequence might occur if a state chose the intermediate step of removing a tax exemption rather than actually requiring the performance of abortions. Examples of such withdrawals in other domains were the Catholic Charities of Massachusetts no longer providing adoptions when the state forbade discrimination based on sexual orientation and the Catholic Archdiocese of Washington stopping foster care placement rather than treating same-sex couples equally.[43] Catholic hospitals in 2000 admitted 17 percent of all patients nationally.[44] We cannot be sure what would replace the existence or control of these facilities if the Church withdrew because abortions were required, but the possibility of such a withdrawal is a serious concern.

When one combines all these various factors and adds to them the basic concept of liberty of religious denominations, it makes sense here to limit the exemptions for institutions to religious bodies whose convictions not to supply abortions are drawn from the understandings of their faiths. An interesting, though certainly debatable, decision by the Alaska Supreme Court provides modest support for this position.[45] A state statute provided a general right of hospitals to refuse abortions. The court ruled that given the constitutional right to receive abortions, the law was invalid unless limited to sectarian facilities. Whatever one concludes about the soundness of the court's precise constitutional conclusion, the case does suggest that there are good reasons both to provide some institutional exemptions and to limit them to religious institutions.

SPECIFIC VERSUS GENERAL STATUTES

Two straightforward reasons indicate why exemption protections that apply to abortions cannot be left simply to general statutes such as RFRA. The first is that these laws concern rights held against the government. Standing alone, they do not affect what private employers may do with respect to their own workers. If a legislature wants to restrict the range of choice for those employers, it needs to adopt a statute to do that.

Even when what is involved is possible rights vis-à-vis the government itself, the nature of abortions is such that leaving everything to RFRA formulation would be unproductive. A person or an institution whose religious convictions indicate that participating in an abortion is a form of taking innocent life would satisfy the requirement of a "substantial burden" to their religious exercise, but the government definitely possesses a compelling interest in safeguarding the right of women to have abortions. Since that interest demands that many doctors and nurses participate, there is no "less restrictive means" that involves something radically different from that involvement. Often, the individual or hospital could plausibly contend that given the availability of other doctors and nurses, the state has a less restrictive means than insisting that all carry out that duty, but whether this will really work depends on the accessibility of other medical centers and other doctors and nurses on particular occasions. This would require an assessment of the actual location and the time when a refusal takes place. Judges should not have to try to apply a vague statute like RFRA in a manner that depends so heavily on the unique circumstances of a particular situation, and legislators should not expect them to do so.

For both these reasons, what is needed is legislation that directly addresses abortion and our society's conflicting views about its status. Direct legislation also carries certain advantages over the application of broadly phrased statutes.[46] One we have already examined. A general statute, such as RFRA, is likely to be protective of "religious" exercise, but I have suggested that as far as individuals are concerned, a powerful basis exists not to restrict their claims for an exemption here to ones grounded in religious convictions.

Objections to RFRA and similar laws that have recently been made by those who advocate same-sex marriage and the guarantee of available contraceptives are that they allow violations of law, fail to provide adequate notice, impose costs on third parties, and defeat or delay social progress. In respect to "violations," if I possess a RFRA right not to fulfill a generally cast duty, I am not actually violating the law from which it compels the exception; but that will not be definitely known in advance of a judicial decision. I may be *perceived* as actually violating the law and may actually be uncertain whether I am doing so. A specific law can effectively eliminate this concern by making clear from the outset just what privilege I have. Relatedly, the law can give notice to those who seek abortions that certain hospitals, doctors, and nurses may not be willing to participate. Of course, most people will not know the exact dimensions of the law or which individuals will withhold assistance, but nonetheless notice is more adequate than with a statute like RFRA. And a specific law could well require institutions to provide public notice of procedures they will not undertake.

When the claim for an exemption involves a right to refuse to provide what patients or others perceive as a significant benefit, this can be a concern with both general and specific statutes. But a specific statute can at least deal with this more directly by trying to assure that the needed service will not actually be sacrificed.

A special, related, feature when the important interests of others are at stake is what symbolic message an exemption will send. We will explore that in somewhat greater depth in regard to same-sex marriage, but one can fairly see the right to abortions as involving the status of women. Does conferral of a right to refuse signal inequality and involve moral condemnation of those who seek abortions?[47] Whatever may be the complex historical bases for such views, those who are unwilling to participate in abortions are concerned about innocent life; they do not balk *because* they regard women as unequal. One can rightly see the dispute over abortion as involving some conflict between the rights of women and the possible intrinsic rights of fetuses, but labeling all opposition to participation as simply denying women rights equal to those of men is definitely too simplistic.

Related to this point is how opponents of abortion perceive the women who seek them. Within our culture, the vast majority of those who believe that abortions should not be sought do not regard women who want them as deeply immoral persons. Recognizing both the division of opinion and the basic legal right to obtain abortions, they may feel that the women who seek them are misguided in doing so but not morally blameworthy in some more general way. This sharply reduces any negative symbolic message that nonparticipation carries about the women who undergo abortions. And of course in terms of practical effects on individuals, it is also relevant that most people have no idea whether any woman to whom they are not especially close has ever had an abortion.

The point about symbolic message is somewhat related to the issue of social progress, which also involves a special dimension here. Most citizens would now regard movements toward racial and gender equality as clear instances of social progress, and most, including a much higher percentage of those in the younger generations, see equality for gay people, including same-sex marriage, similarly. Although we shall examine this in more detail in Chapter 8, one might see exemptions, whether general or specific, as impeding that progress. Matters are significantly different with specific exemptions concerning abortion. Given the uncertainty about the beginning of life and what protection fetuses at various stages should be accorded, being certain about what really constitutes social progress here is much harder. But even if one strongly believes that the answer definitely favors both legal and moral acceptance of abortions, significant reasons remain to provide exemptions.

One practical point in this context is clear. If a law specifically forbids medical enterprises from dismissing or disciplining not only those who decline to participate in abortions but also those who choose to perform abortions in other locations, this can actually increase their availability. The second consideration about effects is less obvious and more contestable. If the opposition to participation in abortions is very powerful for some doctors, nurses, and for some religious hospitals, they may be willing to accept widespread availability for women who seek them *if* exemptions are granted. If no exemptions were provided and these personnel and institutions were effectively compelled to participate if they continued in medical practice, this could lead to increased intense opposition to any right of women to receive abortions. That could actually delay social progress seen as acceptance of abortions. In any event, an exemption provision passed by legislators who take the social progress consideration into account may impair that development less than would a Supreme Court decision that an exemption of a particular kind is required under RFRA (a particular worry if the existing Court is seen as inclined in favor of conservative outcomes).

The following section looks at some of the legal standards that have been enacted about abortion. These provisions show that the line between the general and specific statutes need not be absolute; a legal formulation can occupy a kind of intermediate range.

ACTUAL PROVISIONS

An early federal requirement of some accommodation to religious beliefs and practices was the Title VII part of the Civil Rights Act of 1964.[48] That required employers to accommodate the religious beliefs and practices of their employees unless doing so would create an "undue hardship" on the employers.[49] An acceptable accommodation had to be reasonable and not yield an "undue burden" on the employer or coworkers. While focusing on a particular problem, the statutory standard was cast in general terms, leaving it up to employers and judges to determine just what needed to be done and when. Although designed to protect against basic discrimination along racial and other lines, the law's language could support a nurse's claim not to participate in abortions if her doing so burdened neither her fellow nurses nor her hospital. In a significant case, the Supreme Court construed this accommodation requirement in a manner that actually demanded very little of employers—or unions, which were also subject to the act. Dealing with a worker's religious claim not to work on Saturday, the Court said that Trans World Airlines did not need to "bear more than a *de minimis* cost."[50]

Shortly after the Court's establishment of a constitutional right to obtain abortions, Congress adopted a statute directly focused on that medical service. The Church Amendment, supplemented by the Hyde Amendment adopted three years later, bars federal agencies and courts from relying on federal funding of medical facilities to impose requirements that abortions be provided.[51] The law provides that those who on the basis of "religious belief or moral conviction" believe they cannot "perform or assist" with abortion or sterilization cannot be required to do so. In practice, the assertion of such a conviction is sufficient; no deep examination takes place of whether one is really sincere, and no attempt is made to assess the intensity of a person's objection. The breadth of this privilege to refuse was based partly on the sense of many members of Congress, or their constituents, that the Supreme Court had gone too far in creating a constitutional right to obtain abortions. But the act also contains a protection for doctors and nurses who choose to participate in abortions away from the premises of a hospital that declines to provide them. They cannot be dismissed or disciplined on that basis. The language of the act does not qualify the privilege not to participate because someone's involvement in an abortion may be strongly needed in certain circumstances.

The Church Amendment's barring of using federal funding as a basis for requiring the performance of abortions does not entirely preempt state law that provides more or less protection.[52] Various states have adopted similar statutes, though with somewhat different phrasing. Louisiana, for instance, does not allow a person whose "conscience" would be violated to be required to "participate" or not to "participate" in a health-care service, "to the extent that patient access to health care is not compromised."[53]

COVERAGE THAT IS JUST AND WISE

The conclusions that legislatures need to address the range of abortion protections explicitly and that exemptions limited to religious bases make sense for institutions but not individuals do not themselves resolve a number of other issues, at least one of which carries great practical significance.

One question is just how the right of conscience or moral conviction should be formulated. Given the effective self-execution of claims in this context, as contrasted with the kind of serious appraisal involved for claimed pacifists, the formulation carries limited significance in operation. It may, however, have some symbolic force; the more extensively it is cast, the more it may convey the message that even a weak moral objection suffices. A second question is what exactly should be the connection between a person's role and his qualification for an exemption, an issue that takes on even greater importance in respect to other kinds of exemptions. The third question, how far should any such right be qualified by the competing needs of those seeking medical service, carries the greatest practical importance here. We next explore the latter two questions and briefly mention approaches in some other countries.

Any exemption from requiring involvement definitely should include those who have some actual participation in an abortion procedure—not only the doctors who would perform them but also nurses who would directly assist. This coverage is captured by the federal statute's language of "perform or assist." Some countries have a privilege not to be engaged that is limited to those who directly participate, but that seems too restrictive.[54] The language of "assist" in the law does not tell us what amounts to relevant assistance. What should count, and should this be specifically addressed in the statute or left to determination by hospital officials and by courts? And should the degree of protection depend at all on the form of involvement?

Not every person in a hospital who has any contact with a patient seeking an abortion or with facilities used for them should be seen as "assisting."[55] If all a clerk does is register incoming patients and send them to their rooms, he should not be able to turn a woman aside because he is aware that she has come for an abortion. Nor should a janitor who cleans operating rooms be able to refuse to do this job in a room that is used sometimes for abortions.

An involvement could be closer than these in one of two ways. A nurse or another worker could be asked to be directly involved in preparing the facilities for an abortion, providing the necessary equipment for that operation, and so on. We could reasonably see this as assisting with the abortion, even if the person never sets eyes on the patient and is not present when the operation takes place.[56] Another involvement is with the patient herself before or after the operation. Should a nurse, rather than just checking on all the patients on a floor, be required to give concentrated attention to a woman who has come for and received an abortion? One could fairly say that this is not assistance in the performance of an abortion, but it is assistance for the woman's obtaining of an abortion. My own sense is that a nurse who would either get equipment ready for the abortion itself or give concentrated attention to the woman who will receive one should be able to claim nonparticipation. Neither of these claims is likely to be frequent and, when honestly asserted, they do represent a conviction that performing those duties is helping in the taking of innocent life. However, a qualification to any such privilege should be cast in terms of the degree of overall inconvenience within the hospital.

Given the vast range of degrees of possible involvement and the infrequency of claims by those whose involvement is peripheral, legislatures need not try to set more precise boundaries, instead leaving to the medical facilities, and occasionally to courts, the question whether a person's duty involves the degree of assistance needed to support a valid claim.

The issue of whether and when an initially valid claim may nonetheless be rejected is more troublesome. The Church Amendment contains no explicit exception to its privilege for nonparticipation. This is obviously troubling if a woman's life is actually at stake[57] or if nonparticipation will make it very hard to get an abortion anywhere near the locality in which she lives. Although one reason Congress may have declined to add a qualification is that many members simply disapproved abortions, for our purpose we need to assume that women really do properly have the right to obtain them.

On this basis, the right to nonparticipation does need to be qualified *unless* legislators have very solid reasons to suppose that very often those who run facilities will force participation by ostensibly relying on such a qualification when it does not really apply. Not surprisingly, various states have added qualifications like Louisiana's, but a number of other state statutes have no such limits.[58] In cases arising under both the Church Amendment and state laws, in which individuals have objected to institutional denials of their refusals to participate, responses have been that no one has otherwise been available to provide the service. Courts have been strongly inclined not to acknowledge a right of individuals to refuse in those circumstances.[59] Despite the absolute language of its relevant statute, a case in New Jersey was settled in a way which acknowledged that temporary assistance could be required if no one else was available.[60]

When one reflects on this issue, an absolute right to refuse any assistance is unwarranted for genuine emergencies in which no one else is readily available. In other countries and under the European Union, a balance does have to be struck that protects women's receiving abortions.[61] But given the sense of the objector that he is contributing to the death of an innocent being, institutions should definitely make strenuous efforts to assure that others are available, at least when, as normally required, those objecting to assistance have provided advance notification of their convictions.

It does make sense here that the necessary degree of hardship that will allow an employer to decline a claim not to assist should depend partly on the degree of assistance. The need should have to be extremely pressing if those with conscientious opposition are told they must directly perform an abortion or provide crucial, intimate assistance. If as I have suggested, even those with less close connections should be allowed to claim nonassistance, the degree to which the institutions must tolerate hardship and inconvenience should decline somewhat as the tie to the abortions themselves becomes more remote. Just how much is required and exactly when is not something we should expect legislators to specify; that question of judgment must be left to those operating facilities, and, when actual legal disputes arise, to courts. Although it is definitely arguable just how far hospital managers and judges should be left to make assessments based on balances of considerations, something along these lines is definitely preferable to granting a right to refuse participation in all circumstances.

A different issue about the relation of institutions and workers that has been raised by Elizabeth Sepper is worth considering.[62] What she suggests is that if doctors and nurses can decline to perform the treatment their institutions require, why, based on similar conviction about what is morally right, should they not be able to perform, even within the facility, a medical procedure to which their employers object? Her position is based partly on skepticism about institutional conscience, but the primary argument here is that the right to perform should be viewed similarly to the right not to perform. Although this is hardly a decisive answer, I believe there is a basic difference in principle. If individuals know that a person can get a benefit that they believe is warranted from other sources, they do not typically feel a moral duty to be the providers. On the other hand, if they know that if they refuse the person will still get the service, they nevertheless feel a moral duty not to provide it if they have a powerful moral objection. Put generally, a sense of religious or moral obligation not to perform is broader than a sense that one must perform. Two exceptions can be when no one else is available to provide a service or the person in need of it is someone to whom one feels extremely close, such as a family member. When one reflects on these considerations, the present set-up of favoring refusals to perform is not somehow illogical, but legislators might do well to consider whether the privilege that Professor Sepper recommends is ever warranted.

Conclusion

The latter part of the chapter addresses one of the most troubling circumstances of sharply different perceptions of what is morally right, involving competing conceptions of the beginning of life. In contrast to the earlier half, which discusses rights to refuse needed medical treatment, the central question here is when participation and help should be required, given a clearly established right for women to receive abortions. Yet despite the special features of each part of this chapter, many of the reasons for and against exemptions are not so different from those in prior and later chapters. These reasons need to be recognized as genuine and carrying force by those whose own perspectives are sharply at odds with each other.

6

Contraceptives and the *Hobby Lobby* Case

Introduction

Closely related to the subject of the last chapter is the provision of contraceptives. This chapter focuses on that practice and an appropriate range of exemptions. It also concentrates on the 2014 *Hobby Lobby* decision, which addressed the statutory requirement of companies to provide insurance and concluded that the Religious Freedom Restoration Act (RFRA) generated an exemption for closely held for-profit corporations.[1] That decision has given rise to intense disagreement over its result and over religious exemptions more generally. I contend that it does sharply raise questions about the range of exemptions and the interpretations of vague statutes but is not a helpful guide to the most core questions about exemptions.

The contraceptives that generate the greatest reservations about use and supply are those that sometimes may operate after the moment of conception. For some people, this is when life begins, and they do not want to be involved in the possible destruction of a fertilized egg. What varies here from the previous chapter, which concentrates largely on abortion, is that this type of contraceptive use is not an ordinary "medical procedure"; it involves either the ingestion of a particular pill by a woman who chooses to take it or the implantation of an intrauterine device at her request. The object is not to correct or change her existing condition but to prevent a pregnancy from occurring. What has become highly controversial is not whether actual medical practitioners should be required to engage in the desired insertion of the intrauterine device but how far others should be compelled to support these choices by women. That question was sharply presented in *Hobby Lobby* by the claim for an exemption from having to provide such insurance to employees. The case concerned fundamental issues about how RFRA and similar statutes should be interpreted and about just how far exemptions should extend to indirect assistance. It also implicitly raised questions about the desirable roles in this context of specific statutory and executive determinations, as contrasted with judicial constructions of open-ended general statutes or similarly construed free exercise constitutional provisions.

Contraceptives and Their Supply

The position taken by the companies in *Hobby Lobby* and many other evangelical Protestant groups is not based on opposition to all contraceptive use, only to those that can operate after fertilization. It is worth mentioning here that there is a broader position, notably one contained explicitly in Roman Catholic Church doctrine, that the use of any contraceptive is wrong. The justifying reason has been that sexual involvement is for married couples to produce children. This stance has even been supported by claims of certain Catholic natural law theorists who do not themselves depend on religious premises; but their particular argument about the implications of natural reason is wholly unpersuasive for almost anyone who does not subscribe to the basic religious doctrine.[2] In fact, the majority of a papal commission set up by Pope John XXIII had in 1968 actually recommended the Church's acceptance of the use of contraceptives, but Pope Paul VI reiterated that condemnation. Nevertheless, the great majority of Catholic women who engage in sexual intercourse do sometimes use contraceptives. And in contrast to its views about abortion and sexual activity outside marriage, a statement by U.S. Catholic bishops in 2006 did not indicate that men and women who used contraceptives should decline to take communion unless they have first received the Sacrament of Penance.[3]

Because the use of most contraceptives is so widely accepted, whether pharmacists are given a general duty to sell them, and, if so, whether any exemptions should be granted, does not carry much practical importance. Perhaps no requirement is really needed, since a pharmacy would almost certainly suffer a genuine financial loss if it never made them available. On the other hand, maybe those who run pharmacies should be ready to supply all basic standard drugs to their customers. If so, any exemption might be regarded as too far out of line with the general practices and understandings in our culture. Having noted that opposition to all contraceptive use is conceivable; this chapter concentrates on the question of the much more practiced concern in our era, one that touches only a few contraceptives.

The serious problems arise over procedures and pills that may work after fertilization; these are intrauterine devices and one or two oral contraceptives taken after sexual intercourse. Of those two contraceptives, the prevailing evidence now is that Plan B may work only to prevent fertilization by delaying ovulation so that no eggs connect with sperm but that ella probably does sometimes prevent implantation of fertilized eggs and also destroy fertilized eggs after implantation.[4] Intrauterine devices usually prevent fertilization but occasionally preclude implantation.[5] Because some believe that pregnancy begins at fertilization and others at implantation, the word "conception" is a bit imprecise in distinguishing these two stages.[6] However, I use that term in what follows because if a drug may work both between fertilization and implantation and after the latter, which of these stages someone sees as the beginning of pregnancy is not crucial. What matters is that he perceives the drug as sometimes effectively ending a pregnancy and constituting an early form of abortion.

When pharmacists or their employees believe that drugs can have this effect, should they be able to refuse to sell them, should hospitals be able to decline to supply them, and should employers be able to not include them in otherwise required insurance? For pharmacies, as noted, one could defend the absence of any requirements about what they supply, so long as other pharmacies are easily available for customers. However, in some localities, people may not have multiple pharmacies in close range, and even within a major city, if a woman regularly uses a particular drugstore and learns it does not sell a drug, she may feel some insult to her dignity if she is told at the pharmacy that because of the convictions of those who run it, a common drug is not available. She may be at least annoyed with having to go elsewhere, especially to a place without a prior record of her insurance coverage. If she does not see her need as critical, she may just do without the drug, and if she feels she needs it badly and quickly, she may become distressed at having then to go to what is for her a novel pharmacy. These are strong enough reasons to require the supply of standard drugs unless those running the pharmacy have a genuine and deep objection. Since such objections will almost always be connected to religious convictions, a privilege not to supply the drugs could sensibly be limited to those, although given that "natural" reasons could be seen by some as indicating that human life begins at this early stage, a broader privilege of conscience would also make sense. In fact, state statutory provisions vary about this. As of 2015, only seven states specifically protected pharmacists, but more general formulations of "health care providers" may also be seen to reach them.[7] Some of these laws and other proposals were cast in terms of religious convictions; others referred to conscience more generally.[8]

Such exemptions from legal liability should fairly extend to individual pharmacists within drugstores in the manner that applies to abortions. If a pharmacy itself provides the drug, it should not be able to require that of an individual pharmacist who objects in conscience if another pharmacist who is present can do it at that time. Probably the connection of others, such as clerks who hand drugs to customers, is not close enough to warrant any exemption from direct legal requirements or from discipline by their own organizations.[9] Overall, exemptions from required supply may well be warranted here, but they should be carefully constrained so that those who want the drugs suffer no genuine inconvenience or embarassment.

The Insurance Question

The crucial question presented by *Hobby Lobby* is whether a company under a general requirement to provide insurance that covers intrauterine devices and ella and Plan B for its employees is entitled to an exemption under RFRA because of the religious convictions of its owners that these contraceptives sometimes operate as a form of abortion. For three aspects of this basic question—the wisdom of an exemption, the desirability of specific or general provisions, and how RFRA should be interpreted—we need to start with some legal background. This includes the Supreme Court's rejection of a claim for a tax exemption, the basic context of the 2010 Patient Protection and Affordable Care Act (ACA), and steps taken by the Obama administration toward religious accommodations relating to the act's requirements.

Legal Background

As earlier chapters explain, prior to 1990, the Supreme Court employed a standard of application for the Free Exercise Clause that people did not need to conform to a general legal restriction if doing so imposed a substantial burden on their religious exercise and did not serve a government interest that was both compelling and could not be achieved by less restrictive means. As also indicated, the compelling interest test here was really one of intermediate scrutiny, not one that was sharply restrictive of what the government could do.

In addition to its implausible distinction between the force of hybrid claims and the application of single constitutional provisions, Justice Scalia's majority opinion in *Employment Division v. Smith* stressed that the Supreme Court had actually applied its free exercise approach in only two kinds of cases.[10] A few of these decisions had upheld claims for unemployment compensation and for damages from the loss of employment made by those whose religious convictions barred either a certain kind of work or work on a particular day that their religion maintained was holy and must be free from that nonreligious activity. What the Scalia opinion does not tell us, or even refer to, is how often employers and officials aware of Supreme Court doctrine had made accommodations to workers' claims, how often state and lower federal courts sustained such claims, and how often the Supreme Court declined review of those cases. In short, *Smith* really gives almost no insight into how effective the standard it abandoned had been. As noted earlier, some states still interpret their state constitutional free exercise provisions in accord with the Supreme Court's pre-*Smith* jurisprudence.

Among the cases decided prior to *Smith,* one that is especially relevant for how we should see insurance coverage is *United States v. Lee,*[11] in which an Amish employer with only Amish workers claimed a right not to pay the Social Security tax, since it is contrary to the Amish religion to accept government benefits such as Social Security. This case followed the decision in *Wisconsin v. Yoder,*[12] which a decade earlier had sustained the constitutional right of the Amish to withdraw children from school after the eighth grade, given Amish beliefs and training in cooperative practices within the Amish community to help the children prepare for their lives there. Despite *Yoder,* the Court, with only one dissent, rejected the claim in *Lee.* The government had a compelling interest in collecting taxes, without a less restrictive means of accomplishing its objectives. If one focuses on the precise issue in *Lee,* one can easily imagine two feasible alternatives to requiring that genuine objectors actually pay Social Security taxes. The first is obvious. So long as these objectors are an extremely small minority of those required to help their employees in this way, the government could simply bear the cost. In fact, Congress did supply just the exemption sought by *Lee* after the Supreme Court's rejection. Of course, such a privilege might lead to some outright fraudulent claims by employers who just wish to save money. Even if limited to religious convictions, it might also encourage some employers with weak religious reservations to formulate those as based on strong religious conscience. An independent reason to reject this option for the *Lee* case also could matter. Insofar as Lee's claim was partly based on the fact that all his employees were Amish, a right limited to similar circumstances could strongly encourage the using of religious membership as a basis for hiring, not a practice the government should assist.

The second possibility of a less restrictive means is another "alternative" I believe has never actually been used for taxes and other requirements to pay legal fees. If someone strongly objects to how a particular tax or general taxes may be used, let them indicate what government objectives they do consider legitimate and pay money that will be used only for those purposes, so long as they pay something like 5 percent more than the normal tax would entail. Since the government can finance the purposes to which they object out of the general payments made by others, this concession will cause only a very slight administrative task and thus will not interfere with any government purposes. And the extra cost will definitely discourage anything less than claims based on sincere and strong objections. In rejecting the possibility of less restrictive means, the Court in *Lee* did not actually delve into the viability of either of these possibilities for the government to grant the accommodation without undercutting its Social Security policy. Lurking in the background of *Hobby Lobby* is the relevance or irrelevance of the decision in *Lee.*

In 1993, with virtual unanimity, Congress adopted the Religious Freedom Restoration Act (RFRA).[13] The law states that the "government shall not substantially burden a person's exercise of religion even if the burden results from a rule of general applicability . . . [unless] it demonstrates that application of the burden to the person (1) is in furtherance of a compelling government interest; and (2) is the least restrictive means of furthering that . . . interest." As other language in the statute makes explicitly clear, the aim of the law was effectively to reintroduce the free exercise standard that preceded *Employment Division v. Smith* and to overturn the significance of that case. As we have seen, the Supreme Court did not accept RFRA's application to the laws of states, on the basis that Congress lacked this power, but it did rule it effective in respect to federal laws. Thus, the country has a federal statute, as well as nineteen similar state statutes,[14] that embody the rather open-ended general approach that had earlier constituted part of constitutional free exercise law.

When Congress later adopted the Religious Land Use and Institutional Persons Act (RLUIPA), whose force we will consider in the next chapter, it made a modest revision or clarification of what the RFRA standard, initially adopted by Congress, was designed to do. Aiming to counter weaker judicial interpretations, it provided that RFRA applied "whether or not" an exercise of religion was "compelled by, or central to, a system of religious belief" and that it was to be "construed in favor of a broad protection of religious exercise."[15]

The question in *Hobby Lobby* was whether RFRA's language provides a privilege for a closely held for-profit corporation not to provide insurance for contraceptives to which the owners strongly object on religious grounds. The case raises not only the question of how that law should be construed in such a circumstance but also whether a more direct legislative focus would be preferable.

Should RFRA be taken to create an exemption from the requirement under the federal Affordable Care Act (ACA) that companies of substantial size must supply for their workers insurance that covers contraceptives? To understand the claim of *Hobby Lobby,* and the Court's resolution, one needs to grasp other features of the act itself and what the Obama administration had done.

The regulations issued under the ACA, which had been amended by the 2010 Health Care and Education Reconciliation Act,[16] provided that companies with fifty or more employees had to provide extensive insurance for their workers, including intrauterine devices, and also Plan B and ella. The mandate did not apply to companies with fewer than fifty employees or to those with grandfathered plans in place. It exempted religious organizations such as churches but not religiously affiliated hospitals, social service agencies, and universities. Although some opposed all religious accommodations, the more intense objections were to the narrowness of the scope of those provided. In response, the Obama administration indicated that it would not require religiously based enterprises such as hospitals to pay for insurance for contraceptives for which they have religious objections. However, their employees remained entitled to this coverage, to be provided by insurance companies.

According to rules set in July 2013 and amended in 2014, a nonprofit entity that holds itself out as a religious organization and has a religious objection will be free of the contraceptive coverage requirement if it self-certifies that it meets those requirements.[17] Given the effect of the self-certification, no active review takes place about whether an organization is truly religious or has stated its convictions sincerely. Under the rule initially set, the organizations did have to submit an EBSA Form 700 to qualify for the exemption. Some religious universities and other organizations objected that even filing the form violated their convictions. Although various lower courts rejected this argument, in *Wheaton College v. Burwell,* the Supreme Court declined to rule that organizations had to fill out the form, prior to judicial resolution of the merits of the college's claim not to do so.[18] In response, the government issued a rule allowing religious nonprofits to inform the Department of Health and Human Services of their objection in some way other than formal submission of Form 700.[19] As a consequence, a question not yet resolved is whether having to file a particular form, or even providing a direct request for an exemption in some other way, can amount to a substantial burden; and, if so, whether the government's need for such a notice overrides the burden. Various nonprofit entities have asserted that even any such requirement violates their convictions. Although seven courts of appeals have rejected their claim that RFRA protects them,[20] a district court has determined otherwise.[21] This is actually an interesting analogue to the long-standing requirement of draft laws that young men must register, which led to a significant number of pacifists ending up in jail.

Given the effect of the ACA statute and its implementing rules, the contraceptive coverage paid for the insurance companies and not financed by employers who have offered religious claims can happen in one of two ways. If a hospital provides insurance benefits through an independent company, that company simply bears the costs directly. Since contraceptives reduce the number of pregnancies and births, it has been assumed that insurance companies would actually be better off providing the coverage than if they did not do so. Of course this would still cost a company more than if the employer had actually paid for that coverage; and this could conceivably affect how much it would charge the employer to pay for the rest of its insurance. Things work out somewhat differently for religious institutions that directly provide their own insurance. They need to have an administrator get an insurance company that provides this coverage under Federally Facilitated Exchange Insurance. That coverage alone is, of course, not going to save this insurance company any money, but the company is then allowed to pay the government less for the privilege of participating in the federally facilitated exchange.

The *Hobby Lobby* Claim and the Supreme Court's RFRA Interpretation

The owners of Hobby Lobby and another closely held for-profit corporation claimed a right under RFRA not to comply with the ACA regulations insofar as they cover contraceptive drugs and devices that may prevent a fertilized egg "from developing any further by inhibiting its attachment to the uterus."[22] Under their religious convictions, when an egg is fertilized, it is a human life that deserves protection. Not having an exemption under the issued regulations, the companies claimed a right under RFRA. To win, they needed definitely to succeed in two respects and also in at least one of two others. What they had to establish was that they counted as a "person" exercising religion under the statute and that their compliance with ACA would constitute a substantial burden on that exercise. They then needed to show that the government either lacked a compelling interest or had available a less restrictive means. A succinct explanation of these issues can both clarify the debatable ways in which a broadly worded free exercise standard may be interpreted and suggest why in this context a more specific legislative or regulatory focus would be desirable. In what follows, I offer some critiques of how individual standards were taken, but my main difficulty with the opinion in *Hobby Lobby* is that it treats those standards as separate and in a formal way, rather their considering what will make sense in terms of the statute's overall objectives.

QUALIFYING ENTITIES UNDER THE ACT

In terms of ordinary language, one does not conceive of companies as engaged in "a person's exercise of religion." Justice Alito's opinion relies on the broadness of RFRA, its clarification or extension by RLUIPA, and the existence of an earlier free exercise case in which most justices seemed to accept that a for-profit company could make a claim that is should be able to be open on Sunday, contrary to the law, because of its religious conviction that it must close on Saturday, its Sabbath.[23] Writing as if the answer to the coverage question is patently clear, Alito also gives considerable importance to a federal statute that explicitly provides that with acts of Congress "'person' include[s] corporations, companies, associations, firms, partnerships, societies, and joint stock companies, as well as individuals . . . , unless [the] context indicates otherwise."[24]

In truth, the answer is far from straightforward.[25] When the Free Exercise Clause was being interpreted to provide some protection against general laws, little focus was addressed in either judicial decisions or scholarship on the extent of protection, if any, for corporations engaged in seeking financial profits. This was not given serious attention either when RFRA was adopted or when the coverage of protected exercise was made clearly broad by RLUIPA. Justice Alito is definitely correct that RFRA interpretation should not seek to replicate the exact range of rights afforded earlier in specific situations as a matter of constitutional law; no account of constitutional rights is that rigid. But legislators *were* aiming to provide essentially similar protections. Given how an "objective person" and an actual human being would likely understand RFRA's language, an argument that the "context" here indicates a more common reading of "person" has considerable force. On this language point, a plausible counterargument in favor of the Court's conclusion is that no one doubts that basic religious organizations do have rights under RFRA,[26] so this itself shows an expansive sense of "person." However, even if one concludes that "person" may include some organizations, the particular "context" may well suggest distinguishing among the kinds of organizations. Corporations out to make money, whose owners are granted by the government the privilege of not being personally liable for business expenses or bankruptcy, should be seen as not possessing all the rights of individuals and nonprofit religious groups. That, of course, does not itself settle whether for-profit businesses, closely held or not, should ever be granted exemptions from duties imposed on others,[27] but it does constitute a fairly powerful reason not to apply the vague, open-ended language of RFRA, which was not focused on that question.

A further difficulty with the Court's determination is its comparison with large corporations that have public holders of stocks. Assuming that they will be unlikely to make RFRA claims, Alito does not try to resolve whether they are free to do so. But we can imagine two intermediate situations. In one, those initially running a company make clear their contemplated religious limits on maximizing profits. Members of the public considering a purchase of these stocks are thus provided this warning. Even if they fail to make such limits clear, the originators may hold on to a majority of the stocks and sell only 40 percent to the public. In that setting, they will control company policy and may be able to impose restraints. In brief, we can conceive circumstances in which those controlling a company may refuse to comply with legal requirements in certain ways, even if some members of the public holding their stocks do not share their views. If a line is to be established between ordinary large corporations and those that are closely held, it is not yet clear exactly how this line will, or should, be drawn.[28]

Justice Alito's opinion treats the question about qualifying entities and the following three basic inquiries as if they are essentially separate from each other. If, however, the answer to the application of RFRA to for-profit corporations is not clear from the statute itself, a much more sensible approach is to ask how an overall evaluation of such coverage is likely to work, not only in this particular context but more generally. Since eligibility for coverage raises much broader concerns, this is a situation in which the question about what entities are reached should not be decided merely formalistically based on the meaning of "person" or on the appropriateness of application in this single circumstance. The right answer depends significantly on how appraisal of the standards of recovery will operate in practice.

SUBSTANTIAL BURDEN

On the question of whether Hobby Lobby suffered a substantial burden, the majority was sharply divided from Justice Ginsburg's dissent. For Justice Alito, that depends fundamentally on the religious convictions of those making the claim.[29] Justice Ginsburg urges a more general, objective standard based on how direct is the relation of a claimant's religious exercise to the activity that conflicts with his convictions.[30] We have considered in Chapter 5 what should be done about relatively peripheral involvements concerning abortions. The *Hobby Lobby* case directly poses the status of such involvements for application of a law like RFRA, and more broadly it highlights the question of whether specific legislative or regulatory decisions are preferable.

As a matter of simple principle, Justice Alito's approach seems sound, at least when religious convictions rather than standard practices are at stake. After all, if people genuinely feel they are being asked to do something that would be deeply wrong given their obligations to God, is that not a burden on them that is substantial? But how workable is this approach for other officials and for judges? "Substantial burden" means that one must honestly feel performing the act would be deeply wrong, not just less preferable from a religious point of view than the alternative. Thus, if we are concentrating on actual convictions, the concept is not so different from the "conscientious objection" one needed to be excused from a military draft. How is that level of force to be determined? If no exemption has yet been granted, and a person who seeks one may or may not succeed, we have some intrinsic assurance that she really feels very strongly. Otherwise, she would not undergo the risk of a penalty and the inconvenience and financial cost of making a challenge. This presumably was true about the owners of Hobby Lobby.

But what if an exemption has clearly been established for those who suffer a substantial burden? Especially if one advantage of the exemption is that it may save money for the claimants who qualify, someone would now have an incentive to make an outright false objection, or, more subtly, to state her genuine opposition to performance in a way that conveys much more intensity than she actually feels. Remember the nurse in the last chapter who would prefer morally not to help with plastic surgery designed only to preserve youthful appearance. If she knew she could be excused with no negative consequences, might she not be inclined to state the burden on her as substantial? When it comes to the coverage of insurance requirements, no one is going to interview all the owners of companies to see if their objection is both fully sincere and adequately intense. In short, the fact that once an exemption is established, the Alito approach does not really allow serious assessment by others provides a strong reason to make the "substantial burden" assessment depend at least partly on how most people would perceive the connection between the convictions and the degree of involvement.

This raises the specific status of providing insurance, and the question of its similarity to, or difference from, paying taxes. An employer whose insurance covers contraceptives does not actually provide them for use, nor does it encourage any of its workers to use them. An individual worker who herself decides to pay for and use the contraceptives needs only an easily obtainable prescription to do so. Is affording insurance coverage that provides money for a choice and physical consumption made by a free individual very different from paying taxes that are either specifically targeted for purposes to which one objects, such as Social Security, or that fall into a general pool that some people use for such purposes? The difference does not seem all that great, especially for taxes that go to a single kind of benefit that an employer's payment makes his workers eligible to receive. Thus the claim in *Hobby Lobby* bears a significant resemblance to that rejected by the Supreme Court of the Amish employer not to pay Social Security taxes.[31] The nonacceptance of that claim in the *Lee* case was nearly unanimous, and although Alito's opinion in *Hobby Lobby* regards that case as rendered under a no longer applicable free exercise doctrine, he also remarks that the result would be the same under RFRA.[32] It should be noted here in defense of his opinion that the Court in *Lee* does not rely on the absence of burden but rather the unavailability of less restrictive means, an issue we will examine shortly. However, one might well conceive *Lee,* at least implicitly and partly, as based on a sense that paying taxes to the government cannot be seen as a genuine violation of religious exercise to which the law should respond. This could lead to perceiving insurance payments similarly, or at least demanding a really careful analysis of why they differ.

By the way it interprets "substantial burden," the *Hobby Lobby* Court has essentially eliminated it as a real test for claims for certain exemptions of kinds already established. If company owners are willing to assert a grave violation of their serious religious convictions, those applying the law are not going to be in a position to deny that. That consideration, along with the analogy to tax payments, suggests that the treatment in the Alito opinion is too simplistic and hasty. And, like the questions of who qualifies as a "person," that issue should have been considered in light of the broad scope of claims likely to be raised. Such an analysis, along with the tax analogy, might well have suggested that what counts as a substantial burden should depend significantly on just how close is the connection between one's convictions and the behavior to which one objects.

COMPELLING INTEREST

The "compelling interest" question turned out not to play an important role in the decision. In her dissent, Justice Ginsburg emphasized the great importance of contraceptives for the health and welfare of women.[33] Justice Alito did resist casting the crucial interest in broad terms such as public health. He insisted, citing RFRA and the case involving the importation of hallucinogenic tea, that the "Government . . . [must] demonstrate that the compelling interest test is satisfied through application of the challenged law 'to the person'—the particular claimant."[34] One cannot take such language quite literally, since it will rarely be the situation that the government's interest is sacrificed if only one "person" is exempted. Rather it makes sense that the compelling interest is met if the claimant and all those similarly situated are to be treated the same way. More importantly, Alito did note the other employers who were free of the insurance requirements, but he did not really challenge Justice Ginsburg's assertion that the provision of some exemptions from laws is not itself sufficient to undercut the government's strong interest in their broad application. Alito finally concluded that "We find it unnecessary to adjudicate this issue,"[35] relying instead on the availability of less restrictive means. Since the division on the Court was 5–4, and Justice Kennedy in a concurrence made it clear that he thought the compelling interest element was satisfied,[36] he and the four dissenters constituted a majority of justices who reached that conclusion.

LESS RESTRICTIVE MEANS

Justice Alito's opinion throws out one possibility but relies essentially on another to conclude that the government does possess a less restrictive means. On analysis, the first option seems to play more of a role than he acknowledges and sharply raises the issue of whether a serious difference exists here from tax payments for specific benefits like Social Security. Alito initially declares that the least restrictive means standard is "exceptionally demanding."[37] This generalization does not fit well with the Court's stressing nine years earlier that when prisoners made claims under RLUIPA, "due deference" should be given to prison officials about maintaining order and safety,[38] although of course the prison context can be seen as special enough to warrant a much weaker standard of review.

The broad possibility Alito suggests is that the government could pay for contraceptives without much financial sacrifice;[39] but the opinion actually relies on the narrower ground that the Obama administration had already granted an exemption for nonprofit religious employers, without their workers being deprived of the insurance or having to bear the costs. If this alternative could work for nonprofit organizations, without depriving the employees of anything, it could do the same for closely held, for-profit corporations, thus constituting a less restrictive alternative that would satisfy the government's objective.[40]

We need to look more closely than Alito did at the two ways this could work. As already noted, if a religious organization provides insurance itself for workers, the objected-to contraceptive insurance is to be given by an independent insurance company, which is recompensed by paying less to the government for participating in Federally Facilitated Exchange Insurance.[41] I am not sure whether many for-profit companies do directly provide insurance payments for their own workers.[42] If they do, we might see this as slightly more direct involvement than financing independent insurers to make the payments. But the important point here is that with this scheme, under which the objecting owners get a separate company to provide the insurance without providing any direct financing, the ultimate cost is borne by lower payments of the insurance company to the government. This differs from relieving some entities from tax payments only in that those involved are paying a reduced amount to exercise a kind of government privilege. In both instances, the general public finally bears the costs.

Matters are less simple when one considers insurance companies that are contracted by employers to provide all the insurance payments for their employees. How can their paying for objected-to contraceptives not involve costs for them? To illustrate the idea here, and its limitations, I will put aside insurance company profits and use some imaginary and artificial numbers. Let us suppose that C (a corporation) needs to spend $700,000 for insurance on matters totally unrelated to the contraceptives to which its owners might object. Covering these contraceptives would cost an extra $50,000, but that would also render unnecessary another extra $50,000 that would otherwise have been needed for extra pregnancies and their costs. If they had a simple choice of coverage or noncoverage of the contraceptives, they would in either event need to pay $750,000 for insurance. Now, suppose C gets an exemption and need not cover the contraceptives but is assured that its insurance company will do so. If the contraceptives are available for all their workers who wish to have them, and their use is not affected by who provides the insurance, C's insurance costs will now be $700,000. This outcome could save C some money and could provide an incentive for others to make similar claims.

The insurance company (IN) that provides for contraceptives will still be paying $750,000. IN would bear the same cost because of extra pregnancies if no company financed the contraceptives and the women either chose not to use them or could not afford them. But, in contrast to the initial circumstance, what would be the amount it got from C? If either it set a general fee for covered companies and did not adjust what C paid because of C's noncoverage of the contraceptives *or* it set the cost for C based on its awareness that it still needed to pay the extra $50,000, the effective cost would ultimately be borne by C. If IN did not charge the $50,000 to C, it would bear that cost in a way that would not be true if C had paid for full coverage. What all this comes down to is that either the insurance company will itself bear an extra cost in a crucial sense, or it will return all or part of that cost to the company whose owners object to providing insurance for the contraceptives. The latter reality is highly similar to persons paying taxes to the government which are used partly for purposes to which they object.

As this analysis of both situations shows, the analogy to tax payments is not nearly as remote as the justices seem to assume in *Hobby Lobby*. This bears strongly on whether the indirect form of supporting the contraceptive use should be seen as sufficient to raise a RFRA claim and whether allowing nonpayment should be seen as required by this less restrictive means, if such claims are not available in tax cases. Reasonable disagreement exists over whether the decision in *Hobby Lobby* was basically sound.[43] My own sense is that the Court should have not applied RFRA, but my most central critique is of the formalist approach of Justice Alito's opinion.

HOW SHOULD SUCH CLAIMS BE TREATED?

This section so far has suggested that, when deciding the coverage of a statute like RFRA, the Supreme Court should be attentive to wider circumstances in which similar claims might be raised, taking into account considerations of possible insincere assertions and administrability. I do not mean that the standards the Court sets for specific applications should themselves be vague or very general. They need to provide a fairly clear guide to the status of closely held and other for-profit corporations and to what kinds of connections may be too indirect to sustain claims.

When we think about the problem of contraceptive insurance, application of RFRA is less desirable than a more specific legislative focus.[44] A practical concern is that despite the scope of various penalties, whose practical severity for many employers is debated, some companies denied an exemption *and* left with the choice of covering everything or nothing might choose not to provide insurance at all. That would significantly disadvantage their employees. As with abortions, this is itself one reason to afford an exemption.

Because, although nonreligious objections to providing insurance for these contraceptives are conceivable, their rarity renders it appropriate here to cast any privilege of noncoverage in terms of religion. The justification for an exemption in these circumstances is supported by the fact that the negative view about emergency contraceptives does fall within the mainstream of public opinion, which is fairly evenly divided.[45]

As with certain other issues involving possible exemptions, legislators and others should consider possible alternatives.[46] This possible approach can seem even more appealing when what would otherwise be a desirable approach to an exemption seems too difficult to administer fairly. Here the government might itself supply contraceptives for most women. This would be fairly expensive, but it would be a small amount in comparison with the total national budget. Doing so would provide the benefit most women want and need, eliminate the possible violations of religious and other conscience of some owners of enterprises, and sharply reduce what has become a matter of intense controversy.

Conclusion

This chapter's exploration of the specific concern about contraceptives that sometimes operate after fertilization has concentrated on the indirect assistance provided by insurance coverage. When it comes to how RFRA is properly interpreted, I have urged that much in the majority opinion in *Hobby Lobby* is too simplistic in its analysis. The concern about indirect forms of aid plays an important role in the preceding chapter's treatment of abortions and in Chapter 8's discussion of same-sex marriage. As with difficult questions explored in many other chapters, we can perceive reasons for fairly specific legislative forms of exemption, or even for alternatives that open up choices more broadly in ways that are simple to administer.

7

Prisons and Land Use

Introduction

THIS CHAPTER CONSIDERS two exemption issues that differ a great deal from most of those analyzed in prior chapters and from each other. What mainly connects them is that they are the two topics that are addressed by the Religious Land Use and Institutionalized Persons Act (RLUIPA),[1] the federal statute adopted in 2000 after the Religious Freedom Restoration Act (RFRA) was held to be invalid as it applied to states. Both provisions are also interesting examples of how far more specific legislative attention to discrete kinds of impairments of religious exercise and freedom of conscience are feasible and politically realistic. Together with preceding law, they also show how the same, or closely similar, general standards are often treated differently by officials and judges in different contexts. Notably, the way the substantial burden, compelling interest, and less restrictive means standards have been applied for prison claims is strikingly different from how the Supreme Court cast those tests in the *Hobby Lobby* case.

This book is not about the distribution of federal and state power, but for readers unfamiliar with certain nuances about this, a brief explanation of why RLUIPA covered its two subjects may help explain this odd combination. Recall that the earlier RFRA with its broad coverage had been enacted to apply to states as well as the federal government. After the Supreme Court declared that Congress lacked the authority to do this in respect to states, because Congress could not override the Court's construction of constitutional rights, members of Congress and outside advocates sought more limited domains for which such state coverage might be regarded as legitimate. Following analysis, discussions, and debates, and after a political compromise, institutionalized persons and land use were the two topics settled upon, with particular language applying to each. In essence, the three basic grounds were that federal regulation of interstate commerce was relevant for both subjects, that federal financial assistance for the running of state prisons and other institutions warranted setting constraints, and that the number of discriminatory decisions against religious institutions generally or particular disfavored ones, which were often hard to identify with confidence, warranted a general protection in respect to land use. This third ground is one example of how the unconstitutionality of the favoring some religions over others, or the disfavoring of religious groups in comparison with nonreligious ones, can sometimes lead to a broader statutory protection of religious practices.

Before tackling the two aspects of RLUIPA in more detail, it is helpful to note some comparisons with exemptions the previous chapters have covered. The claims of prisoners and other persons within institutions are typically based on religious conscience to be free of generally applicable requirements or to receive special benefits, such as kosher meals. With a few exceptions, the competing grounds for denial to prisoners are not concerns about whether other prisoners will suffer deprivations or discrimination but the need for prison security and the avoidance of excessive expenses. With land use, the bases for regulations and their administration are also mainly ones of public welfare, not the making services available for those who need them and treating others fairly, although what religious groups are allowed to do can in various ways affect to a degree the value of the properties of surrounding residents. Claims about land use for religious purposes typically involve organizations, not individuals. Some, such as the ability to feed the poor, may be based on a kind of conscience, but more common is the asserted need for the group to function effectively. In this core respect, issues about land use resemble those central to decisions about tax exemptions and deductions.

In this chapter, we look first at claims of religious freedom in prisons, the institutions in which the vast majority of claims arise, and then turn to zoning regulations and other constraints on uses of land.

Basic Issues About Religious Exercise in Prison and Its Evaluation

Life within prisons, like that of military personnel, is obviously far more restricted in respect to what occupants are at liberty to do than is true for ordinary civilians. Given the vast number of such restraints, questions arise over whether exceptions should be granted in respect to matters that would be completely up to personal choices for the rest of us. When should we gather for worship, should we shave, what food shall we eat? A special feature of life within prisons is that the "residents" are perceived as persons who have done wrong and are not to be trusted. Not surprisingly, this strongly affects what prisoners are generally forbidden to do,and what exceptions may seem warranted. Given the harshness of many sentences now authorized and imposed and the relative lack of concern by both the public and most members of government about the quality of prison life,[2] we should expect neither much focused legislative attention to particular aspects of prison life nor active judicial sustaining of individual claims in genuinely doubtful cases.

Not until January 2015 did the Supreme Court render a decision that actually explicated how the standards of RLUIPA should be applied in a prison setting. The case involved the denial of an inmate's claim of religious exercise to grow a beard one-half inch in length.[3] If one reflects on *Hobby Lobby* and most other Supreme Court cases involving claims of religious exercise, one might expect a serious division among the justices, but if one looks at the facts of this dispute, the right answer is transparently clear, and the unanimous resolution is hardly surprising. Understanding just how such a case made it to the Supreme Court and how the Court's stated approach strengthens standards of review can benefit from a brief account of prior law, including a comparison with a significant military case and of the actual content of RLUIPA.

Prior to RLUIPA, judges generally afforded broad deference to the decisions of prison officials, and at least in many litigated cases, those officials often took positions that were unaccommodating to religious claims for special treatment. In 1987, the Supreme Court basically accepted this practice and judicial deference when a claim of Muslim inmates to be free from outside work in order to attend a weekly prayer service was rejected, on various grounds including the assumption that requiring that work helped simulate the work conditions of society.[4] Although the constitutional free exercise standards of *Sherbert v. Verner* and *Wisconsin v. Yoder* had not yet been abandoned, the justices stated, "To ensure that courts afford appropriate deference to prison officials, we have determined that prison regulations alleged to infringe constitutional rights are judged under a 'reasonableness' test less restrictive than that ordinarily applied to alleged infringements of fundamental constitutional rights."[5] Not granting an exemption from a neutral rule was sufficient if that was "reasonably related to legitimate penological interests."[6]

Just one year earlier, the Court had rendered what was an effectively similar resolution about military life, though that majority opinion was a lot less explicit about the standard of review. For military life, similar to prison life in sharply restricting what individual soldiers, sailors, and Marines are free to do, a crucial factor is the notion that a high degree of discipline is required for an effective armed force. Understandably, judges have been hesitant to declare that any exception from a general requirement is definitely warranted; but *Goldman v. Weinberger* was an incredibly extreme decision along these lines. The basic issue was whether an Orthodox Jewish rabbi who served as a psychologist in a mental health clinic could wear a yarmulke, in accordance with his belief that he should cover his head before God, despite an Air Force regulation that forbade the wearing of headgear indoors.[7] The two justifications behind the uniform dress regulations were that they help to reinforce the sense of a united force and preclude styles and qualities of clothing that reflect highly divergent social backgrounds. Officials refused to make an exception for the rabbi.[8]

Not clear about the exact standard of review, the majority opinion by Justice Rehnquist did state clearly that "courts must give great deference to the professional judgment of military authorities."[9] Even with appropriate deference, how plausible is application of a strong government interest standard here? How much would an interest in uniform dress be undercut by allowing a psychologist in a mental health facility to wear a yarmulke? None of the reasons for the general rule would preclude an exemption here, and the argument in favor of rigid application was little supported by any worry that other Orthodox Jews might want to wear yarmulkes indoors or by the possibility that members of other religions might make parallel claims. Whether it would have made sense to indicate that these other claims could also succeed or to draw a line based on likely effect may be debatable, but that resolution could have awaited future cases. Another strong reason to reject the asserted grounds to deny the rabbi's claim was that other exceptions to standard clothing requirements had been created to accommodate certain Christian supplements to apparel. That generates a strong equality argument for similar treatment. In truth, a highly likely explanation for the *Goldman* result and the succeeding prisoner case is that most of the justices in the majority were really disaffected with the *Sherbert* free exercise test, which they rejected outright a few years later in *Employment Division v. Smith.*

After *Goldman,* Congress responded by authorizing members of the armed forces to wear apparel that is "neat and conservative" and would not interfere with military performance.[10] When RFRA was enacted seven years later, it contained no general exception for the military or prisons from its requirement of exemptions, thus sharply raising the question whether the compelling interest test should then apply in the same way for duties of the military and treatment of prisoners as it does in the contexts of other claims for religious practice. Yet between the passage of RFRA and its declared unconstitutionality as applied to states, apparently prisoners lost all but nine of ninety-nine RFRA claims that led to reported decisions on the merits.[11]

A broad issue for legislative wisdom about prisons is how far statutes should set out somewhat more specific standards for considering claims of special treatment, as Congress did for military dress after the *Goldman* decision.

THE RLUIPA STANDARDS FOR PRISONS AND INSTANCES OF APPLICATION

In its basic coverage for prisons and mental institutions, RLUIPA closely resembles RFRA, which itself was grounded on the pre-*Smith* free exercise law. It provides, "No government shall impose a substantial burden on the religious exercise of a person residing in or confined to an institution" unless there is "a compelling governmental interest" being served by "the least restrictive means."[12] Regarding the burden on free exercise, the statute, largely in response to lower court cases that were overly demanding on claimants in this respect, provided both for itself and RFRA that "religious exercise" need not be compelled by, or central to, a system of religious belief.[13] During the legislative hearings, Congress had evidence of frivolous or arbitrary barriers. As noted in the subsequent Supreme Court opinion in *Cutter v. Wilkinson,* a joint statement of Republican Senator Hatch and Democratic Senator Kennedy had said, "Whether from indifference, ignorance, bigotry, or lack of resources, some institutions restrict religious liberty in egregious and unnecessary ways."[14] According to the Senate Report, the members of Congress expected judges to apply RLUIPA with "due deference to the experience and expertise of prison and jail administrators in establishing necessary regulations and procedures to maintain good order, security and discipline, consistent with consideration of costs and limited resources."[15]

In *Cutter,* its first RLUIPA case, the Supreme Court reviewed a fundamental challenge, which judges on the Sixth Circuit had sustained, that the law violated the Establishment Clause by giving a preference to religious claims over nonreligious ones. Justice Ginsburg's unanimous opinion sustained the law against that "facial challenge," ruling that Congress may enact religious accommodations. The *Cutter* opinion left a great deal open. It did not resolve whether in specific contexts, treating a nonreligious prisoner claim like a religious one would be wise or even constitutionally required. Nor did it address in any detail just how judges should apply the RLUIPA standard. On the first point, the focus in this book is primarily on when a religious–nonreligious distinction is warranted, not exactly what the constitutionally permissible range should be. On the second point, we shall examine a few actual cases that help reveal how far the standard has been applied fairly and sensibly, or instead taken too restrictively or too permissively. I also address two different, related considerations: Would legislators do well to develop more specific guides for certain kinds of practices within prisons?; and How should those setting prison rules themselves respond to various proposed practices and legal constraints that have been set? As I have suggested, in this area, expecting careful evaluations of competing considerations by either legislators or prison officials may not be realistic, but asking what these might be is nonetheless warranted.

It is important to understand at the outset that, supported by empirical research, penal authorities are aware that inmates who are involved in religious practices generally create fewer disciplinary problems and have a greater chance of not again being involved in criminal activity.[16] Since penal systems in the United States broadly have made various concessions to religious practices of inmates, perceiving that the cases that get to courts show a widespread inflexibility is a somewhat unfair basis to discern general prison practices. Nonetheless, as previously noted, a study some years ago indicated that few claims of prisoners under RFRA that reached courts had succeeded.[17] Unlike RFRA and RLUIPA, certain state statutes explicitly cast prisoners' claims of religious exercise less favorably than those of persons living in the broader society, thus making it easier for courts to sustain the validity of prison regulations with unqualified coverage against claims that religious exemptions are needed.[18]

Just how a standard of evaluation should be cast, whether explicitly in statutory language or by judicial construction of a general language like that of RLUIPA, is hardly simple. The need for prison security is obviously very important, and judges may be less able to assess contested accounts of what will work than when they deal with ordinary civilian society. On the other hand, judges should be more capable of evaluating many arguments about what is needed to make prison life work effectively than what degree of uniformity in the military is needed to prepare soldiers to reliably act on orders and risk their lives in armed conflict. Another possibly relevant factor is what we are told about how many prisons operate. Putting aside concerns about inadequate protection of women against sexual offenses, we hear relatively little about abusive practices within the military, but apparently harsh treatment within prisons is widespread. This could well bear to a degree on just how much judges should evaluate assertions of needed restrictions and affect their degree of deference to prison officials. Perhaps judges should not only formulate and self-consciously apply viable standards but also take into account the general respect appropriately accorded to the level of prison officials whose determinations they are reviewing.

Under RLUIPA, there have been four major categories of prison cases. These involve challenges to restrictions about (1) grooming and clothing, (2) diet, (3) group worship, and (4) access to religious literature and devotional items.[19] I shall begin with a brief history of beard restrictions, before turning to the Supreme Court's 2015 decision about that and the problems raised by other kinds of claims for exemptions.

BEARDS, GROOMING, AND DRESS

A number of prison cases over time have involved claims to wear beards, with prisoners offering a religious conviction that they are required to maintain one, which prisons have not allowed. Prior to the Supreme Court decision in early 2015 sustaining a prisoner's claim to wear a beard slightly longer than prison rules permitted for medical reasons,[20] preceding cases by lower courts had varied. Some reflected an extreme judicial deference to the prison authorities that was grossly opposed to even an intermediate scrutiny, much less a genuinely strict one.

One example was *Friedman v. Arizona,*[21] a decision of the Ninth Circuit Court of Appeals in which the opinion's analysis was pre-*Smith,* although the decision was handed down two weeks after *Smith.* At the time, eighteen out of twenty-nine states surveyed allowed beards for prisoners. Arizona did not, with the exception of a quarter-inch beard needed for medical reasons. The state urged that its rule allowed rapid and accurate identifications needed for ordinary activities such as meals, for controlling disturbances, and for catching escapees. Were an exception made for two Jewish prisoners, others might want a similar exemption. The strength of this justification certainly appears thin. If a relatively few prisoners have beards, they will not complicate identification very much, and requiring at least a plausible claim of religious convictions to grow one would prevent any vast increase in beards. If identification of individual prisoners in ordinary circumstances is increased by a few seconds, that hardly constitutes a major impairment of efficient security. Nevertheless, the court rejected the prisoner's claim, stating, "When a prison regulation impinges on inmates' constitutional rights, [it] is valid if it is reasonably related to legitimate penological interests."[22]

A dissent in the 1985 case *Hill v. Blackwell,*[23] which preceded *Friedman,* suggested a less deferential judicial scrutiny. The majority rejected a claim of a Muslim prisoner to wear a beard. Not agreeing, Judge Arnold urged that the officials had failed to show the need for their strict approach; he relied on obvious exaggerations and flippant remarks by the warden, the only defense witness, as showing that no serious attempt had been made to balance the religious needs of prisoners against security concerns. When the Supreme Court upheld RLUIPA against a formal challenge in *Cutter v. Wilkinson,* Justice Ginsburg indicated that prisoners deserve the degree of judicial evaluation of asserted prison necessities suggested by Judge Arnold.[24] In subsequent cases, at least some courts did not afford prison officials the exaggerated deference reflected in the *Friedman* decision.[25] A district court in California ruled that RLUIPA precluded the disciplining of Muslim inmates who wore half-inch beards since the state had failed to show a compelling interest in grooming regulations that precluded these beards.[26] Considering a claim of a Native American inmate to wear long hair, "an essential part of his Native American beliefs and practices," another district judge did not deny that the state might have a compelling interest in grooming regulations but could probably not show that it had to bar long hair for someone with a religious belief who was not a significant security risk.[27]

This brings us to the Supreme Court's 2015 decision in *Holt v. Hobbs.*[28] In contrast to thirty-nine other states and the District of Columbia that permitted exceptions from their grooming standards for religious claims or had broadly permissive approaches,[29] Arkansas maintained a strict rule against prisoners wearing beards, except quarter-inch ones allowed for medical reasons. Petitioner, though believing his religious faith requires him not to trim his beard at all, was willing to compromise by wearing a half-inch beard. His request to do so was rejected, on the basis that allowing such beards could permit the hiding of contraband and create problems of identification if the beards were shaved. Although skeptical of these reasons, a magistrate judge recommended dismissal of a preliminary injunction on the grounds that the petitioner could exercise his religion in other ways and that prison officials should receive deference. After the district court adopted this recommendation, the court of appeals affirmed, emphasizing deference to the "expert judgment of prison officials who are familiar with their own institutions."

The Supreme Court unanimously decided to the contrary. Although Holt's Muslim religion indicated a longer beard, it did not follow that his claim to compromise with a half-inch beard was not a genuine religious conviction. Writing for the Court, Justice Alito emphasized, as he had in *Hobby Lobby,* that section in RLUIPA which provides that an exercise need not be "compelled by, or central to, a system of religious belief."[30] Given the sincerity of Holt's claim, the Court remarked on the irrelevance of the fact that not all Muslims believe they must grow beards and stated that in its application of "substantial burden," the district court had "misunderstood the analysis that RLUIPA demands."[31] RLUIPA does not render alternative means of practicing religion as relevant for the burden in the way suggested by pre-RLUIPA cases. Although some lower courts had been taking approaches similar to what the Supreme Court rejected in this case, most had already recognized that RLUIPA made clear that the burden test should not be highly demanding.[32]

Having determined the presence of the "substantial burden," Justice Alito turned to the government's countervailing interest. Quoting his opinion in *Hobby Lobby* that the compelling interest test must be satisfied in respect to the particular claimant and that "The least-restrictive means standard is exceptionally demanding" and requires a show of a lack of other means,[33] Alito considered the department's asserted needs to avoid the hiding of contraband and the disguising of identity. He agreed with the magistrate judge that it was "almost preposterous" to suppose that someone could hide contraband in such a short beard especially since longer hair on top of one's head would obviously be more promising for that. Decisively rejecting a degree of deference that amounts to "unquestioning acceptance," the opinion remarks that the contraband argument is "hard to swallow."[34]

The Court next dismissed the argument about disguising identities.[35] All that needed to be done was to photograph the prisoners before they grew their beards, thus providing a picture of how they look without one.

The Court also rejected a contention that a half-inch beard created risks any greater than the quarter-inch beard allowed for medical reasons. Among other things, the Court relied on the fact that "the vast majority of States and the Federal Government permit inmates to grow half-inch beards, either for any reason or for religious reasons. . . ."[36]

Unless one believes deference to prison officials should be absolutely extreme, the unanimous result in this case is obviously correct. An interesting feature of Alito's opinion and a concurrence by Justice Sotomayor concerns the strictness of scrutiny. Alito at points emphasizes the rigor of RLUIPA and its rejection of accepting whatever prison officials assert. Sotomayor concurs with his opinion but asserts that it neither abandons deference when a chosen policy has a plausible explanation nor requires a department to demonstrate that there is no conceivable less restrictive means.[37] Almost certainly the justices are actually divided on just *how* rigorous or deferential the RLUIPA rights should be taken for criminal incarceration cases. We will need to see how they and other judges react when faced with more genuinely contestable restrictions than that imposed here. Given that all justices did join the Alito opinion, the Court clearly does regard the statutory standard as stricter than the one widely taken to control before RLUIPA and used by some lower courts since then.

The Court's approach to grooming under RLUIPA obviously applies to claims of a need to wear clothing with religious symbols. In two earlier cases, courts had concluded that a prisoner's wearing crosses did not present a sufficient danger of thefts or use as weapons to justify a prohibition[38] and that a Native American should be able to wear a spiritual necklace that was no more dangerous than Christian symbols that were permitted.[39] In a case after RLUIPA, a district court favored a claim of a Jewish prisoner to wear a yarmulke while being transported for medical treatment.[40]

In respect to regulations of beards and of what prisoners wear, one issue is how prison authorities should treat circumstances in which religious claims are likely to succeed. An alternative to considering whether a particular religious claim is sincere is simply to accept the assertion made. A yet more convenient approach, say to beards, is to relax the general restriction so that anyone may grow a beard of the kind those with religious convictions seek. The wisdom of this alternative to an exemption approach depends on exactly what is involved and whether a broadening of those whose wishes may be satisfied would actually create any substantial additional hardship or cost within the prison.

FOOD

A different sort of religious claim in prisons sharply raises the issue of a limited exemption or more general availability. Most Orthodox Jews consider eating pork as forbidden by their religious convictions, and some persons are vegetarians based on similar convictions. One might respond that people will not starve if they just decline to eat part of what is served, but of course simply refusing some food does not fully satisfy the religious exercise for those whose diet needs to be kosher. At least in a prison of any size, it is feasible to provide alternative meals. Doing so does constitute an added cost, perhaps twice or more than that of ordinary meals,[41] but this is not an unmanageable expense. Those costs are substantially greater, but typically manageable, if what is involved are the ritual meals of Seder for the eight-day celebration of Jewish Passover.[42] Insofar as expense is the government's basic competing consideration against religious exercise, that should not, given all the expenses of prison management, typically amount to a compelling interest. And most courts have sustained claims for kosher meals.[43]

There can be genuine concerns about aspects of equality and occasionally about security. The possible risk to security is if a group of gang members decides to claim a common religious conviction about food that will bring them together when those meals are eaten.[44] This is rare and identifiable enough not to constitute a justification for denying most such claims of religious exercise.

The equality concerns are a bit more subtle. One worry is that those who are without established backgrounds of such practices,[45] or who belong to disfavored groups, such as Muslims, will not be treated as well as others.[46] On the first point, although fake claims of religious convictions can be made, officials and judges definitely need to recognize that some prisoners may honestly want to become involved in what is for them a new commitment.[47] In respect to novel or disfavored groups, those making judgments about them need to self-consciously avoid appraising claims with extreme skepticism. As in a great many domains involving claims to religious exercise, meeting the aspiration of genuine neutrality may be impossible, but efforts to move in that direction are much better than simply ruling out all such claims altogether. Foreclosing all of these can in this and many other contexts be a deeper denial of treating people equally than drawing less-than-perfect boundaries of exemptions.

The other equality worry is that, especially with food, some prisoners may resent the special treatment afforded to others getting special meals; but this needs to be accepted as a minor cost unless prison authorities choose a simpler alternative. Once they determine what foods some cannot accept for religious reasons, and what is a feasible alternative, they may then simply make that available for any prisoner who chooses it over standard fare. This is one circumstance in which the alternative to an actual exemption strategy is clearly sound, and it has been adopted by many prisons.[48] This approach has been characterized as "neutral accommodation"; religious needs are met by granting all prisoners a generic option.

RELIGIOUS PRACTICES AND MEETINGS

Prisoners may want to engage in religious exercises and meetings that do not fit what is generally permitted within their facilities. When individual practices are concerned, the considerations are basically similar to those regarding grooming and food. Cases have often been less accommodating about what constitutes a "substantial burden" than RLUIPA itself seems to provide and that the Supreme Court opinion in the *Holt* case directs. Among cases suggesting that such a burden may not exist were these: a conclusion that a prisoner believing in "Judeo-Christianity" may be barred from Jewish worship services because Protestant ones were adequate for him;[49] a determination that a Muslim's claimed need for "full ablution" before weekly prayer meetings was not really valid for the Muslim faith;[50] and a suggestion that a prisoner did not, for ritual salutation as a Celtic Druid, need items worth more than the permitted $25.[51] The Fifth Circuit's decision in the last of these cases rested partly on the absence of sufficient evidence of a burden on the prisoner's religious exercise, reflecting the basic difficulty that those who present odd and unusual claims can have in convincing others.[52]

In a case that fits much better with RLUIPA's approach, the Third Circuit held that, absent a showing of no less restrictive means, an inmate should not have been disciplined for conducting an afternoon prayer while in the corner of the prison kitchen.[53]

Perhaps the most difficult questions about prison exemptions involve religious and other desired meetings. In contrast to the rights people have outside prisons, inmates are not allowed to meet whenever they choose for virtually any reason. They are, however, allowed to participate in standard religious services, many of which are run by prison chaplains, who are often paid by government. Among the questions about meetings are these: If the claim to have a religious service or meeting is genuine, need it rest on an assertion that what is involved is mandated by the religious faith, or is it sufficient that it is seen as important from the religious point of view? If standard services are allowed, must less typical ones also be allowed? If religious meetings need to be accommodated, what of nonreligious meetings?

Especially given RLUIPA's clarity that relevant exercises of religion do not have to be compelled by or "central to a system of religious belief,"[54] courts have rightly not imposed such a condition. To take an example that occurred prior to RLUIPA, the Seventh Circuit ruled that a claim by members of the Moorish Science Temple of America not to be forbidden to have a banquet on the founder's birthday did qualify as involving a substantial burden, although the prison's basis for refusal was powerful enough to sustain its denial of the claim.[55] The opinion of Chief Judge Posner made clear what is very often implicit but rarely stated—that different stages of analysis are not completely independent of each other. In these circumstances, when they assess the needed strength of the government's asserted compelling interest and the availability of a less restrictive means, judges should be partly guided by the strength of the religious claim involved.

Another pre-RLUIPA case involved a claim about particular religious services made by prisoners who wanted "full Pentecostal services," which include such practices as "speaking in tongues" and "laying hands on each other."[56] The prison did not permit these, rather having "interfaith" Christian services, although it did allow Pentecostal literature and a Pentecostal volunteer for Bible study classes. The Ninth Circuit denied the claim on the basis that the failure to show that the services were mandated by the faith fell short of a substantial burden. A considerable concern here is that traditional forms of service were being favored over less common ones. Anyone who has participated in or witnessed a Pentecostal service realizes it is radically different from standard Protestant worship, involving not only different activities but also degrees of emotional intensity and movements well beyond ordinary behavior. Unless it can be shown that such involvement somehow increases the risk of violating rules of prison discipline, an accommodation to it, and other untraditional forms of worship, should be made, as RLUIPA clearly indicates.

The issue of nonreligious gatherings presents complexities I shall mention but not explore in any detail. These do also concern land use and some of the subjects of prior chapters, such as tax benefits. Although other exemptions raise questions about nonreligious convictions, few concern nonreligious meetings. When the government is involved in permitting meetings in public facilities or providing financial benefits for the publication and distribution of materials, it cannot, at least in general, favor religious gatherings and publications over nonreligious ones since the general protection of freedom of speech, as well as the Establishment Clause, can bar favoring religious expression over other forms. A notable example of this was the Supreme Court's striking down of a state law that relieved religious publications from sales and use taxes that were imposed on other publications.[57]

The complexities begin with the fact that prisoners do not have broad First Amendment rights to state publicly all that they wish, nor are they allowed to meet for any purpose that is not itself illegal. This might suggest that nonreligious claims lack any grounding here. However, one might think *some* nonreligious meetings are not so different from religious ones, involving reflection on human values and a good life, and that these should be allowed so long as religious services are permitted. An obvious response is that various meetings might well threaten prison discipline or involve hostility against fellow inmates. (This can also be true about some meetings that are, or are claimed to be, based on religious convictions.) Without trying to resolve what exact boundaries might be constitutionally set, there is a strong argument that prison officials should permit some nonreligious gatherings if their purposes are as consistent with the need for prison discipline as religious services. Officers could attend such meetings, and recordings could be made to provide substantial protection from ostensibly desirable meetings being used in reality for illegitimate purposes.

On some issues we have covered, such as the use of alternative means that do not demand estimations of religious sincerity and burden, specific legislation or regulations may sometimes be desirable. For a variety of kinds of requests, prison officials would do well to be a bit more expansive in what they allow rather than granting only what they take as legally required. They should also make a consistent effort not to disfavor claims that are unusual in their content.

Land Use

When it comes to the use of land, many matters, as suggested in Chapter 1, are significantly different than those that bear on the other forms of exemption or special treatment that we have examined. A sharp contrast with the vast majority of prison claims of religious exercise is that the typical assertion of a right to build or to use property in a certain way is almost always made by an organization, not an individual. And often the claimed burden is not a direct contradiction with the settled convictions of an organization or those who run it, of the kind involved in refusals of hospitals to provide abortions or of businesses to insure the use of some contraceptives. Rather the burden is one of monetary cost or practical inconvenience. And the most common competing government interests are not safety, health, and fair treatment, but environmental congeniality and potential tax resources.

As with various exemptions from tax requirements, another important feature of land use is that historically in the United States and other Western democracies, churches have been treated as special. In residential areas in which commercial enterprises and buildings with many stories have not been permitted, exceptions for churches, synagogues, and mosques have been common. A modern example of the long-standing favoritism toward religious uses of property are decisions by New York state courts that municipalities cannot exclude those uses totally, or from residential districts, or from 90 percent of the community.[58] This kind of protection has been provided in many states by courts rather than specific legislation.[59] However, whether religious uses are favored, and, if so, how much, varies greatly among states and localities. California, for example, allows municipalities sometimes to exclude churches from residential areas.[60]

Earlier developed under common law nuisance standards,[61] the typical modern constraints on the nature of acceptable structures and the uses of property are zoning regulations, as well as other state and local laws that preclude certain activities. An underlying question about these is how far religion should be given special advantages, be subject to particular restrictions, or be accorded only an equal status to what else is permitted or foreclosed. As with respect to other aspects of government involvement and restraint, it is clearly impermissible to favor some religions over others. Because many zoning decisions are based on particularized assessments by local administrators, determining how far an unacceptable form of discrimination has generated them is often very difficult.

Given that the Supreme Court had struck down RFRA's application to states and localities on the basis that Congress could not decide coverage of the Fourteenth Amendment, the underlying basis for the land use part of RLUIPA was that it was designed to counter real dangers of constitutional violations. Zoning ordinances, which originated early in the twentieth century,[62] are typically local and largely subject to discretionary administration by local officials[63] rather than clearly specifying what is allowed and what is not. Both state and federal courts have generally deferred substantially to these administrative decisions.[64] The lack of substantial involvement by federal courts and by other federal officials can be viewed as a healthy aspect of federalism,[65] but it raises concern about uncorrected violations of the federal constitution. Over three years, Congress apparently acquired "massive evidence" of religious discrimination; land use regulations were enacted or enforced "due to animus or hostility to the burdened religious practices."[66] The evidence relied upon involved statistics, judicial decisions, and testimony about examples and their breadth.[67]

For land use, RLUIPA contains not only its basic standards of "substantial burden" and "compelling interest" and "least restrictive-means" but also four more distinct criteria of impermissible government action: no institution can be discriminated against on the basis of its particular religion; and religious institutions cannot be treated worse than nonreligious ones; and religious assemblies cannot be totally excluded from a jurisdiction, and unreasonable limits may not be placed on religious assemblies and structures.[68] These provisions are an example of an intermediate approach that lies between a highly general standard and a standard that contains detailed instructions about what is or is not allowed.

Although the Supreme Court has not yet directly stated that the land use part of RLUIPA is constitutional, the statute's basic justification, its application for a decade and a half by lower courts, and the Supreme Court's declining so far to review constitutional challenges, render it virtually certain that its coverage will be deemed acceptable. What is that coverage?

It is striking that in its general formulation, RLUIPA is not significantly different from the free exercise test that was set in *Sherbert v. Verner* and not abandoned until 1990 by *Employment Division v. Smith.* Nor does it vary greatly from the standard seen to be relevant between the adoption of RFRA in 1993 and the Supreme Court's holding of that law as invalid as applied to states four years later. In contrast to this close resemblance in formulated standards of review, courts have generally treated RLUIPA as more rigorous than what preceded it.[69]

Despite the language of *Sherbert v. Verner,* courts usually treated both the validity of land use regulations and their applications with great deference. According to one study, between 1980 and 1990, only in one case did a federal court of appeals give a plaintiff a free exercise exemption that would not have been granted even under *Smith.*[70] And during the time RFRA apparently applied to states, plaintiffs had won in only nine of fifty reported federal court cases not involving prisons.[71] A 2007 study indicates that under RLUIPA, courts have been much more receptive to religious claims; this modest but clear success for the statute suggests that Congress's re-involvement may be the primary explanation. Three relevant cases certainly do not show that the compelling interest standard is as rigorous here as for racial categorizations and interferences with speech, but they can well be regarded as employing an appropriate intermediate scrutiny.

Given this book's concentration on the bases for exemptions and on which existing and proposed exemptions make good sense, rather than on judicial developments over time,[72] my treatment of decisions rendered before and after the enactment of RLUIPA will focus on the appropriate understanding of religious exercise, substantial burden, and compelling interest.

A striking example of explicit or unacceptable implicit discrimination was provided in 1988, when faculty and students at the University of Mississippi wanted to construct a Muslim house of worship. To build in an area close to the university, they needed a special use permit. Based on concerns about traffic congestion, parking, and neighborhood opposition, the board of aldermen kept denying the applications for the Muslim facility, although they had granted all similar requests by Christian groups. The Fifth Circuit Court of Appeals had no difficulty concluding that the aldermen were not applying the permit process neutrally and that this rejection served no legitimate zoning interest.[73] Of course, this outright discrimination was unconstitutional and did not need a RLUIPA statute to be overturned.

In a more recent and difficult case, decided after RLUIPA was adopted, a majority in a Seventh Circuit court upheld certain zoning restrictions that applied to churches in commercial areas. It did so in Civil Liberties for Urban Believers v. City of Chicago (often referred to as C.L.U.B.), over Chief Judge Posner's dissent that the rules favored traditional religious groups over new groups that might rely on storefront churches.[74] A case like this presents a delicate question about what should be seen as unfair treatment. Of course, if it can be established that the adopters of a restriction self-consciously meant to favor traditional religions, that would violate both the Constitution and RLUIPA. But what if the adopters had no discriminatory objective in mind but would probably not have imposed the restriction if it had impaired major faiths? Given the language of RLUIPA, which requires equal treatment, perhaps this alone would not constitute relevant unequal treatment, but, as Posner suggests, such restrictions should be allowed only if the burden on the religious group is slight or if the government's reasons for the restriction are very strong and not accomplishable by alternative means. In limiting a "substantial burden" to a showing that a "direct, primary, and fundamental responsibility for rendering religious exercise . . . [has been made] effectively impracticable," a formulation that did not reach scarcity of affordable property,[75] the court's majority required more than it should have.

Although hardly decisive evidence, it is interesting that up to 2005, fifteen of the twenty-five land use cases decided under RLUIPA were brought by groups representing no more than 4 percent of the adults in their state.[76] This *might* simply be the result of the fact that newer groups were seeking to build in the relevant areas, but it likely indicates that at least some decisions occur as they do because groups are not major denominations. During the first ten years of RLUIPA, 64% of the Department of Justice investigations concerned negative treatment of racial and religious minorities.[77] If the aim is to preclude both self-conscious and implicit discrimination—and each is often hard to discern with confidence—providing, as RLUIPA does, protections that do not depend directly on that showing is highly important.

When one considers the construction of houses of worship, how should "substantial burden" and "compelling interest" be understood? A religious organization is unlikely to assert a religious conviction that it *must* build a church or synagogue within a certain physical area.[78] It may, however, have a financial interest in doing so where property is not highly expensive. Even more importantly, it can consider it very desirable to be near the residences of its members. This can be crucial for Orthodox Jewish groups that hold some services on days on which members must walk rather than ride in cars, buses, or subways. In a 1983 case sustaining a denial by the board of zoning appeals of an application by Jehovah's Witnesses to build a Kingdom Hall in a residential area, the Sixth Circuit Court of Appeals declared that because owning a church is just an "accessory of worship, not a fundamental tenet of the Congregation's religious beliefs," it need not construct one in a residential district.[79] This approach is definitely too limiting about what should be taken as a "substantial burden" on a religious organization in this context. It should be sufficient if the group shows that its religious endeavors would be seriously compromised by the restriction.

This issue has arisen in two cases involving requests to build houses of worship within an agricultural zone. In 1988, prior to *Smith,* the Tenth Circuit sustained a denial of such a request, although the permit procedure allowed the granting of some exceptions.[80] In 2006, the Ninth Circuit, in *Guru Nanak Sikh Society of Yuba City v. County of Sutter,* did sustain a claim for a conditional use permit to build a Sikh temple within such a zone.[81] In cases like these, significant disadvantages of being unable to construct should amount to a substantial burden. And the locality should lack a compelling interest unless the granting of an exception will directly undermine the zone's quality or be genuinely likely to lead to multiple claims that will do so.

A different form of constraint on building structures involves historical landmark preservation. Because some of the oldest and most distinguished buildings in the country are churches constructed long ago, this is a relatively small domain in which the percentage of religious groups restricted in what they can do is much higher than the overall percentage of covered enterprises. That in itself does not amount to unequal treatment. Exactly how compelling is the government's interest in landmark preservation is debatable, and courts have thus far reached various conclusions. In one pre-RLUIPA case, for example, the Second Circuit rejected a claim by St. Bartholomew's Church to demolish its community house in order to build an office tower that would generate income;[82] it upheld what it considered a neutral rule of general applicability. In another case, the district court in Maryland did not sustain a city's refusal to allow the Catholic Church to demolish an old monastery in favor of new church facilities. The judge in that case characterized a historic preservation ordinance as not neutral and generally applicable and regarded historic preservation as less than a compelling interest.[83] In fact, the treatment there by the city of Cumberland of a whole district as historic is more obviously neutral and general than the singling out of particular structures, such as St. Bartholomew's. However, the strength of the interest in historic preservation can vary hugely, and the Maryland church's wish to directly enhance religious purposes may have seemed more appealing than the perceived need of the New York church to rent facilities and raise money. Even under RLUIPA, just how to treat various restrictions made by historic preservation laws can be far from simple.[84]

When one focuses on the building of houses of worship, no other groups are seriously disadvantaged, although those living very close by may experience mild disturbances from traffic or noise at the time of services and could perhaps see a modest drop in the value of their own property. The same absence of important negative effects on other groups or individuals applies to some but not all accessory religious uses of property. These uses may or may not be tied to the presence of houses of worship.

One use that is neither accessory nor attached to houses of worship is the carrying out of religious services in ordinary facilities not designed for that purpose. In one such case, the Eleventh Circuit denied a rabbi's claim to use his garage for religious services, resolving that the City of Miami Beach had a compelling interest in making no exceptions to its zoning plan for single-family houses.[85] That the city would actually suffer in any significant way from allowing this kind of exception is implausible. Using a more nuanced evaluation under RLUIPA, a district court ruled that New Milford, Connecticut, had failed to show a genuine absence of less restrictive means to ensure traffic safety that could justify a zoning commission's ruling that weekly prayer meetings within a district of single-family residences could include no more than twenty-five persons.[86]

When claims involve running schools or day care centers as adjuncts to houses of worship, the right approach to evaluation becomes more complicated. Although some may raise doubts about whether such activities, and others such as food banks and homeless shelters, are based on sufficiently strong religious reasons,[87] the answer is that assisting and educating others are seen by many churches as important elements of what they are called to do. As two members of the Becket Fund for Religious Liberty have emphasized, over time large variations have occurred in how religious groups see themselves and their functions.[88] Crucial performances in helping others should be sufficient to satisfy the substantial burden test if the capability to perform these tasks is being seriously curtailed. Since these efforts typically benefit society in important ways, it is hard to see a compelling interest in precluding them unless their existence will severely disturb the quality of a neighborhood. But at least for schools and day care centers, nonreligious groups may also be trying to provide similar services; it may be unfair to allow a church to use a location that is denied to these other groups and could give it a significant advantage in attracting participants. If this is a concern, perhaps the best resolution is to broaden an exception from ordinary zoning requirements for all nonprofit schools and day care centers, but equality for nonreligious groups in this respect *might* sometimes justify denying the claim of a religious group.

Many of these controversies about buildings and uses of property are not subject to any simple, uniform disposition. Unlike with some exemptions, here it is hard to arrive at specific legislation that will sharply reduce the need to balance competing considerations. The granting of these exemptions must depend significantly on contextual evaluations, made initially by a body such as a zoning board and then reviewable by courts under RLUIPA and relevant state standards. A promising suggestion about how to make all this work better is that much greater uses of mediation should be encouraged during earlier stages of disagreement.[89]

A particular question about RLUIPA is whether it should be applied to local condemnation of land for which compensation is paid. At least if the condemnation covers more than religious property, religious groups should generally have no special basis to challenge it. If, however, the condemnation appears to be a way of getting around the limits on zoning or other restrictions on the uses of religious property, judicial review of its legitimacy appears to be an appropriate use of RLUIPA. Nonetheless, Christopher Serkin and Nelson Tebbe offer a subtle analysis, based largely on the compensation requirement and the publicity that accompanies condemnation, that things will work best if this is simply left to the political process.[90]

A much more general issue that we have explored in other chapters is whether religion should really be treated as special. Here this is not fundamentally a matter of conscience. If the law forbids more than twenty-five people in residences, it should not be enough for a home owner to claim, "My conscience tells me that I must have a party in my home every week with fifty or more invitees." As with certain other organizational concerns, the kinds of similar claims we can imagine here are ones offered by groups that are organized to convey important messages to those who are involved and to outsiders. Nonreligious arguments in favor of uses of facilities should perhaps be available to nonreligious promoters of fruitful lives and advocates of particular practices and legal rules, such as greater government assistance to the poor.[91] Constitutional claims for treatment similar to that given religious beneficiaries can be mainly based on freedom of speech and association.[92]

Conclusion

This chapter explains some fairly detailed aspects of what the provisions in RLUIPA aim to do and how they are best understood. More generally, this statute is a clear illustration about how statutes, even ones that often require comparative balancing, can helpfully address certain specific subjects regarding exemptions and provide more protection than relevant officials may otherwise be inclined to accord. Although the two features of the law protect religious exercise, when we look at the reasons for those protections, we see that some of them do really apply to certain kinds of nonreligious convictions and practices.

8

Same-Sex Marriage and Sexual Relations

Introduction

THE MOST CONTROVERSIAL modern issue about exemptions in the United States today is same-sex marriage. At the start of 2015, as a product of statutory reforms and lower court judicial decisions about unconstitutional discrimination, couples of the same gender could get married in thirty-five of the fifty states and in the District of Columbia. On June 26 of that year, the Supreme Court ruled that the Fourteenth Amendment's guarantees of liberty and equality in its Due Process and Equal Protection Clauses protect such marriages.[1] These marriages are now available in the other fifteen states. Not everyone may recognize that the constitutional right by itself does not settle how private individuals and enterprises can treat those who engage in such marriages. Broad requirements of equal treatment depend on federal or state laws that bar relevant forms of discrimination. A number of our politically liberal states do have statutes forbidding discrimination based on sexual orientation.

Absent specified qualifications, such laws cover discrimination against gay married couples. But many states do not have such laws. Within those states, a general requirement of equal treatment for same-sex married couples will depend on new legislation, such as occurred recently in Utah.[2] Within a high percentage of these states, compromises including exemptions may be necessary for such nondiscrimination coverage to be passed. And the same may well be true if the crucial legislation comes mainly from Congress rather than state legislatures. Ideally, the working out of such compromises can be grounded in a genuine understanding of why those with divergent outlooks see things as they do.

Here are the basic issues in play. Assuming such marriages are legally protected, should laws aimed at equal treatment afford any exemptions to those whose convictions tell them that these marriages are wrong? If so, should similar exemptions be granted to laws barring discrimination based on sexual orientation? If exemptions are granted, who should qualify, and how far should their special right extend? Should objectors, for example, be able not to participate in some form in such marriages? Should they be able to later refuse to grant those married couples the same treatment they afford to traditional married partners? Should they be able even to treat differently anyone engaged in sexual relations with a partner of the same gender? These questions concern what various organizations, such as churches, adoption agencies, and service-providing businesses should be allowed to do. They also bear on permitted individual behavior and employer treatment of current and potential workers. Should employers be forbidden to afford negative treatment to same-sex couples, and should they also be required to grant objectors forms of nonparticipation from the ordinary duties of equal service? Among individuals, special questions arise respecting those who work for federal, state, and local governments. These include clerics who are military personnel or hired by prisons.

Other central questions are ones explored in earlier chapters. These are how peripheral involvements in what a person or an enterprise believes is wrongful should be treated, whether any granted exemptions should extend to those with nonreligious objections, and how far exemptions should be formulated by specific legislation or left entirely to vague general provisions such as the Religious Freedom Restoration Act (RFRA).

Before suggesting what range of exemptions is wise in this context, the chapter first looks at basic arguments for and against creating a privilege not to afford equal treatment. That discussion includes analysis of the force of arguments that objections to same-sex marriage are closely similar to those about interracial marriage. Another more complex argument against most exemptions here is also explored, namely that unequal treatment in regard to same-sex marriage really comes down simply to discrimination based on sexual orientation. Although I contend that things are not so simple, it is true that many forms of discrimination against gay married partners cannot be persuasively distinguished from those based on sexual orientation.

After coverage of these broader issues, the chapter turns to specific controversies that have arisen and suggests exemptions that should be granted or denied, acknowledging that with certain borderline circumstances, the arguments on both sides are of considerable strength. As with other subjects, the overarching objective here is to reveal the force of various reasons and their complexity, not to convince the reader that he or she should agree with each proposed resolution.

Basic Arguments Against Any Exemptions Respecting Same-Sex Marriage and Responses to Those

A fundamental contention by many of those who oppose the granting of any exemption is that a rejection of same-sex marriage is a clear form of unacceptable unequal treatment of gay people, that allowing an exemption authorizes effective discrimination against them and encourages its continuation. This point is frequently supported by the contention that few now believe any exemption should be accorded to those who do not believe in interracial marriage and that an objection to same-sex marriage is fundamentally similar. After addressing the general grounds for opposition to exemptions, I respond to the racial analogy.

The previous chapters have said little about the laws that create the general duties from which exemptions are granted. Because of the significance of the Supreme Court's decision establishing a constitutional right, and because the genuine controversy over the value of same-sex marriage itself bears on the acceptability of exemptions, I shall briefly sketch the bases that moved the Court's majority. What is relevant here is not the soundness of its constitutional conclusion that a bar on same-sex marriage violates both the Due Process and Equal Protection Clauses, but the force of its reasons for why such marriage is warranted. Justice Kennedy stresses a fundamental right to marry, based partly on individual autonomy, which seeks an enduring bond in a two-person union that promotes expression, intimacy, and spirituality. Marriage is a keystone in our social order, carrying many "rights, benefits, and responsibilities." A marriage union is beneficial for children being raised by couples, and roughly 200,000 children in the United States are now within the custody of same-sex couples or individual homosexuals. Given the importance of this marriage right, and the absence of any strong reason to bar equal treatment, same-sex couples have a right to basic equality to marry.

Whether one agrees with the Court's conclusion, which is definitely based on an evolutionary approach to the Fourteenth Amendment that I believe is appropriate, the reasons it provides for some form of legal recognition, given modern understanding and values, far outweigh any opposing bases for denying such marriage. This sense, including the core notion of equality, can bear on how one perceives possible exemptions.

If one asks whether allowing exemptions will delay acceptance of same-sex marriage or undercut broader efforts to bar discrimination based on sexual orientation, one needs to distinguish general possibilities from political realities at points in time. Excusing people from performing any duty they would otherwise have to perform may often encourage those who are opposed to the very imposition of the duty itself. Thus, as Chapter 5 explains, permitting nonparticipation in abortions may help reinforce the views of those who believe that abortions are wrong and that women should have no general right to receive them. But in practical terms, the main effect can be exactly the opposite. Had no exemptions been granted for assistance in abortions, the consequence could well have been more intense opposition to the basic right. With same-sex marriage, the evidence is indeed overwhelming that in many states, had no exemptions been included, the legislation providing for such marriages could not have passed when it did.[3] We cannot be sure whether within a few years attitudes would have shifted sufficiently so that the same legislatures would have been willing to adopt such laws without exemptions; but clearly at some moments in history, exemptions can promote adoption and acceptance of new laws guaranteeing a contested form of equal treatment. Of course, once the Supreme Court has declared a constitutional privilege of same-sex marriage, state legislation to establish that basic right is no longer needed. But if one looks back over the past decades, one wonders whether lower courts and then the Supreme Court would have been so ready to create this new constitutional right had not a number of legislatures already acted. Even after a constitutional right is settled, allowing some exemptions may well, as they almost certainly did with abortions, promote public acceptance of the basic legal right more than encourage resistance to it.

A more subtle concern is that allowing exemptions for same-sex marriage may significantly undercut the force of general laws barring discrimination based on sexual orientation. The claim, developed by Douglas NeJaime,[4] actually involves three related possibilities, each of which this chapter addresses. The first is that opposition to gay marriage really comes down to opposition to gay sexual relations, whatever misleading political rhetoric may suggest.[5] The second is that the range of exemptions proposed and formally accorded in regard to same-sex marriages includes many circumstances that are not really about the marriage but about disapproved sexual orientation and involvement. The third is that allowing exemptions in this context may encourage unjustified broader exemptions unrelated to marriage from laws barring discrimination based on sexual orientation.

These various concerns are partly practical ones about how forms of concentration on a supposedly narrow topic may influence broader issues and what is likely to happen over time if a particular legal step is taken now or in the near future. And, of course, within the United States, the answer to these practical questions may vary somewhat in different parts of the country. This chapter, like those before it, does refer to such practical possibilities, but its primary focus is on the basic underlying reasons for deciding whether to grant exemptions and to determine their scope. I first concentrate on whether convictions about same-sex marriage really amount to just one form of views about gay sexual relations and then turn to what sorts of exemptions may sensibly be seen as really concerning marriage, not a broader right to treat same-sex couples and gay individuals less favorably than others.

The fundamental issue of whether objection to same-sex marriage is basically discrimination against gay persons actually turns out to be quite complicated. We can start with the reality that our society has for most of its history discriminated against gay people.[6] For much of that time, sexual acts with persons of the same gender were treated as criminal. Although these provisions were typically not enforced with rigor, and most eventually got repealed, not until 2003 did the Supreme Court actually declare such laws, which then remained in nine states, to be unconstitutional.[7] Although someone *could conceivably* defend such laws as not really involving discrimination but instead the prohibition of undesirable behavior, that possible justification is now rightly seen as implausible (putting aside someone who believes mistakenly that the civil law of a liberal democracy rightly prohibits acts that do not harm others but are wrongful according to the true religion, as he perceives it). A claim of social harm is substantial if what is involved is sex between adults and twelve-year-olds; and adultery, though no longer criminal, can also be seen as likely to be damaging to others. But gay sexual relations are different. Although even a half century ago the medical profession saw homosexual desires as a kind of psychological problem subject to cure, a perception that could support the sense that actual sexual involvement was unnatural and unhealthy, those acts were not barred because they really hurt anyone else. Most of those against whom such prohibitions operated possessed strong inclinations, now seen as likely basic biological or genetic, that strongly attracted them to others of the same gender.[8] Given the great physical desire that most persons have to engage in sexual acts and the powerful emotional ties and benefits that often accompany continuing sexual involvement between two people, to tell someone that he or she can never engage in such acts with those toward whom he or she is mainly attracted is undeniably harsh. Although precisely what amounts to "discrimination" is far from simple,[9] and the term is often used rhetorically to condemn what the speaker disagrees with, we can reasonably say that the laws against basic gay sexual acts were discriminating, as were many forms of unequal treatment others in society afforded to persons known to be gay.

Is opposition to legalization of same-sex marriage or personal nonacceptance of it just one form of such discrimination? Undoubtedly for some persons it is; their disinclination to accept marriage is just one aspect of their condemnation of gay sexual relations. But this need not be so, and it is not so for everyone. An objector to same-sex marriage *may* believe that sexual involvement between persons of the same gender is no better or worse than nonmarital sexual relations between men and women, either because he accepts responsible sexual relations outside of marriage as appropriate *or* believes all these relations are misguided regardless of gender, since only sex within marriage is warranted. Of course, so long as gays and lesbians lacked the option of marriage, a widely shared acceptance of only marital sex was much more restrictive in their lives than for others.

Whatever their views about nonmarital sexual relations, many religious people, based on what they take as scripture or "church" teaching, believe that God has ordained that marriage be between men and women. They can possess this view without necessarily subscribing to a broader condemnation of gay sexual relations or of the people who engage in them. As Douglas Laycock has explained, "The religion that generates most of these claims [for exemptions] in the U.S. proclaims its obligation to hate the sin but love the sinner. . . ."[10] The fact that some people do see marriage as special in this respect bears on the appropriateness of possible exemptions, even if for others nonacceptance of same-sex marriage connects extremely closely to general disapproval of gay sexual relations.

To understand just how far opposition to same-sex marriage actually rests on more general rejection of gay sexual relations, experts would have to undertake various kinds of empirical study. Such inquiries would need to attend not only to historical causation and present opinions[11] but also to differences between what people may say they believe when they answer questions and what they fully perceive and also between what they consciously perceive and what influences them at some subconscious level. Although no attempt is made here to discern how many people have various views about all this, we should recognize that some who regard gay sexual relations as less desirable morally than intergender relations can also perceive extra reasons not to accept gay marriage. For such persons, opposition to recognizing gay marriage would be grounded not *just* on the marriage itself *or just* on a negative view about gay sexual relations but rather on a combination of both factors, an option Professor NeJaime does not really address. This would render their marriage objection actually stronger than it would otherwise be.[12]

As already mentioned, an important distinction exists between a core legal right to gay marriage and typical antidiscrimination laws. People who are legally married have a basic privilege to be treated as such by all those on whom the law prescribes responsibilities toward married persons. Thus, if a law requires companies to provide insurance to marital partners, they must, absent an exemption, do so for married same-sex couples. On the other hand, if no law curbs the basic choices made by individuals and businesses, they may decide, even on the most arbitrary grounds, not to serve or associate with those about whom they have reservations. As Andrew Koppelman has put it, "In most states, most businesses have the privilege of refusing service to anyone for any reason or no reason."[13] What antidiscrimination laws do is forbid various decisions made on the covered grounds, whether by officials or private endeavors, thus providing a broad social standard of equal treatment.

Questions of possible exemptions typically arise with actual or proposed antidiscrimination laws, and often they have been specifically provided. Some of those have been cast in terms of an organization's size or the personal association that would be involved in treating someone equally. Thus, the laws may not reach decisions by very small enterprises,[14] and the Title VII bar on racial discrimination in rentals did not cover owner-occupied boarding houses with fewer than five units.[15] Of course, if an antidiscrimination law about sexual orientation already includes a specific kind of exemption and gay marriage becomes legalized, including the same exemption presents no special problem. It does not then matter whether the inclusion should be perceived as concerning just marriage or sexual orientation in general. It follows that thoughtful consideration of whether, and when, marriage exemptions are really special must include a sense of the appropriate range of exemptions for laws barring sexual orientation discrimination, of whether the range should actually be greater in respect to same-sex marriage, and, if so, how best then to draw the right line between these two when actual negative behavior is involved.

It helps initially to clarify the relationship of sexual orientation to sexual acts. NeJaime rightly emphasizes the connection of one's activities in life with one's identity.[16] Just as a woman's work, family relations, and chosen recreational activities can affect how she sees herself, so also do her sexual relations, whether within or outside a marriage. To bar discrimination based on sexual orientation is not only, or mainly, about a person's sexual inclinations but also about who he or she engages in sexual relations. Thus, any such nondiscrimination law clearly protects those who in their lives are actually engaging in same-sex relations. It follows logically that any such protection includes those who do not keep their sexual involvement more secret than would be expected from people who have sexual partners of the opposite gender.

Whether this right extends to open and public manifestation presents a more subtle question I shall only mention. If many workers in an organization easily accept open embracing and extended kissing between men and women but are "put off" by similar behavior of those of the same gender, particularly men, could a business discourage the latter or refuse to hire someone who is well known to engage publicly in such intimate contact? Whether, at this stage of history, not only the government but private citizens and enterprises should have to treat all open public behavior between same-sex couples just the same as that between other couples is debatable, although the reactions I have described are partly generational and will definitely change as gay marriage and sexual relations become increasingly accepted.

As with respect to abortions, a person's moral view about behavior and what he or she accepts as appropriate legal rights can differ radically. Within a liberal democracy, a citizen may reasonably accept, even welcome, a law that protects certain actions that most or many people want to perform themselves, or definitely accept as not wrongful, even if she personally regards that behavior as misguided and wishes to not actually assist it. A conviction against participation *need not necessarily* signal actual opposition to legal protection of a practice or status. Indeed, the Mormon Church in Utah displayed just such an understanding in its acceptance of the statute that both protected same-sex marriage and included religious exemptions.[17]

Before addressing more specific questions about what are appropriate exemptions, I briefly suggest why, when one considers the reasons favoring some of them the analogy to interracial marriage has force but is actually not conclusive. The Supreme Court's declaration in 1967 that a ban on interracial marriage was unconstitutional[18] came after a history of slavery in the United States, imposed dominantly on those from Africa and of African descent, followed by a century of racial segregation in the southern states after the Civil War.[19] Any broad exemption for those who opposed such marriage would certainly have been undesirable, violating basic standards of fair treatment and further encouraging one form of the racial discrimination that was powerful and pervasive at the time in most southern states and also existed, although less openly and explicitly, in most other parts of the country. Although some perceive the approval of same-sex marriage as essentially similar,[20] three differences may matter. These can be seen as bearing on the intrinsic reasonableness of convictions of those opposed to participation in each of the two kinds of marriages, or, if not, at least relevant to whether an accommodating exemption makes sense at this stage of history, given the understandable perceptions that many people now possess. To be clear, the analysis that follows does not address whether there could be any objection to a form of interracial marriage that really treated all races equally (though I strongly believe no such objection is sustainable). What is important here is how interracial marriage was conceived historically in the United States.

As I have already noted, an opposition to gay marriage does not *necessarily* involve a rejection of gay persons or their sexual relations, and it definitely does not entail discrimination against men or women as compared with each other.[21] Although we could conceive of a ban on interracial marriage that did not favor or disfavor members of particular races, that was not the law in the southern states of our country that prescribed such bans into the 1960s.[22] Instead, those laws, at least in their origin, were designed largely to protect the purity of the "white" race, which was perceived as superior. A fair number of male slave owners had sexual relations with female slaves, leading to the birth of children of mixed race, who were then treated as "other" "Negroes." According to the laws barring "interracial" marriages, if you were one-quarter, or in some states even one-eighth, black, you were considered Negro.[23] Thus, a young woman three-quarters white could marry an all-black man but not a white man. Clearly the two "races" were not being treated equally; instead, blatant discrimination favoring "unblemished" whites was at work. And many states did not have similar provisions forbidding marriage between those of Asian or Native American descent and either whites or blacks. So, rather than adopt a similar approach to all interracial marriages, the laws were mainly cast to keep those partially black in a status subordinate to that of pure whites.[24]

Although Jane Dailey's research indicates that the most common asserted justification for preventing integration, no doubt reflecting the sincere beliefs of many, was religiously based,[25] that hardly explained the historical practice in the United States. Of course, the distinction between a fundamental justification and a historical explanation does not itself show that the justification is unpersuasive. But at least for some people, the religious ground was likely an attempt to support, perhaps even in their own minds, a more complex cultural and psychological view. Three claimed bases for racial segregation were that God had planted different races in different geographical locations, that scientific evidence suggested that blacks were less able than whites, and that the biblical account of Noah's curse made it appropriate to subject blacks to slavery. Both of the first two bases, weak as they inherently are, also had to run smack up against the treatment of mostly white people of mixed race as Negro. On those accounts, shouldn't someone dominantly white be treated as white? If the religious idea was that blacks are condemned by God to inferior status, conceivably even a bit of black heritage is sufficient for that; but the idea that God favors only pure whites is not a defense many made in the 1960's or are now anxious to put forward.

Whereas history does not show a massive rejection of various forms of interracial marriage, matters are different, at least within the United States and dominantly Christian cultures, for conceptions of marriage and gender. William Eskridge has provided a comprehensive account of the many points in history that various cultures have accepted marriage between persons of the same gender, which he takes as including ones involving berdaches, males dressed in female garb. Also accepted have been certain same-sex unions that are not formally marriage but approximate that.[26] However, for several centuries, in accordance with then-dominant religious views, "strict rules regulating gender and marriage [have been] embedded within and enforced by Western culture, in the United States and elsewhere. . . ."[27]

Although perhaps hard to prove, it is likely that historically marriage at its core has been largely about the need for stable relations in the raising of children. Until recent decades, only sexual intercourse between men and women could produce children. Seeing marriage as being largely between the two parents of their children fit with this. And certainly some Christian and other religious people in recent centuries tied appropriate sex to the possibility of conception. That modern technology permits conception without sexual intercourse significantly changes that possible connection, but it is hardly surprising that many people still regard ordinary sexual relations between women and men as the most "natural" way to create children. And, at least for some, this can relate to their religious views about same-sex marriage. Although it has been suggested that the historical absence of any requirement of an ability to have children undercuts the family explanation of marriage, given both the shorter lives of most people in the past and the lack of any test of who could actually produce children, the absence of any such requirement shows almost nothing about the core basis for marriage.

Related to the belief that keeping both parents together matters for the lives of their children may also have been a sense that men and women differ from each other in ways that make it desirable for family relations to involve parents of both genders.[28] Although the emancipation of women in multiple ways has hugely affected the relations and functions of married men and women, some people still believe that the gender differences are great enough to affect parenting. One obvious possibility is that if women bear children and often provide nursing, they have a stronger inclination than men to feel deeply attached to babies. Of course, arguably different inclinations of men and women are not now actually a plausible basis to oppose same-sex marriage, given the modern frequency of both divorces and single parenting, as well as huge variations in parenting by opposite-sex couples. Two loving persons of the same gender will be preferable to many other parents in the raising of children.

Whether one believes that any of these factors constitute a reasonable basis to doubt the desirability of same-sex marriage in comparison with traditional marriage, they were assumed in past decades by a large number of those now in the older generations and are still accepted by many members of religious faiths that have not yet shifted to acceptance of gay marriage. Given all this, that many people still regard such marriage as misguided is fully understandable. On this point, Justice Kennedy is very careful in the opinion sustaining the right to same-sex marriage. He acknowledges that the opposing view is held "in good faith by reasonable and sincere people." (p. 4), that "that conclusion [is] based on decent and honorable religious or philosophical premises," and that "neither they nor their beliefs are disparaged here." (p. 19). Even if one now sees the perception to which he refers as irrational and completely at odds with proper moral and religious principles, the complexities of historical and religious tradition remain a ground not to dictate that people possessing that conviction be compelled to act directly against it.

Does this conclusion hold if one sees religion in general as misguided? Andrew Koppelman has noted that "the longstanding American tradition of accommodating religious objectors . . . has now . . . become controversial, for reasons that are tightly tied to the emergence of the gay rights movement. Disaffiliation with religion has become a cultural marker for solidarity with gay people."[29] One response to this division is that given history and life, people's discarding of all religion would be unfortunate. For many movements toward social equity, religion has played a positive role. For example, religions generally have done much to help the poor, and some religious groups in the United States had a great deal to do with the movement toward racial equality. More broadly, given the core uncertainties of our lives, including the fates of our loved ones who have died and our own existence or not after death, simply rejecting the place of religion in human society is perhaps both unrealistic about what is likely to occur and rather harsh about what should take place.

Even if a critic rejects all these reasons for expecting religion to survive and for believing that its continuation will not necessarily, on balance, be regrettable, he still has to face a present reality. Although religion may have diminished in its force in American life in recent decades, many Americans still maintain religious beliefs and engage in religious practices.[30] Simply condemning opinions that are held by a substantial number of citizens and forcing behavior directly at odds with those convictions can amount to intolerant treatment.

When the wisdom of exemptions based on negative beliefs about same-sex marriage are being considered, it is important, as Chapter 1 indicates, to consider not only the overall soundness of convictions but whether they are at least based on acceptable values, such as what is good for children or a deep religious tradition, and are defensible in principle. Also relevant are how common those conceptions now are in our society and the extent to which insistence on nonobservance will create discontent and conflict. Given the history of the development over time of notions of marriage, it also matters whether "insistence" or "accommodation" is likely to enhance a move to the more desirable understanding. As William Eskridge has shown, religions throughout history, in respect to interracial and same-sex marriage among other subjects, have often shifted their own approaches in response to basic legal and cultural changes.[31] At least at some stage, the best approach can be to create a legal right to equality but not to require that all act against their deep conviction about how they should act.

In regard to the content of possibly appropriate exemptions regarding same-sex marriage, we need to consider both forms of participation in the marriage or its direct support and subsequent treatment of those who have become legally married. This latter category includes such interactions as availability of services and housing, employment decisions, insurance coverage, and availability of children for adoption. Before addressing those subjects, I shall focus on involvement in the marriage itself.

It is worth noting that, in contrast to subsequent relations, this particular form of contact is itself distinct from other unequal treatments based on sexual orientation. A bar on sexual orientation discrimination is not about assisting particular sexual acts. Of course, we could *imagine* an outsider being asked or required to provide direct help for a nonmarital sexual encounter, but, unless one includes hotel lodging I am unaware of many such demands in real life.[32]

Participation and Other Forms of Involvement

Possible exemptions from actual involvement in same-sex marriage present a number of questions. What degree of otherwise required participation or assistance, if any, should be covered? Should both individuals and certain organizations qualify? Should it matter if someone works for the government? Should relevant convictions or organizations need to be religious?

Individuals as Well as Religious Bodies

Although historically the connection between religion and marriage has often been tight,[33] in most liberal democracies, one must have a civil marriage in order to become legally married. That is not true in the United States. Clerics and ministers, defined fairly broadly in most relevant state statutes, have the authority to marry two people.[34] In many states, it is also possible for almost any individual to undergo a quick process to become a "minister" if a couple wants that person to marry them.[35] In most, but not all, states leaders of nonreligious organizations do not have the direct right given to clergy. That the Free Exercise Clause protects religious bodies from having to marry two people they believe should not be joined has long been assumed. That premise receives solid support from the Supreme Court's unanimous decision in the *Hosanna-Tabor* case,[36] which directly concerned the right of a religious body, without legal review, to hire or fire anyone who counted as a "minister" in a very broad sense. If religious groups have this wide authority to make such decisions, however discriminating they may be, it follows that they need not engage in a religious ceremony joining two people in matrimony when they believe that would be contrary to God's will. Perhaps a new law could allow marriages with legal authority to be performed only by those clerics who are willing to marry all those entitled to civil marriage.[37] However, given that most religions do set their own standards for when they should marry persons, the adoption of such a requirement by an American legislature is very unlikely at this stage of history.[38]

Since any couple can choose civil marriage, awareness that a particular religious group will not marry them does not interfere with their ability to join together, although if one or both happen to be members of the group that refuses, that can definitely trouble them emotionally. Because religious bodies and their clerics are usually the only formal organizations outside government to decide whom to marry, the question of whether private nonreligious organizations and individuals should be able to make up their own minds about whom to marry does not often arise. That could change if the privilege afforded to religious marriages was extended to nonreligious groups and their leaders, or to individuals more broadly, a reform some believe would eliminate an unjust favoring of religion. That possibility does not itself settle what scope of choice the nonreligious performers should possess in respect to whom they should marry.

Putting aside individuals who work for the government, the key question about possible exemptions for organizations and individuals involves their degrees of involvement in marriages that do not constitute actual performance of the union. Should any such exemptions exist, and, if so, how direct need the involvement be? Related questions are what does the present law provide, and should it be altered by specific coverage?

The basic questions about these exemptions also concern the breadth of antidiscrimination laws covering sexual orientation and whether more specific provisions should cover marriages. The effective "scope" of existing laws against unequal treatment concerns not only what the language of those laws apparently covers but also whether any exception is required by a general law like RFRA or a perceived constitutional right.

As already noted, the legality of same-sex marriage alone does not itself require equal treatment in the provision of services. That duty is mainly imposed by required nondiscrimination in respect to "public accommodations." Although earlier laws such as the Civil Rights Act of 1964 not only were limited in the forms of discrimination covered, they also had fairly narrow standards of what counted for public accommodation. Current state laws are much broader. New Jersey, for example, includes more than fifty types of places and also encompasses "any producer, manufacturer, wholesaler, distributor, retail shop, store, establishment, or concession dealing with goods or services of any kind."[39] These laws also forbid broader classes of discrimination, including in twenty states and the District of Columbia as of 2015, discrimination based on sexual orientation.[40] For an individual or organization asked to assist in a same-sex marriage in some way, the questions about a legal obligation to do so are the following: (1) Does the relevant antidiscrimination law reach their behavior? (2) Does a specific statute about marriage create an exemption?

(3) Does a general protection of religious or free speech or association rights, either within a RFRA statute or the federal Constitution or state constitution, cover their wish to refuse?

Within this general framework, it helps to focus on some cases that involve these issues. Three notable examples involving the coverage of the existing state laws also sharply pose the question of just how far any exemptions should extend. In Colorado, a baker refused on the basis of religious convictions to bake a cake for a gay couple's wedding celebration.[41] Elane Photography, a New Mexico photography company, declined on similar grounds to photograph the wedding of two women.[42] A religious association in a beachfront community in New Jersey refused to make its Boardwalk Pavilion available for a gay marriage, although it was open for other uses by private citizens.[43] In each instance, private claims were brought successfully against the defendants on the basis that they had violated state laws barring discrimination based on sexual orientation. Although New Mexico, unlike Colorado, possessed a RFRA law, its supreme court declared that it did not apply to private suits. The following chapter argues that this exclusion was misguided; the attention here is on whether an exemption *should* be accorded from general legal requirements in these situations.

When a professional photographs a wedding, she is involved in a way that is not insignificant. Couples want a photographic record as an aspect of the wedding itself, one that will endure for the rest of their lives. Elane Huguenin, the co-owner and head photographer of her company, typically took roughly sixteen hundred photos at a wedding, trying best to capture the event and illustrate it.[44] Although the taking of such pictures may not directly express approval of the wedding, it does implicitly convey a kind of acceptance. Especially since most couples, once aware of the person's actual sentiments, would prefer not to have someone photographing their ceremony if she believes it is deeply immoral, a law that establishes same-sex marriage sensibly includes a specific standard of exemption for participation or assistance of this degree. And a RFRA law, at least one that reaches private suits based on government requirements, should also be taken to protect against this degree of involvement.

The baking and providing of a cake is much more marginal. Normally, those providing cakes may not even be aware of what the cakes will be used to celebrate, and the supplying of food hardly represents approval of whatever the celebration may be. Even if a cake contains a written message such as "celebration," no one supposes this is what the professional cake providers themselves want to convey. (Matters are different, however, if the requested message is directly at odds with a baker's serious convictions, an issue raised recently by requests of those opposed to same-sex marriage to have gay bakers produce strong antigay messages.[45])

As with some of the hospital worker examples in relation to abortions, the involvement here is best viewed as too remote to be protected against.[46] Specific legislation about exemptions can make clear that they do not reach such a connection that does not involve a genuine message of approval, whatever an individual's personal convictions may be. Either in the statute itself or legislative history, it might help to provide a few examples on each side of the line. If a legislator concludes that the degree of participation presents too difficult a line to be drawn, and that any formulation of this sort is inevitably too vague, she might oppose any such exemption or favor granting it to anyone with relevant convictions who in any way is involved in a marriage or its subsequent celebration.

The possible application of a RFRA statute to situations like the baker's is a bit complex. In areas where other bakers are easily available, the government may lack a compelling interest in enforcement that cannot be served by a less restrictive means. However, RFRA initially requires a "substantial burden" on the baker. *If* one accepts the majority's assertion in *Hobby Lobby* that an honest conviction of serious imposition on religious conscience is sufficient by itself to amount to a "substantial burden," that could be present. But it is more sensible to conclude that provision of an ordinary cake for a celebration is simply too remote to legally constitute a substantial burden in respect to the marriage itself, especially since determining actual intensity and sincerity of convictions is usually virtually impossible (a point developed in Chapter 6). Implicit in the preceding paragraphs is the basic assumption that yet more marginal forms of aid, such as driving a person in a taxi to her wedding location, should definitely not count as relevant participation or assistance.

The Boardwalk Pavilion case raised special problems. One might suppose that a religious organization should have the general right to reserve its own facilities for those who are engaged in practices that the organization accepts. But the Ocean Grove Camp Meeting Association had received public funding and a special property tax exemption based on its representation that the site would be open to the general public and not restricted to religious use.[47] Although it is arguable that allowing a facility to be used for a particular purpose represents a kind of acceptance of what occurs, one can hardly see a genuine approval if a facility or service is available to a broad public, without any systemic inquiry about what will take place. Especially given the financial benefits of government funding and a special tax exemption, "assistance" here did not seem direct enough to warrant an exemption.

With these examples in hand, it is helpful to face some of the broader issues. Despite powerful sentiments that one side or the other does not really have much at stake, in truth there is a genuine conflict. The values of respect, autonomy, forms of equality, and caring for others exist both in regard to those who seek exemptions and those who want to be uniformly treated without discrimination.[48] The most desirable resolution cannot satisfy everyone, but it can be "live and let live," based on mutual consideration.[49]

Given the competing values in play and the difficulty of resolutions, addressing these situations as far as possible by specific legislation, not leaving everything to RFRA statutes and constitutional claims, is desirable. Of course, even specific legislation will not be able to resolve every particular situation. As we saw in respect to abortion, what counts as relevant assistance cannot always be settled by statutory language. Nonetheless, clear, objective distinctions should be drawn, insofar as possible,[50] because it is hard for officials and judges to evaluate in a highly contextual way the weight of considerations on each side, including the degrees of inconvenience and intensity of feelings.

It is worth pausing here to consider a significantly different approach that also seeks to be sensitive to competing considerations. Andrew Koppelman develops a thoughtful analysis that defends a considerably broader reach of an exemption but only if those seeking it provide public notice of what services they will not provide.[51] For Professor Koppelman, what will constrain unjustified refusals to serve is the economic consequences of such notices, which will discourage the making of claims for exemption except by those with powerful convictions.[52] The persuasiveness of this approach rests on a combination of factors: the practical effects of the notice requirement, administrability, and the core purpose(s) of antidiscrimination laws.

The main worry about notices of refusals of service is that in certain areas of the country, those refusals may actually appeal to a large part of the population and not involve financial sacrifice. Perhaps even in some heavily populated locations that are strongly supportive of same-sex marriage, a small local business might effectively help itself by appealing to a discrete minority that is opposed to such marriage. Koppelman recognizes the general possibility that sometimes financial sacrifice may be absent but, especially given increasing acceptance of gay marriage, he sees it as being outweighed by the dominant negative effect in most locales of publicizing a refusal to serve.[53] Almost certainly, his approach is more easily administrable than attempting to determine what degree of involvement crosses the line of an exemption privilege.

The underlying purpose of antidiscrimination laws is less susceptible to a definite answer. For Koppelman, the overarching purpose is to enhance economic equality.[54] If an odd business here or there refuses services, and people can learn of this in advance, the movement toward such equality is not undermined. Insofar as antidiscrimination laws are seen as being substantially about human dignity, matters look a bit different.[55] One might see the legal privilege of exemption as itself a denial of the equality and dignity of same-sex couples, and at least if the exemption is much broader than granted other bases to refuse equal treatment, one could even conclude that it violates the Equal Protection Clause. When the focus is on notices given in advance that services will not be provided, couples learning that will suffer less humiliation than when they are rejected directly, but it can still be troubling; and widespread notices of nonservice can themselves be seen as a kind of put-down. Even if one regards notices themselves as somewhat related to free speech, that could be seen as a reason to prefer less, rather than more, transparency about intended refusals of service.

All these factors can bear on what one perceives to be the best approach to the scope of exemptions and the publicness of refusals to be involved in equal treatment. The more one sees individual denials of equal treatment and notices of refusals of services as themselves having regrettable effects in respect to equal dignity, the more one will be inclined to believe that the actual scope of exemptions should be limited.

The rather wide range of exemptions that have been adopted or proposed in many states is undoubtedly not only a reflection of the strength of opposing positions but also the complexities of determining what really is fair and sensible in light of genuinely competing reasons.[56] And, of course, what does make the most sense can depend partly on the basic composition of a state or locality. In contrast to Congress, which makes laws for the whole country, legislators in narrower domains do need to give special attention to their populations.

Whether religious convictions and organizations occupy a special space here is a genuinely complex question. As we shall explore later in this chapter, the Supreme Court has sometimes protected a right to discriminate based on free speech considerations.[57] In brief, if involvement really does convey to others a message of approval, people and some organizations should have a right not to do so, even if their grounds are nonreligious. Those organizations should be nonprofit,[58] or at least ones that, though making profits, do not have facilities and services available to the broad public. If the core objection has not to do with involvement that conveys any approval or acceptance of gay marriage, but is viewed as merely being at odds withthe organization's committed practices, a limit to religious groups may be appropriate.

When one turns from organizations to individuals, a particular problem arises in respect to those who work for the government. Should any exemptions be afforded to them and, if so, how extensive should they be? Here it is generally helpful to distinguish those who already have a position when the gay marriage right is legally recognized from those who subsequently apply for positions. Also, military clerics may warrant special concessions.

Some hold the view that if you work for the government, you should simply be willing to provide all the services that connect to your position.[59] But that stance is at odds with various accessions to the religious convictions of public employees that have been embodied in Title VII of the Civil Rights Act and other laws; and, more importantly, it is really too harsh in terms of what one should expect of all those who take government jobs.[60] Although earlier state laws about same-sex marriage did not include such protections, they were an important part of a 2015 Utah anti-discrimination statute adopted after the state's constitutional provision barring same-sex marriage had been struck down as violating the federal Constitution.[61] If the ability to obtain a same-sex marriage is not impeded and those obtaining such a marriage are not seriously embarrassed, and if granting an exemption does not obstruct the functioning of the government, why should one be denied, thus forcing a person to choose between violating a deep conviction of conscience and either losing her job or suffering serious discipline?[62]

In respect to civil officials in bureaus that issue marriage licenses and perform marriage ceremonies, the argument for an exemption is greatest for those already working there who perform the weddings. Many of them have taken these jobs when no one foresaw same-sex marriage in the near future. If their religious convictions tell them that such marriages are deeply wrong, should they have to conduct them? The answer is "no," so long as two conditions are present. The first is that these officials cannot be easily shifted to a different position that does not involve marriages and does not cause them any genuine disadvantage, in salary, prestige, and retirement benefits. If such a shift is available and offered, a requirement to perform all appropriate marriages may not cause any substantial hardship, although one could argue that any undesired change in position is a genuine hardship. A second condition is that the couple to be married suffers neither inconvenience nor genuine embarrassment.[63] Being married is an emotionally central point in the lives of people; if their marriage in a standard office would have to be unexpectedly delayed for more than a few minutes *or* the couple were directly informed that the person who would otherwise perform the ceremony thinks they are acting immorally, an exemption should not apply. That should happen only if no serious delay is involved and the objector can be effectively replaced by a colleague without anyone criticizing or embarrassing the couple. These limits mean that clearly no official should be enabled to deny licenses for his or her entire office, as occurred in the highly publicized Kim Davis controversy in 2015.

It is interesting in this regard to reflect on the limits of free speech rights for government employees. If persons in a prosecutor's office are allowed to refuse to work on capital punishment cases, it does not follow that they can publicly assert that the government's position is mistaken. Nor did I have a right to tell a reporter as deputy solicitor general that I regarded the government's practice of surveillance as deeply unjust. This suggests that if a government worker's declining to perform a duty is otherwise accepted, it should take place in a way that does not communicate publicly the message that the legal right underlying the duty is misconceived.

Whether a privilege not to perform should be extended to clerks who merely issue marriage licenses, which are then used for civil or religious marriages, and to judges and justices of the peace who have the right to marry but may or may not have a duty to perform marriages in general, is difficult. If, in fact, a judicial official at some level has no duty to perform the ceremony and can decline on any basis she chooses, no particular exemption is needed. But if she has a legal duty to perform marriages in general or is, as in Arizona,[64] foreclosed from refusing someone on the basis of a forbidden classification, a specific exemption based on fundamental conviction should be the same as for those performing marriages within a marriage bureau.

How the simple issuing of a license should be regarded is less straightforward. On the one hand, this could be regarded as a kind of formalistic step, like admitting someone to a hospital, rather detached from the marriage itself. On the other hand, a couple does have to obtain a license in order to get legally married; that is a necessary part in the process, and an officer believing same-sex marriage is deeply wrong may feel she cannot provide it. Given that at least some in those positions do have that conviction,[65] it makes sense to extend an exemption to them if doing so will cause no inconvenience or embarrassment.

A rather different setting is when someone applies for a government job that is largely about marriage licenses and performances and whose standard requirements involve performing gay marriages. Should he or she be ready to undertake that responsibility? Here an exemption seems, on balance, warranted only if those to be married and others in the office will suffer no inconvenience whatsoever. Alternatively, rather than outright forbidding or protecting the exercise of the conviction of applicants not to assist same-sex marriages, those decisions might be left to the discretion of supervising officials, as in the examples noted in Chapter 1.

The considerations regarding military clerics are special in certain ways. Although ministers and others who apply for this job are subject to various requirements that do not apply to clerics in the general society,[66] they are not expected to violate the basic tenets of their religions. Especially when one considers forces in combat areas, having clerics who actually represent the major religions is very important. Any requirement that a cleric act directly against his religious faith in respect to marriage raises a genuine question about the scope of the constitutional ministerial exception to antidiscrimination laws. Taking all this into account, not requiring those clerics who are already committed to a term of office within the military to perform marriages only recently legalized makes sense. For clerics who apply for a position after the new legal requirement, perhaps they should be granted an exemption only if the form of marriage is barred by their religious denominations. These matters could desirably be addressed by specific rules concerning the hiring of military clerics, although both RFRA and the constitutional ministerial exception lie in the background as possible grounds to argue that no requirement can be placed on clergy to perform marriages that violate their religious convictions.

Subsequent Treatment and the Relationship to Laws Barring Discrimination Based on Sexual Orientation

When a same-sex couple becomes married, can others treat them in ways less favorable than their interactions with men and women married to each other? Of course, once the government has recognized a marriage as valid, its agency officials cannot act toward the partners in a discriminating fashion, whatever may be possible for those opposed to participating in the wedding. Therefore, the main question here concerns private enterprises and individuals.

What exemptions might be appropriate concerning equal treatment of already married gay couples is closely related to what, if any, exemptions are warranted in respect to laws barring discrimination based on sexual orientation. Figuring out just why the relationship between the two bars on unequal treatment should, if ever, matter, and, if so, why and in what way, turns out to be fairly complicated. One concern is rhetorical effect, emphasized by Douglas NeJaime,[67] which raises the question of whether advocacy and adoption of privileges regarding gay marriage will tend to undercut the broader coverage of antidiscrimination laws. Closely related is the categorization itself, which brings up the issue of whether unequal treatment for gay married couples is *really* about sexual orientation and behavior, not essentially about their marriage. The third question, which I shall emphasize here, involves when, if ever, exemptions in respect to treatment of already married gay couples should extend beyond that appropriate for a more general bar on sexual orientation discrimination. Before tackling these concerns, I note again the basic distinction between limits on government officials and those that reach private citizens.

The federal and state constitutions, and statutes such as RFRA and RLUIPA, are fundamentally about what those in the government may or may not do themselves or require of others. Just as I am free to provide certain services to and invite into my apartment whomever I choose, when private employers and businesses are free of antidiscrimination legal restraints, they can do the same, even when their choices deviate sharply from those allowed public officials and from broad social values. It is statutes that matter here. They may require that services be granted for all those who need them *or* request them or they bar discrimination in public accommodation and services, providing that enterprises not preclude availability based on certain characteristics. Thus, a hospital cannot refuse to admit a person who desperately needs medical help, and restaurants cannot refuse to serve members of racial minorities. Within states whose statutes bar discrimination based on sexual orientation, discrimination against already married gay couples would constitute one form of that discrimination based on sexual orientation. It would be forbidden *unless* a special privilege were present in the broader law or were granted in respect to marriage. A key question is whether such a privilege that would not extend to other negative treatments of gay individuals can ever be warranted for married couples.

As we have already seen, the argument for a special exemption is strongest if the form of interaction involves in some way a direct participation in the marriage itself.

The worry emphasized by Douglas NeJaime is that the advocacy and granting of exemptions in respect to married couples will reach what is really not about the marriage but rather sexual orientation. An earlier section suggests that a person *can* sincerely be opposed to gay marriage without accepting broad discrimination based on sexual orientation or can be troubled by both gay marriages and gay sexual relationships more generally but perceive some special negative aspects of the marriages. That conclusion alone does not take us very far in how to see negative treatment that occurs once the marriage is in place.

In two kinds of circumstances, it does not really matter whether such treatment is really about the marriage or sexual orientation. If an exemption is justified in both contexts or in neither context, the classification of a borderline instance as falling into one category or the other is insignificant.[68] Although the framing of borders may influence people's outlooks in some way, when the concern is about what *should* be done, distinguishing the marriage situation becomes crucial only if a basis exists for believing that an exemption for it should be more (or conceivably less) extensive than that in respect to equal treatment of gay individuals. For purposes of wise legislation and judicial decision, drawing the distinction in borderline instances should then rest primarily on the basic justification for an exemption.

I shall say relatively little about the provision of ordinary goods and services and the availability of housing. Title VII of the Civil Rights Act did allow racial discrimination by those who rented only a few apartments and who lived within the same facility as their tenants. A similar privilege makes sense in respect to rentals to same-sex couples, but it is hard to imagine that a renter would be allowed to preclude such married couples but not those openly attached but unmarried. Similarly, with standard services available to people generally, no reason presents itself why married couples should be treated worse than nonmarried ones. People have many ideas about who should or should not get married but, putting aside their direct involvement in the marriage, no enterprises refuse services to people its leaders believe should have refrained from marriage. For the provision of ordinary services broadly available to the public, no exemption is justified from laws barring unequal treatment of gays.

With the expansion of state laws on what counts as public accommodation, some covered services may now involve a kind of personal involvement that should not be required if that would offend the provider's convictions. Elane Photography would be an example of this. Although one possible way to eliminate this concern would be to curb what counts as public accommodation,[69] a state might better provide instead that for these instances, differential treatment should be allowed *only* if it is based on genuine convictions. Rather than broadly restricting its category of public accommodations, it could thus provide a privilege limited to those with genuine contrary convictions. But even here, putting aside the direct participation situations, it is hard to imagine that someone has no problem with personal contact with openly gay nonmarried partners but cannot accept similar interaction with a married couple.

I am not claiming that such a view is inconceivable. A person might regard same-sex marriage as so misguided, he should treat anyone who undertakes one negatively in the years that follow. However, many people do believe adultery, divorce, sex outside marriage, or some other behavior is deeply immoral. We do not see common claims to be able to treat all those who have so behaved unequally in unrelated contexts. Not perceiving a reason why same-sex marriage should be regarded differently in this respect, I do not think any distinctive exemption should extend broadly beyond aspects of involvement with the marriage itself.

In summary, for ordinary services and facilities, few if any particular exemptions from sexual orientation antidiscrimination provisions are justified,[70] *and* no substantial reason presents itself why those in respect to married gay couples should be any broader.

More complicated and debatable issues are raised by adoption agencies and certain forms of equal treatment generally required by employers. The most notable example of how subsequent treatment of same-sex married couples might differ from treatment based on more general sexual orientation may be a nonprofit organization that cares for children and puts them up for adoption. That practice is a kind of actual involvement in the basic married life of a couple seeking to adopt. If a religious organization providing this service believes that same-sex marriages are both contrary to God's will and a less promising setting for young children, it may not want to allow the children for whom it cares to be adopted by such couples. This has, indeed, been the position of many Roman Catholic adoption agencies. This conviction provides a fairly strong argument in favor of an exemption from a general requirement of equal treatment, as might an agency's insistence on favoring Roman Catholic couples over those of other religions, based on the belief that these couples are most likely to enhance the lives of children they adopt. This comparison provides one example of when considerations of the legitimacy of exemptions regarding same-sex marriage can benefit from reflecting on the permissibility of drawing distinctions directly based on people's religion.[71] A practical argument supporting this particular privilege, drawing upon what happened in Massachusetts,[72] is that if religious organizations are not permitted to draw such distinctions, they may drop out of providing the services. Of course, that may or may not reduce the availability of the services in general.

The competing reasons against an exemption here are also undeniably strong. Should couples seeking to adopt be disadvantaged because of their common gender or their religious practices? And should the children up for adoption be denied a couple that might be more suitable judged by neutral standards? Each of these negative reasons on which a state could rely might well be seen as serving a compelling interest. Whether fairness to the potential adopters could be otherwise achieved might depend on the number of adoption agencies within their locality; in terms of protecting a child's interest in getting the best parents judged by a neutral standard, there may be no less restrictive means.

In respect to the balance of considerations, one might draw a distinction between children whose birth parents choose a religious adoption agency that represents their own convictions, as contrasted with children whom the government assigns to the agency.

A rather different response by an organization that provides adoptions might be that the law's accepting same-sex marriage does not really represent a determination that that is equal in all respects to the marriage of men and women. After all, discrimination based on age or economic status may be generally barred by law, but adoption agencies do not have to treat poor couples in their fifties the same way they treat economically secure couples in their thirties. Of course, this approach, whether sound or not, would lead only to a general favoring of intergender couples, not a complete exclusion of same-sex ones.

The adoption example differs from many others because, in contrast to most services, it is widely assumed that agencies will prefer married couples over individuals. However, the issue about comparative discrimination with that regarding sexual orientation could present itself if the state required, or an organization chose, that married couples not be favored over nonmarried couples, or, even though preferring married couples, did also provide some adoptions for nonmarried ones and for single individuals. In any of these instances, should it be able to favor heterosexuals? If a primary basis were a debatable view that having parents of both genders is a positive feature for children, that might count as a favorable element but would not preclude the allowing of adoption by otherwise very well-qualified gay couples, married or not.

This all raises the issue of how far the simple religious conviction against same-sex marriage should be able to count. What seems obvious is that an adoption agency should not be able to treat a couple worse because it has chosen to marry than it would treat an unmarried couple. Although adoption does involve a kind of participation in a marriage, the right to treat negatively gay married couples in comparison with other couples should not be greater than any right to treat gay unmarried couples less favorably than other unmarried couples.[73] It may well be that absolute exclusion, as compared with counting as one relevant factor, should not be allowed. That distinction carries special force if the child up for adoption is an older child with a disability and the only couple available to adopt is one of a single gender, otherwise well qualified. The child should not have to suffer because of the organization's distinctive view about same-sex marriage.

The various competing considerations on the general adoption issue are powerful enough that legislators should directly address the issue, providing an answer that probably makes relevant whether in particular locations other public and private organizations are putting children up for adoption. Although this is debatable, I do not believe statutes such as RFFA should be construed to provide an exemption here.

When it comes to ordinary employment decisions and insurance coverage, an argument for any exemption based on a couple's same-sex marriage is much weaker. Any law barring discrimination based on sexual orientation is going to preclude standard hiring decisions grounded in that feature. If partners in a law firm within a state that bars sexual orientation discrimination are opposed to gay marriage, they cannot refuse, even on the basis of religious conviction, to hire secretaries or legal staff because those applying are gay or are partners in same-sex marriages. Nor should they be able to deny insurance coverage that would generally extend to the marital partners of their employees because the partners happen to be of the same sex. As Douglas Laycock has written, employers should not generally be allowed to "occupy choke points that empower them to prevent same-sex couples from living their own values."[74] Here legal status of the couple should control. These forms of "support" are too indirect to justify a denial of equality to the partners in a same-sex marriage. This conclusion would only be magnified if the law already requires similar treatment for nonmarital partners, as is true in some localities.[75]

When it comes to employment decisions, positions that convey a message that is at odds with the basic convictions of an organization raise a serious concern. The ministerial exception gives religious organizations a constitutional right to fire and not to hire clerics they believe are acting contrary to the principles of the organization, and they can do so without any basic judicial review of their sincerity. In the *Hosanna-Tabor* case,[76] this principle was applied to a teacher who had achieved the status of a "minister," although her functions mainly involved education of children at a religious school. What of a teacher who does not qualify as a minister? The religious school still has an important interest in not having messages sent to students that are contrary to the basic premises of its religion. Such a school would not need to hire as a teacher someone publicly supporting atheism. If the religion is opposed to same-sex marriage, an open participant in such a marriage would be sending an implied message at odds with that conviction. Whether religious or not, an organization whose purpose is to educate children or convey an important public message should not have to hire someone for a position whose important tasks include conveying its basic premises, if that person is obviously living a life directly contrary to one of those premises. The Supreme Court effectively adopted this approach when it allowed the Boy Scouts, despite contrary state law, not to keep an avowed homosexual in the position of leading young members.[77] The Court ruled that such a decision was protected by the rights of free speech and association covered by the First Amendment. Thus, even if the organization's basic message is not religious, it can have a right not to hire someone in an important position who is living at odds with what it attempts to convey.

When it comes to same-sex marriage, it would be desirable for legislation to indicate the range of such an exception to equal treatment. But clearly here, if persons whose lives apart from marriage are at odds with the organization's tenets need not be hired, a similar privilege should exist in respect to marriage.[78]

Conclusion

This chapter strongly supports some exemptions in respect to equal treatment of same-sex married couples but also urges that these should be decidedly limited. More broadly, it powerfully illustrates the book's basic theme; here we have genuinely complex, strong, and competing considerations, which need to be recognized and carefully evaluated. Both strong supporters of equality for gay marriage and persons moved by the religious conviction that marriage is best seen as between men and women need to try to understand, respect, and care for each other. And they need to try to do this even if they see those with a contrasting view as fundamentally misguided in their basic perception.

9

Religious Bodies and the Role of Common Law

Introduction

THIS CHAPTER BOTH explores a range of practices engaged in by those within religious groups that may warrant exemptions from ordinary legal requirements and asks whether any such exemptions should reach others who engage in similar behavior. The first two sections address the confidentiality of communications between parishioners and their clergy and then turn to possible liability for failures to give adequate advice. After that, analysis focuses on various practices such as the shunning of deviant members and the boycotting of outsiders that might generally be grounds for legal liability.

For many of these questions, restraint derives from potential tort recovery by a person who suffers rather than from a duty directly owed to the government itself. As Chapter 8 mentions, the supreme court of New Mexico determined that its Religious Freedom Restoration Act (RFRA) law did not apply to private suits, and other courts have adopted a similar view.[1] This raises not only the question of how RFRA laws should be construed, but also whether more generally potential tort liability under the common law—and also private forms of recovery that statutes specifically authorize—should be regarded differently from a direct statutory obligation owed by individuals and organizations to the government. I shall address those questions briefly before turning to more specific topics.

The crucial language of the federal RFRA is that "government shall not substantially burden a person's exercise of religion even if the burden results from a rule of general applicability . . . [unless] it demonstrates that the application of the burden to the person (1) is in furtherance of a compelling interest; and (2) is the least restrictive means. . . ."[2]

The ordinary meaning of this textual language is indecisive about whether it reaches ordinary common law tort actions or private suits based on statutes. The federal RFRA does say the "*government* shall not substantially burden" unless "*it* demonstrates" the needed interest. If a statute creates an obligation leading to a private recovery, that should be seen as a burden the government imposes. In a private suit, the party seeking to reject the religious claim, not the government itself, would need to show the government interest, though it might well seek input from some government authority. One *could* take "it demonstrates" as including only the government as a party.

However, the conclusion that the law has no relevance for private suits would be very odd. If a law adopted by the legislature would not, in light of a contrary religious conviction, create a direct obligation to perform, the beneficiary of the religious exemption should not be subject to substantial damages in a private suit for exactly the same behavior. Especially since RFRA was enacted to reinstitute the previous free exercise constitutional approach, "it demonstrates" is better not taken literally. This conclusion is strongly supported by reflection on the 2012 decision in *Hosanna-Tabor Evangelical Lutheran Church School v. E.E.O.C.*, in which the Supreme Court conferred an absolute right of religious groups to be free of penalties for employment discrimination when they fire "ministers" broadly conceived.[3] In the last two sentences of the opinion for a unanimous Court, Chief Justice Roberts explicitly states that the conclusion would be the same if a fired minister "sues her church. . . ."[4] If this is the obvious conclusion about basic free exercise rights, it also makes sense for statutes which, like RFRA, are enacted to protect religious exercise. To take the example of the *Hobby Lobby* case, discussed in Chapter 6, once it is determined that the government cannot require employers to provide insurance for certain contraceptives, employees who want that insurance should not be able to sue their companies for failing to provide it.[5]

What of tort suits that rest not on statutes but on common law? These suits do not involve the government in the sense of the political branches as the source of a duty. However, if a general statute does not render a particular religiously motivated action criminal, or impose a direct civil penalty for a failure to perform because doing so would impose a substantial burden on religious exercise, does that not relate implicitly to tort recovery as well? Tort law is indisputably an aspect of how the entire government treats its citizens. If those who suffer from performance or from a failure to perform can recover financially, that clearly imposes a "burden" on those whose adherence to their religious conviction is the cause. In brief, if a statute would not impose direct liability or authorize private recovery for behavior, allowing tort damages that effectively penalize the same actions and discourage their future performance would be incongruous. Even if in a few contexts plausible arguments might favor having tort liability despite the unacceptability of an imposed statutory duty, that distinction generally is misconceived in terms of what the government imposes.

The conclusion that allowing tort recovery can amount to a genuine burden strongly affects how an existing RFRA statute should best be interpreted, unless either its language or the clear intentions of its enactors definitely point in the contrary direction. To take the federal law, courts should regard standards providing tort recovery as a relevant burden imposed by the government. The problem about private recovery does suggest that it would be desirable for legislators to adopt language that is clear about this when they pass such statutes. With these observations, I turn to the specific issues, focusing on what exemptions are warranted and assuming that a RFRA law would provide them for tort liability as well as direct statutory requirements.

Clerical Privilege Not to Reveal

Should clerics be obligated to provide information about what they have learned, to the same extent as ordinary citizens or nonreligious professional counselors? During confessions or other communications, apart from the standard interchanges that occur within healthcare facilities and educational institutions, a cleric may learn of serious criminal behavior or other harmful acts. Should he or she have to disclose this? One source of potential obligation is compelled testimony. When people generally are called upon to testify, they are legally obligated to reveal the truth if questioned about what they have learned from others. The one standard exception to this involves marital partners; they typically need not testify against each other. Since the requirement to testify is general, and a failure to fulfill it can lead to incarceration until one is willing to talk,[6] or even a form of punishment for contempt of court, any special treatment of clerics here definitely amounts to an exemption.

A different legal issue concerns certain classes of people who are now under statutory obligations to come forward and directly reveal specific kinds of information, for example that parents or others have physically abused children. In respect to child abuse, all fifty states, partly as a consequence of a federal law, have mandatory reporting requirements.[7] Most of these designate particular groups, such as social workers, teachers, and physicians, that must report, but some are cast more generally.[8] The crucial question about clerics is whether they should be included among those with a duty to inform officials. Given the strong concerns both about some Roman Catholic priests and other clergy members involving youngsters in sexual relations, and about those relations not being revealed or sharply disciplined within the denominations, the concern about a clerical privilege here is particularly sharp.[9]

In order to understand the basic exemption from required testimony for clergy, it helps to begin with the Roman Catholic view about confessions and the responsibilities of priests. Roman Catholics are required by church doctrine to confess their sins to individual priests in order to receive Holy Communion, the fundamental sacrament. At least since 1215, the church has given priests an absolute duty not to violate the confidential seal of confessions.[10] Even if a penitent has confessed to a murder for which an innocent person is likely to be convicted, the priest, without risking excommunication, is not allowed to reveal what he has been told. If secular law demanded that he testify about what has been confessed to him, a faithful priest would refuse, thus bringing to bear the potential application of ordinary sanctions without the state's accomplishing its basic purpose of acquiring the information.

This example reveals the two powerful reasons that have supported the "priest–penitent" privilege. One is the overall effects regarding what best serves the public interest; the other is freedom of religious exercise.[11] However, the extreme possibility of protected silence leading to an unjust conviction of an innocent defendant as well as concerns about particular practices such as child sexual abuse raise questions about the reach of any such exemption. What forms of communication to clergy should qualify? Who should count as a member of the clergy? How absolute or qualified should an exemption be, and should that determination depend on the convictions of an individual clergy member or on those of his denomination? Should an otherwise available exemption be qualified if the public need for information is very great? How far should any such exemption replicate or differ from one available to other professional counselors, such as lawyers, doctors, and psychotherapists? Those trying to answer these far from simple questions can reasonably reach different conclusions. I will briefly explore various possibilities and offer proposals about desirable resolutions.

This is definitely an area for which legislators should give specific statutory attention rather than leaving everything to a RFRA or a state constitutional requirement. If a crime is serious and officials have reason to believe a suspect may have made a relevant confession, could the government nevertheless lack a compelling interest? Perhaps if evidence of guilt is overwhelming, a priest's lawyer could plausibly contend that the state does not really need a revelation of his parishioner's confession, given a less restrictive means of proceeding without it. But suppose other evidence is inconclusive, or the confession may have revealed that a different suspect, perhaps already being tried or even convicted, is really innocent? Then a judge could discern no less restrictive means to satisfy the government's interest in convicting the guilty and not the innocent.

Every U.S. state maintains a statutory privilege for clerics, and, although Congress has failed to approve one, the Supreme Court has ruled that federal law also includes such a privilege,[12] which federal courts have developed "in the light of reason and experience."[13] Some states have adopted language like that which was proposed for a federal statute; it covers "a confidential communication by the person to a clergyman in his professional character as a spiritual adviser." This language definitely reaches beyond formal acts of confession. The phrasing in other states could well be taken more narrowly. Arizona, for example, refers to "any confession made to . . . a clergyman or priest in the course of discipline enjoined by the church to which he belongs."[14] This wording could be taken to cover only formal confessions made within a religious group whose doctrine requires them; that would not include most non-Catholic religions, including the vast majority of Protestant churches, which rely on group confessions in religious services and personal confessions in prayers. However, the modern trend has been toward liberalization of the priest–penitent privilege, and even rather narrow language has typically been interpreted expansively.[15] Given the help that conversations with clergy can provide members facing practical and psychological problems, this more generous coverage makes sense, but whether it should exceed a privilege available to licensed secular therapists is debatable. Clearly it should not include every communication to a cleric. Some ministers may be relatives or personal friends to whom one speaks for that reason; and some interchanges are over business matters, such as whether a treasurer has misspent the church's money. To qualify for an exemption, the communication must be to a cleric in his or her special role in that capacity.

Privileges accorded to secular therapists, doctors, and lawyers not to disclose what clients have communicated to them are qualified in various ways. These professionals have no right to decline to testify about certain information they possess, which can include both orally revealed secrets and the kind of physical evidence doctors acquire, such as gunshot wounds or the bruises of a child violently assaulted by a parent.

The exact scope of the privileges and their exceptions differs among various jurisdictions.[16] The privilege in respect to lawyers typically covers only confidential communications related to legal advice for clients and does not apply if the client has waived the privilege or if his communication was made for the purpose of committing a crime or fraud.[17] The patient privilege in respect to doctors, legislatively enacted in forty-four states, does not cover acknowledgements of commissions of crimes or plans to engage in one.[18] Physicians and psychotherapists are generally permitted to reveal disclosures which indicate that a patient poses a threat to himself or others.[19]

The setting of these nonreligious privileges, and their limits, involves a balancing of considerations—the desirability of people feeling free to get medical, legal, and psychological help without having everything revealed, against the critical public need that certain information not remain secret.[20] Those who undertake these professions are expected to accept what the law indicates about how far they should remain silent or reveal information.

A privilege for clerics is supported by similar values but also by extra ingredients. A Roman Catholic who reveals damaging information to her priest *may* believe God requires that she do so, and both she and the priest may understand that he must remain absolutely silent. Thus, at least in some circumstances, direct religious convictions of both clergy and confessing members could be at odds with possible secular requirements of disclosure. This reality could undercut the effectiveness of a requirement to reveal.

These factors sharply raise the question of how far a legal privilege not to speak should depend on the convictions of particular clerics or their denominations. If a minister and his church are as open to disclosing crucial information as secular counselors, should their privilege not to speak be any broader?[21] A possible argument against drawing distinctions based on actual convictions is that this would favor some religions over others, but one can see good reasons not to provide a special exemption that extends beyond what a cleric perceives as an actual substantial burden on his religious exercise.

A possible argument against *any* exemption for clerics that extends beyond that afforded secular counselors is that, given the sound judgments of prosecutors, clergy will rarely be called to testify, since government officials do not want to generate conflicts between their enforcement efforts and the claims of religious groups. If prosecutors limit themselves to extreme cases of need, perhaps all could be left to their judgment. This argument, however, faces three large obstacles. First, not all prosecutors exercise sound judgment, and second, their restraint is likely to be much less if the religious group is an unpopular minority, as contrasted with a dominant Christian faith such as Roman Catholicism. Finally, if no legal exemption applies, a cleric may be called to testify by defense counsel in a criminal case or by a party's lawyer in a private civil suit, decisions not controlled by government officials.

When one assesses these competing reasons, the basis for a specified exemption is powerful, and at least sometimes should extend beyond that offered to lawyers, doctors, and psychotherapists. This by itself does not resolve who exactly should qualify, how an exemption should be formulated, and whose claim against reliance on it should control, questions to which I now turn.

In terms of those who qualify, a cleric should be understood as a leader of the religious community, with a special role of hearing admissions of sins or consulting with members about their problems in life, or both. This would mean that if a religious group somehow regarded all members as clergy, that would not be sufficient to safeguard against testimony regarding any admissions made to a fellow member. In contrast to lawyers, doctors, and psychotherapists, clergy do not receive a government license to practice, but the exemption should extend only to those who do occupy a special position. They could, like Catholic nuns, have such a position, although not ordained as clerics.

The issue of how the privilege should be formulated is more complex and debatable. The two basic questions here are whether to draw distinctions that are based on the convictions of religious groups or individual clergy and whether to set any limits on the exemption in terms of specific features or a balance of considerations. Although distinguishing among different religions is somewhat troubling, it nonetheless is warranted here. Given the Roman Catholic doctrines about confessions and the duty of priests to remain silent, an exemption for its priests should not be qualified. This resolution is supported by the reality that requiring testimony about Catholic confessions will be much more likely to generate ineffective efforts at coercing testimony than to produce valuable information. But if a religion does not subscribe to any such doctrine but rather sees clergy as having responsibilities like those of ordinary counselors, a legal exemption should not afford its individual clerics a privilege to decline to testify simply because that is their preference. Because the range of an exemption should be related substantially to what members of the religious group can expect of their clergy if they reveal damaging secrets to them, any cleric who relies on a broad exemption that does not apply to all clergy should need to present a plausible claim that he is supported by the doctrines of his faith rather than rely simply on individual convictions. Civil judges should determine only whether such a claim is reasonable, not exactly what is the prevailing religious doctrine if this is contested.

In respect to limits on exemptions for those who do not have a distinctive religious ground for a more extensive privilege, a statute should not just refer broadly to a balance of considerations but should, as for doctors and lawyers, indicate what specific kinds of information fall outside a privilege not to reveal what has been discovered.

Just who should be able to rely on the privilege to remain silent is tricky. In the Roman Catholic example, and with other religious faiths, the priest or other cleric will see a refusal to reveal as an exercise of his or her religious responsibilities. But what of a person who confesses to a priest? She sees herself as engaging in a required religious exercise that is protected by the priest's obligation of silence. When a Protestant consults with her minister, she may not feel she is under a direct religious obligation to confess, but she may well believe that seeking this religious guidance is one aspect of what their faith calls for, and she may rely on her minister's keeping their conversation in confidence. Of course, in the typical situation of a damaging revelation, both the member and cleric may desire silence, but two kinds of circumstances can raise the issue about whose wish should carry priority for legal purposes.

Suppose the confessor has actually revealed information that stands in her favor. Of course, she is free now to disclose the same facts, but, if she lacks independent evidence, she may think that a priest testifying that she told him this a long time ago in a circumstance in which lying was highly unlikely would provide her with substantial support. In such a circumstance, a cleric should not be able to rely on protecting the individual confessor, but if he fairly asserts that his church doctrine and individual convictions bar testimony even in such circumstances, that should not be overridden by the member's wishes, at least if the church doctrine was apparent to the member.

The opposite situation is one in which a cleric decides that he should reveal information that the member believes she made relying on his silence and wants to be kept secret. Here, if the member can show that the cleric is departing from the doctrines of their religion, she should be able to assert the exemption successfully *if* her attempt to do so precedes the cleric's testimony. (Of course, once the cleric has revealed information, it cannot be retracted or totally disregarded, though the member might have a potential tort claim.) If the religion itself is indecisive or fuzzy about what a cleric can reveal, he should be free to rely on his best judgment about that and not be stopped by the member's desire for his silence, possibly based on her misapprehension of what might be done.

Failing to Give Adequate Advice or Engaging in Improper Activity

A different problem arising with respect to counseling is whether a cleric should be liable for giving bad or inadequate advice or for improper practices. The most common improper practice is sexual involvement, with persons using their positions of influence to engage in such intimacy with those who are vulnerable to their authority. The most publicized examples of such involvement have been about Roman Catholic priests who have had sexual relations with minors.[22] Insofar as the law bars sexual relations between adults and minors, no exception should be created for clerics. This is obviously so if their religion itself forbids or frowns on such relations, but it should also be true regardless of the religion's doctrines. The protection of minors from their elders enticing or pressuring them into sexual involvement is an important enough public objective not to call for exceptions. That conclusion does not itself tell us who exactly should count as adults and minors for this purpose. The age of consent in the United States is set within states between sixteen and eighteen, and most make exceptions from the crime of statutory rape when older teenagers involved are roughly of the same age as their partners.[23] But none of these formulations create exemptions for clerics, and no one suggests that they should.

A harder question about the legal acceptability of sexual relations arises when both consenting partners are adults. Although such involvements are generally allowed, they may provide a basis for tort recovery, or conceivably even criminal penalties,[24] if one party has exercised authority improperly to achieve the connection. Extreme examples would be a doctor or psychological counselor informing a patient that her physical or mental health will be served if she engages in sex with him, or a lawyer telling his potential client that he will represent her only if they have sex. Were a cleric involved in similar urging, he should have no exemption from what would otherwise be liability. Should there be an exception if the cleric or counselor honestly believes that the sexual relations will promote good health? Partly because determining sincerity is so difficult in such a situation, no exemption either for religious or secular counselors should be based on that. However, if in an unusual case, church doctrine actually approves such relations and its members are fully aware of this, that would appropriately be a basis not to allow recovery for an adult member who is both aware of this religious view and chooses to engage in clergy consultation that leads to consensual sex.

A different kind of possible exception is a counselor claiming that he did not attempt in any way to rely on his general status or his authority in consultation to engage in sexual involvement. He might say to his client, "Look, I know you've been seeking my advice, but what I tell you now has nothing to do with responding to the general problems we've discussed. I've actually fallen in love with you, and since we are both single adults, I'd be delighted if we could be an involved couple." On the one hand, it seems harsh to render any counselor potentially liable because of sexual involvement with a client, especially in our modern culture in which the social acceptability of sexual relations outside marriage has increased radically. On the other hand, distinguishing clearly between independent attraction and someone's being drawn to a person because he has a kind of authority and is providing help is nearly impossible, and the client herself may not understand just what is affecting her. What should be done legally here is arguable, but I would be inclined not to create liability if no effort has been made to rely on one's special position in order to create a relationship.[25] Whatever one concludes about this, a cleric should be treated in this respect no better or worse than other counselors.

Questions concerning inadequate forms of advice are a bit more complicated. Like doctors, lawyers, and secular therapists, clerics occupy a special position, and what they say to a member seeking counsel may carry considerable weight. What if they offer advice that is generally regarded as undesirable, or what if they fail to give needed advice? An example of the first might be a recommendation that a man move away from his spouse for reasons, such as religious convictions, that standing alone would not constitute an appropriate basis according to general social norms. An illustration of failure might be not telling someone with a physical ailment that she badly needs to see a doctor or not advising a person inclined toward suicide that she needs psychological help. In an actual case, parents sued a cleric who, they claimed, had told their son that living a life of sin was genuinely worse than committing suicide, which he had subsequently done.[26]

Three variations here distinguish clerics from secular counselors. The state neither licenses them nor sets standards for their practice. Second, in a liberal democratic society, much wider disagreement exists both about the roles of clerics *and* what are relevant appropriate forms of behavior for those consulting them than is true for doctors, lawyers, and psychotherapists. Third, two important aspects of the free exercise of religion are that minority groups should be able to act according to their convictions and that what is spiritual harm and competent spiritual leadership are not the state's business. These strong reasons support not holding clerics to the same standards as nonreligious counselors.

On a particular point, if the question is what is right to do in God's eyes, a cleric should be able to advise that even an illegal act may be appropriate, so long as he does not positively instigate its performance[27] and the act will not cause direct harm to others. Thus, he should be allowed to say that not submitting to a military draft because of an unjust war, or engaging in a demonstration calling for trespass, is acceptable. It may well be that secular counselors, and perhaps even lawyers, should also have a similar privilege.

On the failure to give needed advice, a privilege should partly rest on what the cleric genuinely sees as appropriate behavior according to the religious convictions of his group. When a simple *failure,* not itself grounded in any religious conviction about how someone should act, is involved, a good deal should depend on how the religious group and the cleric portray the role of clergy consultation. If they make clear that the cleric cannot be relied upon to give ordinary secular advice about medical welfare, the consulting member should not be able to recover for failing to get such advice. However, if the clergy have presented themselves as providing comprehensive expert advice, recovery for a definite failure would be sound.

Carrying Out Religious Practices That Are at Odds with Specified Legal Requirements or the Law of Torts

Various practices engaged in by religious groups and their leaders may conflict with ordinary standards of what people are allowed to do. These include treating existing or recent members in ways that, in other circumstances, would amount to invasions of privacy or "intentional" infliction of emotional distress, engaging in potentially tortious actions toward nonmembers, committing defamation, and recruiting new members with tactics that might seem coercive and that might cause emotional harm.

The majority of actual cases that have concerned such actions have been private tort suits, and I mainly consider them in that context here. That these controversies are mostly grounded in the common law does not tell us whether some of this behavior would desirably be governed by specific statutory provisions that grant or deny exemptions. Nor does the tort status of various claims tell us whether a defendant should be able to raise a claim under a RFRA statute. If a specific statutory prohibition covered his behavior, and a religious claimant could successfully raise a RFRA defense against a government penalty, that same behavior should also be protected against a private suit for damages. Although perhaps slightly more debatable if the only potential legal liability is civil damages, I urge at the start of this chapter that judges providing tort recovery under the common law should be seen as imposing a government requirement to which RFRA's indecisive language should apply. Similarly, if a state retains a flexible interpretation of its free exercise constitutional clause, religious practices that may not be forbidden by statute should also be free from tort liability. As noted earlier, a RFRA statute would do well to specify that it does include protection against tort recovery if it would otherwise apply, unless for particular behavior the legislature has directed differently.

A delicate problem for much of the range of possible tort recovery is the potential conflict between free exercise for a religious group and that of individuals who may suffer. The more latitude the group has in various respects, the more the affected person's freedom may be curtailed. This complicates just what should be allowed and what should not. The following analysis assumes that judges should take religious claims, and possible nonreligious analogues, into account when they determine if tort law should be conceived as reaching certain behavior.

Disclosing Highly Embarrassing Facts

The conflict over competing aspects of religious liberty sharply presents itself when religious leaders choose to reveal highly embarrassing facts about a member or former member. The Oklahoma Supreme Court dealt with two such cases roughly a quarter of a century ago and came up with resolutions whose variation makes theoretical sense but is unwise in its likely practical import.

In 1989, the court considered a revelation by elders in a Church of Christ, made to their own members and four surrounding churches in the same denomination, that Ms. Guinn, a former member who had just resigned, had been engaging in fornication outside marriage. She sued, claiming an invasion of privacy and intentional infliction of emotional distress.[28] Despite the term "intentional" in the second of these two torts, an actual aim to accomplish an objective is not required, only an awareness that emotional distress is a likely consequence of an "outrageous" revelation. Thus, a speaker who lacks a substantial enough reason for a disclosure is liable if he is recklessly aware that he may cause that distress, even if that is not his actual purpose. The court, treating the victim's religious freedom as an important state interest, concluded that the elders had no right to commit this tort against a former member. Three years later, the same court concluded that a similar revelation was justified about existing members *and* that if that revelation implemented a previously announced ecclesiastical sanction, the actual communication could occur *after* an excommunication (or presumably a resignation).[29]

Before addressing what revelations really should be protected, I shall mention a crucial difficulty with the court's particular division. If we ask ourselves how we hope things might work, we might well conclude that if a member is acting contrary to what is acceptable behavior within his religion, the elders should contact him, encourage him to reform his behavior, and make clear that if he fails, he will have to suffer whatever consequences of church discipline, if any, will follow. A person involved in a forbidden romantic relationship he does not want to abandon *may* conclude, "Well, I guess I better just resign." Under the Oklahoma approach, if he does so prior to any discipline, the elders will not be able to reveal his "forbidden" behavior. If, instead, they instigate secret investigations and formally resolve to discipline him, they can disclose his behavior even if he resigns as soon as he is aware of what is happening. In short, the court's distinction could well encourage both a failure to warn and the undertaking of a secret investigation leading to formal condemnation before the "guilty" member resigns. For many, both outsiders and insiders, such tactics are hardly how religious groups should treat members who have gone astray.

This brings us to the more fundamental issues. The elders' disclosures could serve two fundamental objectives. The first is the effort to help straighten out the sinning member. Everyone engages in acts that are contrary to the religious convictions of their faith, at least if the faith subscribes to standards about much specific behavior, or the feelings with which one acts toward others. When confessions are made, part of the objective is to encourage reform, and church discipline is imposed for the same reason. For most religious groups, those who actually resign or fall away short of formal resignation are not then totally disregarded. Many individuals rejoin groups they have once left, and these groups often hope to achieve that. Unless "excommunication" is seen as permanent condemnation, even that does not entail that the group no longer has any interest in the life of a former member. For this reason, making the group's privilege to disclose dependent exactly on when a person has ceased to be a member is artificial in respect to its concern about the individual's life.

The group's second objective involves its other members. In many religious denominations, members connect closely with each other. If other members have been confidants of someone who has fallen away and resigned or been excluded, their knowing why that has happened can matter. It will help them understand whether their leaders have had a genuine basis for what they have done and also make them aware of reasons they should no longer closely associate with the former member. To be clear, beyond their encouraging individuals to live in accord with what is spiritually desirable, my own views do not support religious organizations trying to influence and control the everyday lives of their members, but doing so has been a premise of many religious groups over time; and it is not the state's business to decide what is right or wrong from a religious point of view.

If disclosures about personal qualities, even about recent nonmembers, are rightly seen as a religious exercise of various close-knit religious groups, the protecting of such disclosures against potential tort recovery could effectively restrict the religious liberty of existing members who are inclined to engage in forbidden acts and perhaps leave the denomination. Someone aware that such revelations are likely to be made may be strongly tempted to conform to a group's standard requirements or to keep his forbidden behavior secret. Even if he has reached a point at which he no longer subscribes to certain basic tenets of his faith, he may strongly wish not to openly confess that if the consequence will be to sacrifice personal relationships that have become central in his life.

Just how to resolve this dilemma is perplexing, but I believe a crucial factor is how well informed members are about the basic practices of their religion. Let us suppose that it is widely understood that if one fails morally in what the group takes as an extreme way, even on matters now largely regarded as personal in the general culture, one's fellow members will be informed. Such a practice may promote a group's being closely connected, with careful observance by most members of its core requirements. If a person consciously chooses to join such a group and later violates its norms, one might see him as assuming this risk; he has much less basis to complain than if a disclosure is totally unpredictable and unexpected. In brief, the ability of a religious organization to engage in this and other activities that might create civil liability should depend largely on how well it has informed joining members of its doctrines and practices.

Another concern is what exactly is the group's aspiration in making disclosures, insofar as these are determinable. Whatever their doctrines,[30] religious groups should not have a right to injure people simply because they are nonmembers, if that behavior would otherwise be prohibited by statute or constitute a tort. Suppose someone resigned or was expelled two decades ago and moved to a different state. If the chances both of helping to reform him and of protecting existing members have become minimal, the elders should not be able to reveal long-gone or present deviations from what the church prescribes. Although neither judges nor juries should attempt a deep inquiry into actual motivations, any privilege accorded religious groups to do what would otherwise be illegal should depend partly on how recently someone was a member and how closely associated he now is with present members.

An implication of this conclusion is that religious groups should not usually be afforded a special privilege to reveal confidential information about those who were never members, even if their claimed basis is to protect members from harmful involvements. Perhaps an exception to this should be made if the information concerns how those nonmembers are directly seeking to connect to members in a special way, involving more than ordinary services and nonintimate relations.

Related to when disclosure should be permitted is what its ranges should be. Providing members with information is one thing; making it widely available is another. The basic justifications for disclosure concern efforts to reform the sinner and protect those who have been fellow members. The latter justification may cover actual members of the same church and closely related churches, such as the four involved in the initial Oklahoma case.[31] Of course, realism tells us that within a small town or village, information about sexual discrepancy, if provided to members, will leak out to nonmembers as well, and the aim of limiting disclosure becomes still more unlikely with online communication. Nonetheless, a group's justification for disclosure should have to depend on its aiming to reach members, not the general population, and its efforts should be required to reflect this objective.

Should what may be seen as a way of striking the balance between understood likely harm and legitimating reasons that sometimes provides an effective exemption from forbidden disclosure extend to nonreligious as well as religious groups? The basic answer to this should be "yes," but the instances of such a privilege should be highly limited. Disclosures may be either about someone's personal life or about public or quasi-public activities in which he is engaged. A fair number of nonreligious groups are seeking to promote programs they see as benefitting their members or the general public. If a leader within the organization is actually committing a crime, such as bribing legislators, or is promoting objectives at odds with the group's purposes, its leaders have a strong reason to disclose that so that its members and the broader public are not being misled about what it is doing. But here no special privilege is needed because such disclosures, if accurate, would rarely or never be the basis for tort liability.

Rather few nonreligious groups have a special concern about the personal lives of members, but we can imagine examples. Suppose a group is formed to protect marriage in general, or to support marriage between men and women and oppose all sexual relationships between persons of the same gender. If part of their aspiration is to have members dedicated to the lifestyles they support, we can imagine that if a member of the group is consistently committing adultery or is deeply involved sexually with a person of the same gender, the group should be able to tell other members about this, even if in modern times this information would be regarded as private enough not to allow others to publicize it. In this setting, apart from the basic idea that the government should not involve itself in spiritual matters, the reasons applicable to religious groups could apply to how the common law for torts should be construed.

A rather different context might be a dedicated vegetarian organization that learns that one of its members is consistently eating meat. It wants to reveal this unfaithfulness to other members, and perhaps hopes to reform the woman who is violating the group's convictions. Here, since eating meat is generally accepted, the member might have trouble establishing the grounds for invasion of privacy or intentional infliction of emotional distress, but if she could get over that hurdle, the group might again be able to rely on their efforts at attempted reform and protection of other members to avoid liability.

In summary, the privilege to make some factual disclosures that would otherwise be tortious should not be restricted in principle only to religious groups, but its overriding significance will remain there.

One can imagine a kind of alternative that would permit any revelations of true information made with the objective of serving some broader purpose—not to simply hurt the person whose secret is revealed or to satisfy a public that enjoys hearing scandalous facts, but to promote a positive objective to which the disclosing individual or group subscribes. However, given the variations in what individuals see as appropriate aims, the outright oddness of some of these views, and the difficulties of assessing sincere versus insincere statements of what someone is trying to do, such a broad range of permitted disclosures would largely undercut the limited protection we possess from the torts of invasion of privacy and infliction of emotional distress. So long as we believe these torts themselves have a proper place and that some aspects of our lives should be safeguarded against being subjected to widespread revelation, exceptions to the general standards of liability should not be stretched broadly; they need to be circumscribed along the lines suggested here.

Defamation

Does it matter if the disclosure of "facts" is false rather than true? According to the ordinary law of defamation, which includes written "libel" and spoken "slander," a communicator who is sued for making damaging false assertions must prove that what he said is true; if he cannot do that, he may be subject to actual or punitive damages determined by a jury. In the important case of *New York Times v. Sullivan,* the Supreme Court relied on the Free Speech and Free Press Clauses to limit recovery for the defamation of public officials. The plaintiff could succeed then only if the speaker either knew his assertions were untrue or acted with reckless disregard of the truth.[32] As this doctrine has developed, it applies to important public figures as well as to officials.

The question here is whether such a limitation on the range of recovery for defamation should apply to religious and nonreligious groups seeking to protect their operations. One kind of situation involves the functioning of the group. Given that within many churches all members have an actual or potential responsibility for choosing ministers, suppose at a meeting someone says he has been told that a candidate for the ministry has had extramarital affairs at his previous parish. The candidate is not hired and sues the speaker, claiming that the false allegation both cost him the job and hurt his professional reputation. The ordinary law of defamation already protects those who have a responsibility to evaluate the qualifications of candidates, so long as they say what they believe is true, and their mistaken "information" is relevant to the position to be filled. This protection presumably reaches both church members and members of nonreligious organizations who are involved in choosing leaders and thus makes any distinctive exemption from ordinary standards unnecessary.

Of course, what will distinguish religious groups from virtually all nonreligious ones is that a wide scope of a ministerial candidate's personal life will be relevant to his or her qualifications for a position, a reality that also bears on when groups should be able to dismiss ministers from their positions.

A somewhat harder situation is present if the person defamed is not the one who seeks or occupies the relevant position. In a California case, in a church that took a narrow view of acceptable divorces, an administrator had justified a minister's divorce on the basis of offensive behavior by his wife, as well as her opposition to the church.[33] Whether she had or had not been fighting with the church was essentially a matter of opinion, not subject to defamation recovery, but she claimed she had not abused her husband in the ways asserted. Given that the "information" was significant for the status of the minister and did involve his behavior in getting divorced, the court rightly concluded that the speaker should be granted the same latitude as would be accorded statements made about public officials or in the process of evaluating persons who might be hired. Again, if a comparable situation existed for a nonreligious group, the outcome should be the same, although there will be few such groups for which the marital life and divorce of leaders and their spouses will be of central importance.

Shunning

Religious groups may respond to what they take as improper actions with direct behavior that carries serious, negative consequences. This may involve organized shunning, or the encouragement of spouses and other family members not to involve themselves with the person who has done wrong. In many states, organizing a boycott of a business is a tort. And it used to be the law in many states that even an individual urging a person to avoid contact with her spouse constituted the civil wrong of "alienation of affection." That specific tort has largely disappeared,[34] but when leaders of a group urge all members or those within the family to cease contact with a person, that could amount to intentional or reckless infliction of emotional distress.

When religious groups undertake to impose such isolation, should they be subject to ordinary standards or get a special concession? Some religious bodies, includes Jehovah's Witnesses and groups within the Mennonite tradition, believe that shunning can increase an offender's shame and enhance his repentance and restoration and can also protect faithful members from contamination. Barring legislative focus on this discrete problem, something unlikely given that few legal cases actually arise from this kind of group encouragement of disinvolvement, it makes sense to view a special claim to shun from a RFRA perspective. Those engaging in the practice of shunning members who have violated basic church standards may be able to show that forbidding their shunning would constitute a substantial burden on carrying out their religious convictions. Given that if it allows the shunning, the government has no other way to protect the living conditions of the person who is its object, it lacks an alternative less restrictive means. On this analysis, resolution comes down to whether the government has a strong interest in forbidding the practice or making those engaging in it susceptible to damages.

Courts have reached different conclusions. In 1975 the Supreme Court of Pennsylvania implied, by sending a case back to the trial court, that the state had a powerful interest—based on preserving marriages, avoiding alienation of affections, and preventing interference with business relationships—in forbidding a church from encouraging its members, including the spouse, to shun a former member.[35] By contrast, the Ninth Circuit later concluded that the practice did not constitute a sufficient threat to public welfare to justify state intervention.[36] The related questions here are whether the state should ever allow recovery for shunning, whether the quality of life of individuals should count as a strong enough state interest to override a possible privilege for a religious group, and whether aspects of the group involved matter.

As explained in prior chapters, in this domain of RFRA-like laws, the needed government interest is really intermediate rather than compelling in the strongest sense. The government undoubtedly has a sufficient interest in protecting individuals from physical harm even if no threat exists to the broader public. Although shunning differs from physical harm—in that individuals acting alone are free to stop associating with someone whose life disturbs them—given the extreme distress and possible economic disadvantages that group shunning can produce for victims, I believe the government's interest here is strong enough to require a comparison with the strength of the group's claim about religious exercise.[37] It follows that the options of allowing all shunning, or all that is not engaged in for economic gain, should be rejected.

As noted earlier, one argument in favor of allowing recovery by the person who suffers is that this threat against religion-based shunning may help preserve the religious freedom of the individual involved. If a person is aware he may be shunned, that may strongly discourage him from acting with candor if he has come to reject some of his group's teaching. Here, as with a church's disclosure of information, much should depend on how well its informed members are. If they choose to join a group whose practice of occasional shunning of deviant members is no secret, the individual who then becomes subject to that has much less basis to claim he is being treated unfairly. It is also relevant here that one can see the religious freedom of members of the group in general as being protected if they have chosen to join a denomination whose close-knit coherence is partly served by its stringent discipline.

As with some other inflictions of harm on present or recent members, nonreligious groups should potentially have a similar privilege under the common law *if* they could show that shunning relates closely to their group's convictions and its coherence. Such a showing will at most be rare, and these groups will not have the advantage of a RFRA law, but the law of torts should be developed to make such claims at least conceivable. Moreover, whether engaged in by religious or nonreligious groups, shunning and its encouragement could be seen as aspects of expression protected potentially as free speech.[38]

The degree of protected shunning should not include any shunning undertaken primarily to injure those who have left the movement. No group should be able to engage in acts that would normally lead to tort liability, if any aims of reformation of those who have fallen away and of protecting members are overwhelmed by the simple objective of ruining someone. A letter once sent by the founder of Scientology expressly indicated this objective. The church later formally cancelled that policy, but subsequently a court was persuaded that the denomination continued to follow a "fair game" policy of taking away the economic, political, and psychological power of "heretics."[39] Although it is not the government's business to evaluate intrinsically religious claims, public policy should not permit exemptions from general rules for actions for those whose overriding purpose is to harm others. As with some other government practices, such as fighting wars and forbidding racial discrimination, this approach may carry an implication that a particular religious doctrine of a group is not sound, but that sort of indirect judgment is essentially unavoidable.

The conclusion that simple harm is itself an unacceptable objective applies to efforts to boycott businesses and other endeavors that have had no connection to the religion involved. If a business is directly engaged in activities that are counter to a group's religious convictions and practices, leaders should be able to encourage members not to involve themselves with it. The Supreme Court did decades ago establish that expressive groups have a First Amendment right to encourage boycotts that are a matter of political protest;[40] and the same principle should apply to practices that a religious group opposes. If, however, the objection is somehow only to the persons who are running a business, any privilege to encourage noninvolvement should be restricted to messages designed to help members avoid corrupting influences. Simply hurting the nonmembers should not be a justification.

A different question is who should decide if the possible infliction of emotional distress is "outrageous" enough to warrant recovery. In normal circumstances, this determination is one a jury would make in assessing evidence about behavior and its effects, but it is important here that a judge initially undertake a weighing of a group's interest in religious exercise, or free expression, against the kind of harm it is causing. Were all this left to a jury determination, even after its being given appropriate instructions, the danger is too great that the jurors' view of the group involved would dominate, leading to inadequate protection of minority faiths, especially those unpopular with most local citizens.

One may question any exercise in balancing of the sort I have proposed on two grounds. The first is that it is simply too difficult; the second that it will inevitably favor some religious groups over others. The answer to the second concern is that assessing burdens and government interests, which RFRA and similar state requirements require, inevitably makes outcomes partly depend on a group's religious views and the effects of its actions. This is not a direct favoring of particular groups, or a genuine assessment of the soundness of religious doctrines. Although unpopular groups *may* fare less well than those that are widely accepted, the alternative of no exemptions whatsoever will not be better for them but worse. The possible objection that the balancing is too difficult is a genuine concern, but I believe that there is no alternative, more precise approach here that would be both viable and wise.

Internal Community Life

A member of a religious group may find that the group's practices or doctrines cause emotional distress. Should this be a potential basis for tort recovery? Essentially the answer is "no." The practices of certain religions or of subsets of members of those religions may hinder growth of various kinds and could potentially cause a participant to believe she has suffered. A prominent example is the restrictions on how Roman Catholic nuns and monks live their lives, and even more extreme is the rule that Trappist monks must adhere to a vow of silence. If after years, a participant feels she made a misguided choice and now suffers greatly in terms of how she can lead her life, might she maintain a tort claim? The simple answer is that if she voluntarily made that choice at an adequate age, she must suffer any foreseeable consequences. The government can, of course, forbid such a choice if it involves actual physical injury, but beyond that people are able to decide for themselves what restraints they accept on how to live, and religious and other groups can propose what these constraints should be. This includes even an urging that adherents sever family ties, a not uncommon practice among some small religions. The same conclusion applies if someone claims that church doctrine, such as the inferiority of women to men, has caused emotional distress.[41]

A group could potentially be liable for fraud if it effectively guarantees that it will accord members certain secular benefits and then fails to do so.

A particular kind of practice is recruitment for membership. Objections may be raised that this can be coercive or deceptive. In one California case, David Molko, a law school graduate, claimed that the Unification

Church had induced him to visit a farm at which there were lectures, discussions, and exercises; until the twelfth day, it was denied that the group was religious.[42] Given that he could have insisted on leaving at any point and that he joined the church well after being fully informed of its nature, the California Supreme Court affirmed a summary judgment for the church about false imprisonment but indicated that a jury should decide if Mr. Molko had suffered brainwashing. Of course, recovery should be possible if outright coercion, involving physical restraint, is involved, and perhaps also if someone could show a kind of brainwashing that essentially overrode free will. Given his background, liberty to leave, and his joining well after retraction of how he was falsely informed, Mr. Molko almost certainly could not establish that. The latitude afforded religious groups in recruitment should otherwise be largely unrestricted, and juries should not be left free to resolve marginalized cases in light of their sentiments about particular religions. The group's freedom would not apply, however, if the group engages in actual fraud about the basic components about what is required or expected of members and that fraud is maintained up to a person's becoming a member.

As a matter of tort law, other nonreligious groups also devoted to how people may best lead their lives should be understood to have a similar latitude.

Institutional Liability

A concern that arises both with religious and nonreligious bodies is when the organization is liable for the wrongful actions of its leaders or members. Here the general rule for tort liability should apply. The organization can be liable if the individual is attempting to carry out its purpose, even if he is negligent in some way; it is not liable if the individual is secretly violating his responsibilities. The Catholic Church would not be directly liable for a priest's sexual involvement with children, but it could be liable if a bishop assigns a priest with a past history of such abuse to a position that involves contact with children, especially if the bishop does not provide information to those within the local church of this background. In determining the risk of such an assignment, courts should apply standards that do not depend on religious faith. Thus, neither the bishop nor the church would have an adequate defense if the bishop acknowledged, "By ordinary standards, I should not have done this, but I had faith God had achieved the needed reform of the priest's behavior."

Conclusion

This chapter explores a variety of practices engaged in by religious bodies. It examines whether in matters like criminal testimony, church leaders should be exempted from ordinary legal compulsions and whether in the way they treat members and nonmembers some special privileges should exist to engage in behavior that would otherwise be tortious. As with many other existing and possible exemptions, we see genuine competing considerations that need to be recognized. These do support certain instances of special treatment, which should sometimes, but only infrequently, extend to certain nonreligious groups, and which need to be qualified in various respects.

10

Conclusion

Introduction

This book has undertaken analysis of some radically different forms of exemptions granted from legal requirements. It has also covered legal restrictions on private employers that require them to afford exemptions from duties they might otherwise impose on their staff, such as the performance of abortions. And it has treated some rights, such as the refusal of obviously needed medical treatment and income tax deductions, that are not actually exemptions but resemble them in important ways. As Chapter 1 explains, the book's overarching themes are these: the reasons for and against different exemptions vary in significant ways. Not infrequently substantial arguments present themselves on each side. These arguments need to be thoughtfully analyzed and assessed when legislators or others offer proposals and make decisions whether to create exemptions and how to determine the boundaries of their coverage.

For most of the exemptions considered, I have undertaken to provide a fairly detailed analysis of compelling reasons and of what might be the best resolution of conflicting claims. However, the main point of this effort is not to persuade readers about each specific recommendation; any reader will almost certainly disagree with some of them. Rather, it is to reveal that the unsurprising rhetoric one often hears from each side on controversial issues, such as how those engaging in same-sex marriage should be treated, are not the soundest bases for resolution. Understanding and concern for fellow citizens who differ from ourselves best leads us to consider fairly what counts in their lives as well as our own. Sometimes, such considerations, along with other factors, lead to a fairly straightforward conclusion; pacifists should not be subject to a draft for combatant military duty. But often what should be done is much less obvious.

This concluding chapter reviews a number of the different issues treated in preceding ones. It emphasizes specific comparisons in order to highlight similarities and differences that are a crucial element of the entire book. The subjects covered are these: (1) different bases both for granting exemptions and for refusing them; (2) categories of concern about the consequences of exemptions and of bases for some people not to afford equal treatment to others; (3) deciding what should be the basis for an exemption and who should qualify; (4) who needs to comply with the exemptions granted; (5) what it means for an exemption to be necessary, justified, or misguided; (6) what problems exist about assessing sincerity and making an exemption fairly administrable; (7) when alternatives to exemptions are wise; (8) when, if ever, religious grounds should have a status different from nonreligious reasons, and organizations should have more or fewer claims than individuals; (9) how far exemptions should be created by statutes, constitutions, or the common law; (10) when the standards for exemptions should be specific rather than general; and (11) how to interpret a vague statute. These subjects overlap to a significant degree, and the aim of this chapter is only to highlight features and how they relate to certain exemptions, not to provide an analysis that is nearly as detailed as that in the preceding chapters.

Different Bases for Exemptions and for Refusing Them and Limiting Their Scope

When one considers basic reasons for and against the granting of exemptions from ordinary legal duties, considerations of the general welfare of society almost always play a role. Legal requirements are adopted to serve that welfare, and allowing exemptions may reduce those benefits to a degree. Thus tax exemptions and deductions reduce government receipts, and exemptions from the provision of abortions may reduce their availability. Some exemptions themselves serve general welfare in various ways. Allowing pacifists not to serve in the military may actually help the effectiveness of armed forced and avoid the expenditure of money on jailing people whose confinement does not fit the goals of criminal punishment. Many tax exemptions promote welfare by aiding private enterprises that are helping society in significant ways and are also promoting the organizational autonomy that is highly important for a liberal democracy.

Exemptions often involve a respect for the autonomy of people to act according to their religious convictions or their consciences more broadly. This is plainly a basic reason for allowing pacifists not to serve and not requiring doctors and nurses to perform abortions they perceive as the taking human life. Not infrequently, considerations of dignity and equality actually figure on both sides. If someone who believes that assisting same-sex marriage violates God's prescription about who should marry, he may perceive a legal compulsion to do so as a failure to treat him equally and with dignity; but more obviously, the couple wanting to be married can see such refusals as denying their equality and dignity. And even in respect to autonomy, a conflict can be involved. If a religious group has the autonomy to shun a member who has fallen away, that can definitely reduce the freedom of members to act on beliefs and inclinations that begin to deviate from church doctrines.

Figuring in all this is not only how people are themselves directly affected but what message is sent by the existence of any exemption or its breadth. Couples of the same gender may be understandably troubled by broad exemptions from required equal treatment even if they suffer no setbacks in what they can actually do.

Important Categories Relating to Concerns About Negative Aspects of Exemptions and to Various Bases for Some People to Treat Others Unequally

One concern about exemptions is that other individuals will suffer actual harms if objectors do not perform what are generally prescribed duties. This figures in respect to hospitals and individuals not having to perform or assist in abortions; perhaps women will be inconvenienced, and they may even die if providers are not available when one is necessary to a woman's survival. The refusal to supply or insure for needed contraceptives could generate harm for women wishing to avoid pregnancy. Similarly, a child may suffer if a parent is allowed to refuse needed treatment for religious reasons. And shunnings by a religious group can severely disadvantage those who are its object.

Even when the risk of serious harm to individuals is slight or nonexistent, one may worry about the negative effect of a message of inequality, a central concern about same-sex marriage. For some people at least, the granting of a right not to assist in abortions implicitly communicates an unequal status of women.

For other possible exemptions, the major countervailing reasons are not direct harms to individuals but broader concerns about public welfare. This is true about tax and draft exemptions, although with both the notion that some people or organizations are receiving exemptions may seem to be a form of unfair, unequal favoring of them over others who would like to be treated similarly. Rights for prisoners to grow beards and for religious groups to use forbidden drugs in worship services are other examples of special treatment that does not directly harm nonparticipants.

Related to the negative aspects of exemptions are the discrete categories of reasons some individuals have to treat others unequally. One concerns another's personal characteristics, such as race or gender. Another is the status of persons based on what they have done in their lives. A right not to afford services to people who have chosen divorces or received abortions would fall into this category. Finally, what a person or group can regard as deeply objectionable is actually to assist in behavior it regards as seriously wrong. As suggested in Chapter 8, we are, in our personal lives, generally much more hesitant to help perform what we regard as wrong than generally to afford unrelated benefits to others who have engaged in such acts. Of course, when it comes to assistance, there are huge differences of degree. Actually aiding a performance of an act is not the same as providing insurance to allow someone to pay for it, a crucial distinction that could have mattered in the *Hobby Lobby* case.

The differences in the categories just sketched can matter greatly for whether any exemption is warranted, and, if so, how extensive it should be. The fact that no one is directly harmed by a draft exemption bears on why it seems eminently sensible. Given the power of most people's desires for sexual involvement, when it comes to sexual relations between persons of the same gender, we can hardly distinguish someone's personal characteristics from his or her sexual actions—at least so long as the involvements are reasonable by standards other than the partner's gender. Requiring that those who believe certain acts are immoral actually involve themselves in performance is sharply different from requiring equal treatment in other respects. This bears heavily on who should qualify, and when, for an exemption from an antidiscrimination law. The same could be true in respect to abortions *if* it were a real issue whether objectors should be able to deny equal treatment for women who during their lives have had them.

All these factors can bear heavily on whether, on balance, any exemption is warranted, and, if so, what its scope should be. One implicit theme of this book is that when we address highly controversial claims for exemptions, it is actually helpful to reflect on other circumstances in which the competing reasons bear some resemblance and resolutions have been reached that are now fairly widely accepted.

WHO SHOULD QUALIFY AND WHEN

If fairly strong reasons support granting an exemption, that by itself does not tell us who should qualify and for what circumstances. Assuming that pacifists should not be drafted for combat duty, should they also be excused from noncombatant military service? And what should be done about selective objectors? For those objectors, the arguments for an exemption are powerful, but so also are some competing reasons not to provide one. Should exemptions from prohibitions on drug ingestion include nonmedical individual use as well as group worship services? Should exemptions from having to perform certain duties, such as participating in same-sex marriage, extend to those who work for the government?

For individuals and organizations who might be eligible to qualify, what degree of involvement is sufficient to justify an exemption? This is a central question about same-sex marriage and also has relevance for abortions. As Chapter 6 develops at some length, how far providing insurance for certain contraceptives should be subject to an exemption is a very hard question about degree of involvement. That inquiry includes the subquestion of whether insurance should be seen differently from the payment of taxes to be used for practices to which one objects.

In a number of areas, including a clerical privilege not to testify, religious groups' revelations of secret behavior, and their shunning, as well as abortions and same-sex marriage, an important component clearly or arguably concerns the extent to which objectors have provided prior notice about the practices or refusals of service to which they are committed.

When one brings to bear all the considerations, it often becomes extremely hard to decide just where the boundaries of particular exemptions should lie. In addressing that question, one must ask not only what makes sense in principle but what will work practically. People can often reasonably disagree about both answers.

WHO MUST COMPLY?

With many exemptions, only the government's relationship to individuals or organizations, or both, is involved. Draft exemptions are for individuals; many tax exemptions are for nonprofit organizations. An exemption for a forbidden use of peyote *could* free both some group and individual use from criminal liability. Certain modern legal rights and antidiscrimination laws, notably the federal law regarding abortions and some state laws regarding same-sex marriage, require organizations to exempt objectors from performing covered duties that they could choose generally to require of their employees. Although exactly when is debatable, this kind of requirement is definitely desirable in certain contexts.

NECESSARY, JUSTIFIED, AND MISGUIDED

Certain exemptions are "necessary" in various senses. They may be obviously needed given the weight of competing considerations or politically unavoidable at some stage of history. I have urged that the reasons for exempting pacifists are plainly dominant; when same-sex marriage was initially treated seriously by state legislatures, some exemptions were needed to assure passage.

Exemptions may also be seen as constitutionally required in various senses. Supreme Court doctrine may declare them to be provided, as the Court has ruled about the freedom of religious groups to hire "clerics" on whatever grounds they choose. An outsider, especially one not persuaded by *Employment Division v. Smith*'s curbing of free exercise coverage, may believe that constitutional requirements enforceable by courts should reach more broadly. And one may further believe that legislators should see some constitutional obligations in this area, even if those will not, and perhaps should not, be judicially enforceable.

When exemptions are justified and not misguided is what really counts. Clearly, we should not want an undermining of the effectiveness of ordinary legal requirements, and exemptions that were based on mere preferences or did truly serious harm to others would be misguided. Even if some exemptions are warranted, their extensions to others might be rightly regarded as a mistake, a claim that has been made about some tax exemptions. That judgment can also rest on the degree of harm or basic denials of equality others may suffer.

SINCERITY AND ADMINISTRABILITY

A critical question about a large number of exemptions is how to gauge the sincerity and intensity of conviction of those who seek them and how to administer that and other borders of coverage. With income tax exemptions, all this is fairly simple: What kind of organization is involved? With individual tax deductions, what is a person's income, and what medical expenses has she borne and what contributions has she made? Similarly, if an exemption is to be free to do something virtually no one would wish to do for selfish reasons, such as killing in a special way animals that are to be eaten, sincerity is not a real problem. But when it comes to avoiding the draft, not wishing to have one's children vaccinated, or not helping married couples of the same gender, matters are different. People can have reasons for these choices that fall short of genuine claims of conscience. The most obvious problem for officials is discerning a completely selfish motivation, which a person may fraudulently conceal. More subtle obstacles concern actual moral judgments favoring nonparticipation that for one reason or another fall short of genuine conscientious objection. Thus a draftee might believe not being in the military is morally preferable given the country's present use of its armed forces but not feel he would be acting against his conscience if he submitted to a draft rather than going to jail. When an exemption is not yet clearly established, and a person or group that claims one in a legal suit will undergo considerable expense and the serious possibility of a substantial penalty, the pursuit of the claim itself provides assurance about intensity of conviction. We can see the Supreme Court majority's assumption that this was true for the businesses opposed to providing contraceptive insurance in *Hobby Lobby*. But once the exemption is established, the incentives are much greater to offer disingenuous reasons or to overstate the degree of one's opposition. This can certainly be true when the granting of an exemption will benefit a group financially, and it would also be a significant worry about excusing selective objectors from a draft.

If sincere and intense objection to involvement is important in principle, trying to discern it can greatly magnify problems of administrability, especially in the numerous situations when we cannot expect official administrators to carefully appraise each of a broad range of claims.

A different problem of administrability involves situations in which the treatment of particular kinds of claims or individual outcomes needs to depend on a balance of considerations. When have parents stepped over the line if they decline medical treatment for their children for religious reasons? When does the need for an abortion outweigh reasons not to be involved? What hardships for gay couples being married should preclude exemptions that might otherwise apply? These fundamental problems about assessing honesty and intensity of conviction and about balancing the weight of competing consideration can figure centrally in deciding what approaches to various exemptions are called for. Most obviously, even if one believes that, in principle, eligibility for a particular exemption should depend on actual convictions and a balancing of competing considerations, one may conclude that this is so hard to administer that outright denial of an exemption or a rigid straightforward classification is needed in the law. On this basis, many readers may find various of my nuanced suggestions about the appropriate lines legislatures and courts may draw as impractical.

ALTERNATIVES

All these complications bear on the desirability of legislatures considering viable alternatives. If some exemptions are genuinely justified, and deciding exactly who qualifies is difficult, is it possible to create an alternative of free choice that does not do social harm? I have suggested that the answer is "yes" for military service if everyone is given the choice of two years of military duty or three years of civilian service; it is also "yes" for taxation if people can avoid financing practices to which they object by paying an extra 5% for other uses of their funds. In respect to prisons, why not allow any inmates to grow short beards or choose diets that some insist upon for religious reasons? For many exemptions, such an "alternative" approach is not viable; but those considering exemptions that now exist or are proposed would do well to think carefully about whether an alternative is viable that will neither harm others nor impair general welfare.

When Are Lines Between Religion and Nonreligion and Between Individuals and Organizations Warranted?

Two important questions about many exemptions are whether they should be limited to religious claims or extend to conscience more broadly and whether they should be only for individuals or organizations or both.

SIGNIFICANCE OF RELIGION AND ITS RELEVANCE

As the chapters on draft exemptions, prison privileges, refusals of vaccinations, and drug use reflect, we can often see reasons for limiting exemptions to religious claims but also understand why solid bases support extending them.

We can start here with two relatively straightforward reasons for such a limit. In respect to how one may kill animals for food and to whether one may possess a beard in prison, it is hard to conceive of nonreligious reasons that rise to genuine claims of conscience not to comply with ordinary regulations. Another reason for nonextension, applicable to using forbidden substances for nonmedical reasons, is that doing so would increase the danger of fraud too severely, a concern that in this context also makes a limit to religious gatherings, not individual use, sensible.

The harder questions are whether in some deeper sense religion is special and, if so, how and how much. Here, drawing two distinctions is very important. The first involves whether the nature of religion does or does not present some actual reasons for an exemption and whether, even if it does, a created exemption should be limited to religious claims. The second distinction concerns what someone thinking about all this perceives as genuinely true, as contrasted with what seems to have force in the outlooks of many or most other citizens and in the country's tradition.

For both these distinctions we may start with this country's tradition of religious freedom and nonestablishment and the conviction of many religious believers that we owe responsibilities to a higher power that can carry priority over our ordinary moral obligation to perform duties set by our government. These do constitute reasons for exemptions for pacifists from a draft, from duties to assist in abortions, and from the performance of same-sex marriages, for those whose religious convictions are in direct conflict with a requirement imposed by the law or their employer.

That religious claims carry some force does not itself settle whether any exemption should be limited to such convictions. On the latter point, if there are genuine nonreligious views that are closely similar *and* the dangers of fraud are not increased significantly, the exemption should definitely be broadened. We can certainly perceive such views about killing in war and about when life begins. When it comes to same-sex marriage, it is harder to imagine totally secular views that would reflect a similar intensity of wrongness, though a person might see the joining of those of different genders as generally preferable for the raising of children or for some other reason. As the draft cases reveal, one reason not to draw a line between religion and nonreligion is the difficulty of deciding exactly what constitutes "religion."

It is worth noting three special aspects of lines drawn in terms of religion. One is that singling out or excluding particular religions is usually unacceptable, given the values of non-establishment and free exercise. The second is that, since the disfavoring of religion is often a violation of free exercise rights, it is hard to imagine an exemption that would be limited to nonreligious bases. The third is that a particular claim that certain nonreligious groups must, or should, be treated similarly can rest on the values of free speech and association. Although these free expression values do not figure in respect to most exemptions, when groups that have the objective of conveying messages about what is genuinely desirable are choosing their leaders or dealing with members who are violating the group's basic tenets, they have a special basis to be granted a latitude that religious bodies would possess. This reason does not apply to ordinary businesses, although arguably it does cover businesses that have explicitly set forth objectives related to religious practice or public issues.

A more pervasive and deeper issue is how one should assess the possible value of religious convictions and claims. Of course, a person who herself is deeply religious will see a special value in religion, although she may well regard certain particular religious claims as silly. Some people, and one might acknowledge a considerably higher percentage of scholars than other citizens, regard all religions as essentially misguided and as posing obstacles to a healthy social life. This is a view taken by some advocates of same-sex marriage. Here it is crucial for a person to distinguish between what she perceives as basically sound, what she understands as the views of many others in society, and how far she sees that some accommodation to religious objectors will avoid serious frustration and conflict and may even promote acceptance over time of the practice to which they now object. When it comes to same-sex marriage, these are central considerations; they entail that dismissal of the soundness of all or some widely shared religious perspectives does not itself tell us whether an exemption at this stage of our history is actually unwise.

The need to reach beyond one's fundamental perception of what is sound in respect to religion is illustrated especially sharply in countries in which central groups in the society are essentially connected to different religious traditions and associations. Thus, in India, some respect has to be given to the practices of Muslims and Christians as well as Hindus if serious social conflict is to be avoided. As a consequence, in accordance with its colonial heritage, the country leaves most of family law, as well as other systems of personal law, to these religious groups.[1] That does operate against aspects of women's equality, although various qualifications in the general law, such as allowing "opt outs," counter this to a degree.[2] What this broad approach illustrates is that a convinced Hindu or atheist citizen of India does need to take into account how Muslims and Christians in the country see things. Although in the United States the religious divisions and their ties to discrete cultures are not nearly as sharp, nevertheless, sensible assessments of how to treat members of groups with particular convictions do need to take their views into account in deciding what they should be allowed to do.

INDIVIDUALS OR ORGANIZATIONS

Many exemptions are about individual conscience. These include those concerning the draft, personal assistance in abortions, and the wearing of beards in prison. Tax exemptions and those concerning how to treat present and former members of one's group concern organizations. Certain kinds of exemptions extend to both. Hospitals, as well as individuals, do not have to perform abortions in ordinary circumstances. For certain exemptions, such as the use of forbidden substances for nonmedical reasons, whether they should reach both group and individual use can be seen as a genuine issue. I have suggested that an extension to individuals here would undermine administration of the general prohibition too substantially.

An important issue about organizations is just what kind should qualify. Leaders of organizations, or even members more generally, may have objections, religious or not, to certain practices. The *Hobby Lobby* case sharply raised the question of whether a religiously based exemption did, and should, extend to closely held for-profit businesses.

Legal Bases: Statutes, Constitutions, or Common Law

The typical bases for exemptions in the United States are statutes. As Chapter 9 explains, however, the common law of torts has allowed religious groups to engage in certain practices with members and former members that might otherwise be the basis for civil recovery; and the clerical privilege not to testify developed initially under the common law. The role of our federal Constitution and state constitutions is a bit more complicated. The federal Free Exercise Clause was once seen by the Supreme Court as a general basis for religious claims to be free of certain legal requirements. That has been for the most part abandoned, except for how religious organizations choose and dismiss "ministers," broadly conceived. Some state constitutions are still interpreted to provide more expansive protections. And, of course, the federal Constitution does set limits on how the qualifications for exemptions can be set, most obviously barring the favoring of some religions over others. At least in some circumstances, a plausible argument can be made that an exemption which is much too broad in respect to an antidiscrimination law actually violates equal protection rights of the class protected by the basic law. However, the great majority of decisions about exemptions lie initially with legislatures, and they have exercised that authority in many different ways.

SPECIFIC OR GENERAL

Just how legislatures should exercise this authority is itself hardly simple. The most basic distinction is between general categories, as in the Religious Freedom Restoration Act (RFRA), and specific provisions, such as those that have applied to military service and tax exemptions. Of course, this distinction itself is not always sharp because a granting of a particular exemption may leave some assessments a bit vague. Notable in this respect are what counts as relevant "assistance" in respect to the performance of abortions and what amounts to a powerful enough hardship on others to preclude refusing that assistance. Also "intermediate," in a sense, are general provisions that contain somewhat more specific standards of guidance, as is true of the treatment of property protections in the Religious Land Use and Institutional Persons Act.

A major reason for specific treatment is that vague standards are too hard for officials and judges to apply, and they do not give individuals, organizations, and employers adequate notice about what behavior is protected or not. On the other hand, one cannot expect legislators to foresee and deal with all relevant situations. Some generality is needed to reach those. A related concern about expecting needed specific provisions is that legislators may not care enough concerning some minority groups and unusual circumstances to deal with them fairly. At least about some matters, a somewhat open-ended standard may also enhance desirable evolutionary development.

A strong recommendation in many chapters is that specific provisions are desirable when feasible. A somewhat intermediate approach would be for a legislature to set fairly general standards but authorize one or more administrative agencies to then provide more specific criteria of coverage. Yet another possibility is to leave certain decisions up to the discretionary judgment of officials who are in charge of what those working under them need to do.

INTERPRETING GENERAL PROVISIONS

Two crucial points concern how statutes like the RFRA phrased in general terms need to be interpreted and applied. In contrast to what the Supreme Court majority did in *Hobby Lobby,* attention needs to be given to overall structure and its application. The Court then mistakenly treated each provision as essentially separate and did not really consider how well the application it dictated would work over time with other claimants, instead focusing too narrowly on the particular situation before it. Higher courts considering how things will work when they interpret general laws do, however, need to set fairly specific standards that can be applied by officials and lower court judges without great difficulty in similar circumstances.

Conclusion

This chapter essentially summarizes what the book has developed, reiterating central questions about exemptions and their scope and drawing comparisons that reveal significant similarities and differences among kinds of possible exemptions. The overall message is that context matters a great deal, that many factors are often relevant, and that serious reflection on what should be done requires recognition of actual competing considerations and genuine concern for fellow citizens who differ from ourselves in significant ways.

NOTES

ACKNOWLEDGMENTS

INDEX

Notes

1 • INTRODUCTION

1. 494 U.S. 872 (1990).
2. Burwell, v. Hobby Lobby Stores, Inc., 134 S.Ct. 2751 (2014).
3. 42 U.S.C.A. §2000bb-1.
4. City of Boerne v. Flores, 521 U.S. 507 (1997).
5. Gonzales v. O Centro Espirita Beneficente União do Vegetal, 546 U.S. 418 (2006).
6. 42 U.S.C. § 2000 cc-1(a)(1)(2).
7. 132 S. Ct. 694 (2012).
8. Fraternal Order of Police v. City of Newark, 170 F.2d 359 (3d Cir. 1999).
9. Texas Monthly v. Bullock, 489 U.S. 1 (1989).
10. Church of the Lukumi Babalu Aye v. City of Hialeah, 308 U.S. 320 (1993). Only a plurality joined Justice Kennedy's reliance on the history motivating the enactment. For an explanation of why it is a mistake to understand the case as more broadly protecting animal sacrifice, see James M. Oleske Jr. Lukumi at Twenty: A Legacy of Uncertainty for Religious Liberty and Animal Welfare Laws, 19 Animal Law 295 (2013).
11. See 42 U.S.C.A. §3000 a-7 (2000).
12. Robin Fretwell Wilson, The Calculus of Accommodation: Contraceptives, Abortion, Same-Sex Marriage, and Other Clashes Between Religion and the State, *Boston College Law Review* 53: 1417, 1433–45 (2012).
13. For a systematic defense of why in constitutional law religious convictions should not be considered either true or false, see Paul Horwitz, The Agnostic Age (Oxford University Press 2011).

2 • EXEMPTIONS FOR MILITARY SERVICE

1. Roland H. Bainton, *Christian Attitudes Toward War and Peace,* 53–84 (Abington Press, Nashville, Tenn., 1960).
2. Reprinted in John Locke, *A Letter Concerning Toleration,* in Focus, John Horton and Sam Mendes, eds. (Routledge, New York, 1991).
3. Michael McConnell, The Origin of Historical Understanding of Free Exercise of Religion, *Harvard Law Review* 103: 1409, 1466–71 (1990).
4. Id. at 1469.

5. See Kurt T. Lash, Power and the Subject of Religion, *Ohio State Law Journal* 59: 1069, 1112–14 (1998).
6. Federal adoption of state provisions for exemption preceded this act.
7. 40 Stat. 76, 78 (1917).
8. See generally Mulford Q. Sibley and Philip E. Jacob, *Conscription of Conscience: The American State and the Conscientious Objector, 1940–1990,* 12–14 (Cornell University Press, Ithaca, 1982); Jeremy Kessler, The Administrative Origins of Modern Civil Liberties Law, 114 Columbia Law Review 1083, 1123-36 (2014).
9. United States v. Kauten, 133 F. 2d 703, 708 (2d Cir. 1943).
10. Berman v. United States, 156 F. 2d 377, 380 (9th Cir., en banc., 1946).
11. Section 6(j) of the Selective Service Act of 1948, 62 Stat. 613.
12. This practice and subtle variations within it are described in Kent Greenawalt, *Interpreting the Constitution* 186-88 (Oxford Univ. Pr. 2015).
13. E.g., United States v. MacIntosh, 283 U.S. 605, 633 (1931).
14. Wisconsin v. Yoder, 406 U.S. 205 (1972).
15. These subjects are covered in some depth in Kent Greenawalt, *Religion and the Constitution,* vol. I, Free Exercise and Fairness (2006), vol. II, Establishment and Fairness (2008) (Princeton University Press, Princeton, N.J.).
16. 380 U.S. 163 (1965).
17. Id. at 166.
18. Id. at 164–65.
19. Welsh v. United States, 398 U.S. 333, 342 (1970).
20. Id. at 339–40, 333–44.
21. Id. at 370.
22. Id. at 344–54.
23. A "plurality" opinion represents what constitutes the most justices voting for a particular result but less than a majority of all sitting justices in the case.
24. 401 U.S. 437 (1971).
25. The procedures, and how they shifted over time, are described in greater detail in Kent Greenawalt, All or Nothing at All, Philip B. Kurland, ed. *Supreme Court Review* 31, 42–46 (1971). For the initial (but increasingly unsuccessful) attempt to shield draft classification decisions from judicial review, see Jeremy K. Kessler, *A War for Liberty: On the Law of Conscientious Objection*, in The Cambridge History of World War II, Vol. 3, eds. Michael Geyer & Adam Tooze, (Cambridge University Press, 2015), 467, 473-474.
26. For the acceptance of a draft board's determination of insincerity, see Witmer v. United States, 348 U.S. 375, 396-397 (1955) (finding a "basis in fact" for the appeal board's "inference of insincerity or bad faith").
27. See Donald L. Doernberg, Pass in Review: Due Process and Judicial Scrutiny of the Selective Service System, *Hastings Law Journal* 33: 871 (1982).
28. As a consequence of this requirement, many Jehovah's Witnesses had to serve jail terms during World War II and following. See Nathan Elliff, *Jehovah's Witnesses and the Selective Service Act,* 31 Virginia Law Review 811 (1945). Raymond Franz, a former member of the governing body of Jehova's Witnesses, discusses the Jehova's Wittnesses' stance on alternative service in *Crisis of Conscience: The Struggle Between Loyalty to*

God and Loyalty to One's Religion 123-71 (4th ed. 2004), available at http://khazarzar .skeptik.net/books/franz01.pdf.

29. During the Vietnam War, the susceptibility under the Military Selective Service Act of 1967 to being drafted extended beyond 26, but effective liability to the draft did not reach beyond one's 26th birthday. 50 U.S.C. §454(a) (the Military Selective Service Act) authorizes the President to draft individuals outside the specified age range (18-26) to secure a sufficient number of registrants, but generally registrants outside that age group are not inducted into the Armed Forces. See 53 Am. Jur. 2d Military and Civil Defense §87 (available on Westlaw).
30. According to the CIA's World Factbook, as of 2013 women are now included in Bolivia, Chad, Eritrea, Israel, Mozambique, and North Korea. See Central Intelligence Agency, The World Factbook, https://www.cia.gov/library/publications/the-world-factbook/ (last visted Sept. 5, 2015).
31. However, in South Korea many males not physically or mentally capable of military service are required to undertake an alternative form of government work.
32. E.g., Iran. See Arash Karami, Iran May Increase Compulsory Military Service by Three Months, Al-Monitor (Dec. 19, 2013), available at http://iranpulse.al-monitor.com/index .php/2013/12/3506/iran-may-increase-compulsory-military-service-by-three-months/ ("There are various other exemptions, such as ... for those who work in industries vital to the government or military.").
33. I explore the relevance of various bases for criminal punishment, including incapacitation, reform, deterrence, and vengeance, for conscientious objectors in Accommodation to Selective Conscientious Objection: How and Why? in Michael F. Noone, Jr., ed., *Selective Conscientious Objection* 7, 12–13 (Westview Press, San Francisco, 1989).
34. See Paul Horwitz, The Agnostic Age: Law, Religion, and the Constitution 198–208 (Oxford University Press, New York 2011). See also id. at pp. 238–39, (quoting Steven D. Smith, Our Agnostic Constitution, 83 N.Y.U. L. Rev. 120 (2008)), "[I]nsisting that communities give up any official acknowledgement of what the Founders called the 'blessings of liberty' might 'affirmativelyalienate them and forfeit their full loyalty.' . . . [A] rule of non-establishment can alienate the very individuals and communities whose loyalty we ought to treasure."
35. Reynolds v. United States, 98 U.S. 164(1878).
36. See Jesse Choper, Defining "Religion" in the First Amendment, *University of Illinois Law Review* 579, 598 (1982). I respond to this argument in Conscientious Objection and the Liberal State, in James E. Wood, Jr., ed., *Religion and the State* 247, 259–62 (Baylor University Press, Waco, Tex., 1985).
37. See generally Bainton, supra note 1, at 85-135. See also Michael Walzer, Just and Unjust Wars: A Moral Argument with Historical Illustrations Basic Books, New York, 4th ed. 2006; Brian Orend, Michael Walzer on War and Justice (Cardiff, University of Wales Press, 2000).
38. This is summarized in Greenawalt, All or Nothing at All, note 25, supra, at 57.
39. See United Nations, *Charter of the United Nations* VI & VII (Oct. 24, 1995).
40. Council of the European Union, *Common Security and Defense Policy*.
41. They may well treat this as a "political question," not for courts to decide.
42. See Denis Hayes, *Challenge of Conscience* 52–64 (Garland Publishing Company, New York, 1972). His book provides a detailed account of the development of conscientious exemption in Great Britain from 1939 to 1949.

43. Romanian Law 46 of 1996, Art. 6; Government Decree 618 of 1997.
44. See Ukraine Constitution, 28 June 1996, Art. 35.5, On Alternative (Non-Military) Service; Ukraine Law Resolution 2066/1999, adopted Dec. 1992.
45. HCJ 7622/02, Zonstein v. Judge Advocate-General (Nov. 23, 2002); see http:/www.unodc.org/tldb/showDocument.do?documentUid=7661.
46. See Gil Cohen, IDF Dismisses Intel Reservists Who Refused to Serve Over Palestinian 'Persecution', Haaretz, January 26, 2015, available at http://www.haaretz.com/news/diplomacy-defense/.premium-1.639176
47. For an extensive account of various senses of "conscience" suggested by various writers and a claim that the term is too vague and hard to administer to make it often a desirable basis for an exemption, see Andrew Koppelman, Conscience, Volitional Necessity, and Religious Exemptions, 15 Legal Theory 214 (2009).
48. The granting of such an exemption would raise the question whether those already serving should be able to leave if they object conscientiously to participating in a new war.
49. However, as I indicate in All or Nothing at All, note 25 supra at 86–93, I do not think the extension should have been seen as constitutionally required.
50. United Nations, Commission on Human Rights Resolution 1989/59 (March 8, 1989), Resolution 1998/77 (April 22, 1998). For the roots of the 1989 Resolution in the earlier promotion of selective conscientious objection to military service under apartheid governments, see Jeremy K. Kessler, *The Invention of a Human Right: Conscientious Objection at the United Nations,* 1947-2011, 44 Columbia Human Rights Law Review 753, 770-778 (2013).
51. Recommendation No. R(82)8 (1987).
52. During the Vietnam War, a total of 170,000 men received conscientious objection deferments, whereas during WWII, only 72,354 men applied for conscientious objector status (Albert N. Keim, *The CPS Story: An Illustrated History of Civilian Public Service* (Good Books, PA, 1990); original citation found in *Conscientious Objection in America, Primary Sources for Research,* Swarthmore College, http://www.swarthmore.edu/library/peace/conscientiousobjection/co%20website/pages/HistoryNew.htm).
53. I explore this in more depth in Greenawalt, note 36 supra, at pp. 262–64.
54. Yet another alternative would be to have someone either commit to two years of civilian service or be subject to a lottery that *might* produce two years of military service.
55. Although the German constitution actually requires that the duration of an alternative civilian service not exceed that of military service (German Constitution, Article 12(a)(2)), the alternative service was at times (especially around the 1980s) up to one-third longer than the military service. This was justified by the fact that soldiers could later be called to military exercises and had to work longer and that the will to endure some additional hardship (by conscientious objectors) should serve as a test of conscience (which was ruled as constitutional by the German Constitutional Court in 1985). The difference was decreased over time, and equal length was reintroduced in 2003, and the draft program was suspended in 2011. See Justin Collings, Democracy's Guardians: A History of the German Federal Constitutional Court, 1951–2001, at 211 (Oxford University Press, 2015); Uzgr Heval Cnar, Conscientious Objection to Military Service in International Human Rights Law 31-32 (Palgrave-MacMillan, 2013). The difference was decreased over time, and equal length was reintroduced in 2003, and the draft

program was suspended in 2011. See Alan Cowell, The Draft Ends in Germany, but Questions Quest Ends in Germany, but Quest of Identity Endure, N.Y. Times (June 30, 2011), http://www.nytimes.com/2011/07/01/world/europe/01germany.html?_r=0

3 • TAX EXEMPTIONS AND DEDUCTIONS

1. See Herman T. Reiling, *Federal Taxation: What Is a Charitable Organization*, 44 A.B.A.J. 525, 526 (1958).
2. Act of Aug. 27, 1894, ch. 349, §32, 28 stat. 556.
3. 26 U.S.C. § 501(c)(3) (2006).
4. See John F. Coverdale, The Normative Justification for Tax Exemption: Elements from Catholic Social Thought, *Seton Hall Law Review* 40: 889 (2010).
5. Id. at 892.
6. See Henry Hansmann, The Rationale for Exempting Nonprofit Organizations from Corporate Income Taxation, *Yale Law Journal* 91: 54, 69–71 (1981); Rob Atkinson, Theory of Federal Income Taxation for Charities: Thesis, Antithesis, and Synthesis, *Stetson Law Review* 27: 395, 400–06 (1997).
7. See Coverdale, note 4, supra. For emphasis on the relevance of institutional autonomy for religion clauses and free speech law, see Richard W. Garnett, Do Churches Matter: Toward an Institutional Understanding of the Religion Clauses, 53 Vill. L. Rev. 273 (2008), and Paul Horwitz, First Amendment Institutions (Harvard Univ. Pr. 2013).
8. See Coverdale, note 4 supra.
9. The Exemption of Nonprofit Organizations from Federal Income Taxation, *Yale Law Journal* 85: 299 (1976).
10. Id. at 305.
11. Id. at 307–09.
12. Id. at 309.
13. Id. at 309–10.
14. Id. at 315–16.
15. Id. at 349–56.
16. Id. at 358.
17. See, e.g., Robert C. Clark, Does the Nonprofit Form Fit the Hospital Inherently, *Harvard Law Review* 93: 1417 (1980).
18. However, John Coverdale has written, note 4 supra at 892, "Contemporary scholars approach consensus in rejecting Bittker and Rahdert's theory that the income of nonprofit organizations simply falls outside the normative tax base."
19. Hansmann, note 6 supra.
20. Id. at 54.
21. Id. at 72–75.
22. Id. at 81–82.
23. Bob Jones University v. United States, 461 U.S. 574 (1983).
24. The Case for For-Profit Charities, *Virginia Law Review* 93: 2017 (2012).
25. Id. 2065.
26. Id. at 2065–66
27. See, e.g., Bittker and Rahdert, note 9 supra, at 348–58.

28. See John D. Colombo, Why Is Harvard Tax Exempt? (And Other Mysteries of Tax Exemption and Private Educational Institutions), *Arizona Law Review* 35: 841 (1993).
29. See Garnett, note 7 supra, and Horwitz, note 7 supra.
30. See Joint Committee on Taxation, *Present Law and Background Relating to the Federal Tax Treatment of Charitable Contributions* 10 (2013).
31. Id. at 4.
32. Id. at 14. Somewhat different rules apply to donations of property, clothing, and household items. Id. at 22–24.
33. Id. at 14–15.
34. Id. at 1.
35. See id. at 7. This is $6,100 for individuals and $12,200 for married couples filing jointly.
36. One might see the standard deduction as assuming such contributions in general, but people can, of course, receive that without making them.
37. For this and other proposals for revisions, see id. at 48–56.
38. See Evelyn Brody, All Charities Are Property Tax Exempt, But Some Charities Are More Exempt Than Others, *New England Law Review* 44: 621 (2010).
39. See Colombo, note 28 supra.
40. See Brody, note 38 supra at 623–25, 670–71.

4 ▪ FORBIDDEN SUBSTANCES

1. Kevin Sabet, note 3 infra, writes, at 1173, "Big Tobacco tried for decades to conceal the harm of the drug tobacco and millions of lives were lost as a result." According to the Department of Health and Human Services, mortality among smokers in the United States is much higher than that among similar people who have never smoked. See U.S. Department of Health & Human Services, The Health Consequences of Smoking–50 Years of Progress. A Report of the Surgeon General (Atlanta: National Center for Chronic Disease Prevention and Health Promotion, Office on Smoking and Health, 2014), available at http://www.cdc.gov/tobacco/data_statistics/sgr/50th-anniversary/index.htm. Cigarette smoking alone causes one of every five deaths in the United States each year, or more than 480,000 deaths annually. *Id.* Smokers have a life expectancy 10 years shorter than nonsmokers. *Id.*
2. See Office of National Drug Control Policy, White House, https://www.whitehouse.gov/ondcp/state-laws-related-to-marijuana ("Voters in Alaska, Colorado, Oregon, and Washington state also passed initiatives legalizing the sale and distribution of marijuana for adults 21 and older under state law. District of Columbia voters approved Initiative 71, which permits adults 21 years of age or older to grow and possess (but not sell) limited amounts of marijuana.") (last visited Sept. 4, 2015).
3. However, the great majority of those in prison are those engaged in drug trafficking, not those simply possessing and using. See Kevin A. Sabet, A New Direction? Yes. Legalization? No. Drawing on Evidence to Decide Where to Go in Drug Policy, *Oregon Law Review* 91: 1153, 1159–63 (2013).
4. Id. at 1164–66, 1175–78.
5. Id. at 1159–60.

6. Concerns about these, as well as the troublesome relationship between federal enforcement of prohibitions and state authorizations of medical use of marijuana, are treated in Paul Lewis, A Gateway to Future Problems: Concerns about the State-by-State Legalization of Medical Marijuana, *University of New Hampshire Law Review* 13: 49 (2015). Interestingly, the American Medical Association has not endorsed that use. Id. at 66.
7. People v. Woody, 394 P. 2d 813 (Sup. Ct. Cal. 1964).
8. Id. at 817–18.
9. Leary v. United States, 383 F.2d 851 (5th Cir. 1967), rev'd on other grounds, 395 U.S. 6 (1969).
10. See note 7, supra.
11. 494 U.S. 872 (1990).
12. 42 U.S.C. §§ 2000bb-1–2000bb-4 (1993).
13. City of Boerne v. Flores, 521 U.S. 507 (1997).
14. Gonzales v. O Centro Espirita Beneficente União do Vegetal, 546 U.S. 418 (2006).
15. For a fuller account of this, see Kent Greenawalt, *Religion and the Constitution,* vol. 1, Free Exercise and Fairness 214–32, 236–43 (Princeton University Press, Princeton, N.J., 2006).
16. See Matthew Gibson, Rastifari and Cannabis: Framing a Criminal Law Exemption, *Ecclesiastical Law Journal* 12: 324 (2010). (This proposal would authorize individual use.
17. Gonzales v. O Centro Espirita Beneficente União do Vegetal, 546 U.S. 418 (2006).
18. See Kent Greenawalt, note 15 supra, at 124–56.
19. People v. Woody, note 7 supra, at 817-22.
20. Commonwealth v. Nissenbaum, 536 N.E. 2d 592 (Mass. 1989). The church in question had services three times a day.

5 ▪ RECEIVING AND PARTICIPATING IN MEDICAL PROCEDURES

1. In 2014, Marlise Munoz was kept on life support while pregnant and brain-dead at John Peter Smith Hospital in Texas, despite her parents' and her husbands' intent to honor her wish that she be removed from life support. See Manny Fernandez and Erik Eckholm, *Pregnant, and Forced to Stay on Life Support* (Jan. 7, 2014), http://www.nytimes.com/2014/01/08/us/pregnant-and-forced-to-stay-on-life-support.html. The Texas statute at issue, the Texas Advanced Directives Act, states, "A person may not withdraw or withhold life-sustaining treatment under this subchapter from a pregnant patient." Tex. Health & Safety Code § 166.049. The Texas court applied the statutory definition of "death" to find that the statute did not apply to Ms. Munoz. Seema K. Shah, Piercing the Veil: The Limits of Brain Death as a Legal Fiction, *University of Michigan Journal of Law Reform* 48: 301, 333 (2015) (citing Munoz v. John Peter Smith Hospital, No. 096–270080–14, Judgment (96th Dist. Jan. 24, 2014).
2. See Robin Fretwell Wilson, When Governments Insulate Dissenters from Social Change: What *Hobby Lobby* and Abortion Conscience Clauses Teach About Specific Exemptions, *University of California, Davis, Law Review* 48: 703-790(2014).
3. 406 U.S. 205 (1972).

4. 494 U.S. 872 (1990).
5. To be clear, I do not disagree that the weight of two provisions can matter to an outcome, only that if a provision can sometimes carry that weight, it is illogical to suppose it can never suffice on its own. For a fuller analysis, see Kent Greenawalt, *Religion and the Constitution,* vol. I, Free Exercise and Fairness 75–81 (Princeton University Press, Princeton, N.J., 2006).
6. See Leilani Pino, In the Courts: Recent Decisions Attempt to Balance the State's Best Interest of Children and the Fundamental Rights of Parents, *Children's Legal Rights Journal* 30: 74 (2010).
7. Rebecca Williams, Faith Healing Exceptions Versus Parens Patriae: Something's Gotta Give, *First Amendment Law Review* 10: 692, 719–26 (2012).
8. Prince v. Massachusetts, 321 U.S. 158, 166 (1944).
9. Wisconsin v. Yoder, 406 U.S. 205, 234 (1972).
10. Shirley Darby Howell, Religious Treatment of Exemption Statutes, Betrayest Thou Me with a Statute? *Scholar* 14: 945, 950–55 (2012), explains the faith healing tradition in America, ushered in by Mary Baker Eddy, who established Christian Science. See also Allison Ciullo, Prosecution Without Persecution: The Inability of Courts to Recognize Christian Science Spiritual Healing and a Shift Towards Legislative Action, *New England Law Review* 42: 155 (2007).
11. Id. at 193.
12. See Howell, note 10 supra, at 963–64.
13. Commonwealth v. Twitchell, 617 N.E. 2d 609 (Mass. 1993).
14. See Seth M. Asser, and Rita Swan, Child Fatalities from Religion-Motivated Medical Neglect, *Pediatrics* 101 (4): 625–629 (1988); Williams, note 7 supra, at 693. The authors suppose that the number of actual deaths is "many more" than the reported cases they examined. Asser and Swan, p. 628.
15. The Child Abuse Prevention and Treatment Act of 1974 (CAPTA) contained a regulation that required states to enact a religious exemption in order to receive federal funding of child protection programs. See Williams, note 7 supra, at 694.
16. See Asser and Swan, note 14 supra, at 629.
17. For a collection of state laws, see National Center for Prosecution of Child Abuse, National District Attorney Association, Religious Exemption Statutes (Feb. 2015) available at http://www.ndaa.org/pdf/2-11-2015%20Religious%20Exemptions%20to%20Child %20Neglect.pdf (as reproduced in Appendix to Howell, note 10 supra).
18. See, e.g., Walker v. Superior Court, 763 P. 2d 852, 860 (Cal. 1988); Janna C. Merrick, Spiritual Healing, Sick Kids and the Law: Inequalities in the American Healthcare System, *American Journal of Law & Medicine* 29: 269, 290 (2003).
19. Asser and Swan, note 14 supra, at 629.
20. See Monica K. Miller, Parents' Use of Faith Healing for Their Children: Implications for the Legal System and Measuring Community Sentiment, in James T. Richardson and François Bellanger, *Legal Cases, New Religious Movements, and Minority Faiths* 227–43 (Ashgate, Burlington, Vt., 2014).
21. My fuller account of these purposes is in Punishment, *Journal of Criminal Law and Criminology* 74: 343 (1983), and in *Encyclopedia of Crime and Justice* (1983). Somewhat different categorizations—retributive justice, restorative justice, and therapeutic

justice—are used by Sana Loue, Parentally Mandated Religious Healing for Children: A Therapeutic Justice Approach, *Journal of Law and Religion* 27: 397, 408–15 (2012).

22. See Howell, note 10 supra, at 964–68.
23. See generally Loue, note 21 supra, at 413–22, proposing what she calls *therapeutic jurisprudence: a forward-looking approach.*
24. To be clear, I believe strongly that no exemption should extend to parents who deliberately kill their own children. Actual intentional killing, barring self-defense or protection of others, should always be regarded as unacceptable.
25. *See* Planned Parenthood v. Danforth, 428 U.S. 52 (1976) (holding unconstitutional the state's imposition of a blanket parental consent requirement for a minor's abortion during the first 12 weeks of pregnancy); Bellotti v. Baird, 443 U.S. 622 (1979) (requiring state to provide judicial bypass proceeding in which minors could obtain approval to seek abortion without parental consent). For a discussion of minors' abortion rights, see generally Malinda L. Seymore, Sixteen and Pregnant: Minor's Consent in Abortion and Adoption, *Yale Journal of Law & Feminism* 25: 99 (2013).
26. N.J. Stat. Ann § 26.6A-5 (West 2014) provides such an exception to death determinations, but only for religious claims.
27. See Paul Fine et al., "Herd Immunity": A Rough Guide, *Clinical Infectious Diseases* 52: 911–16 (2011); *Community Immunity ("Herd Immunity"),* Vaccines.gov, http://www.vaccines.gov/basics/protection.
28. See Jennifer Zipprich et al., *Measles Outbreak—California, December 2014–February 2015,* Centers for Disease Control and Prevention (Feb. 20, 2015), http://www.cdc.gov/mmwr/preview/mmwrhtml/mm6406a5.htm?s_cid=mm6406a5_w, which notes, "[a]mong the 110 California patients, 49 (45%) were unvaccinated"; Lenny Bernstein and Brady Dennis, Measles Outbreak Spreads to Three More States and Washington DC; 121 People Now Affected, *Washington Post* (Feb. 9, 2015), http://www.washingtonpost.com/news/to-your-health/wp/2015/02/09/measles-outbreak-spreads-to-three-more-states-121-people-now-affected/ ("the resurgence is mostly caused by a growing number of people who are declining to vaccinate their children for personal reasons, or delaying the vaccinations.").
29. A. J. Wakefield et al., [Retracted] Ileal-Lymphoid-Nodular Hyperplasia, Non-specific Colitis, and Pervasive Developmental Disorder in Children, *Lancet* 351: 637 (1998), http://www.thelancet.com/journals/lancet/article/PIIS0140-6736(97)11096-0/abstract.
30. Cf. Corri Black et al., Relations of Childhood Gastrointestinal Disorders to Autism: Nested Case-Control Study Using Data from the UK General Practice Research Database, *Primary Care* 325: 419 (2002), http://www.ncbi.nlm.nih.gov/pmc/articles/PMC119436/pdf/419.pdf.
31. As of Spring, 2015, among the fifty states and the District of Columbia, all of which have school immunization laws, only two had no exemptions, 29 exempted only on religious convictions, and 20 had what have been labeled "philosophical exemptions" as well. National Conference of State Legislatures, *States with Religious and Philosophical Exemptions from School Immunization Requirements* (March 3, 2015), http://www.ncsl.org/research/health/school-immunization-exemption-state-laws.aspx. The California law, SB 277 was adopted in late June, 2015.
32. As of 2013, for example, only three of the nineteen states with broader exemptions had

over 93% of children aged 19–35 months with ≥ 1 dose of measles, mumps, and rubella vaccine, whereas fourteen of the other thirty-four states did so. See *National, State, and Selected Local Area Vaccination Coverage Among Children Aged 19–35 Months—United States, 2013,* Centers for Disease Control and Prevention, Table 3, http://www.cdc.gov/mmwr/preview/mmwrhtml/mm6334a1.htm.

33. 410 U.S. 113 (1973).

34. The Court's subsequent approach was somewhat less stringent about permissible state regulations of abortion procedures. See Planned Parenthood of Southeastern Pennsylvania v. Casey, 505 U.S. 833 (1992).

35. This can occur, for example, with an ectopic pregnancy in which the fertilized egg implants outside the uterus. See National Health Law Program, *Health Care Refusals: Undermining Quality Care for Women,* 15, 40, 57 (2009), http://www.healthlaw.org/publications/health-care-refusals-undermining-care-for-women#.VeIzyPlVhBc.

36. This has been partly evidenced by recent proposals of "personhood" legislation that life begins at conception, all of which have failed. See Maya Manian, Lessons from Personhood's Defeat: Abortion Restrictions and Side Effects on Women's Health, *Ohio State Law Journal* 74: 1 (2013). The division in public opinion over abortion is explored in Robert D. Putnam and David E. Campbell, American Grace 406-14 (Simon & Schuster, N.Y. 2010). For an interesting account of how abortion actually can serve women's motherhood, see Priscilla J. Smith, Responsibility for Life: How Abortion Serves Women's Interests in Motherhood, 17 Journal of Law and Policy 97 (2009). Stephen G. Gilles suggests that when the technology of artificial wombs develops in the future, women with a right to have an abortion should not have a right to have the fetus destroyed rather than survive. Does the Right to Elective Abortion Include the Right to Ensure the Death of the Fetus, 49 Univ. of Richmond L. Rev. 1009 (2015).

37. In Greenawalt, *Religion and the Constitution,* vol. II, Establishment and Fairness, 501–03, 509–11 (Oxford University Press, New York, 2008), and in Natural Law and Public Reasons, *Villanova Law Review* 47: 531, 532–33, 538, 543 I consider a claim that an early beginning of life is a scientific fact that does not need to rest on religious conviction.

38. In respect to all human embryos, apparently roughly two-thirds fail to develop successfully. About 38 percent of embryos form normal-looking blastocysts. Krista Conger, *Earlier, More Accurate Prediction of Embryo Survival Enabled by Research* (Oct. 3, 2010), https://med.stanford.edu/news/all-news/2010/10/earlier-more-accurate-prediction-of-embryo-survival-enabled-by-research.html.

39. Mario Cuomo, a devout Roman Catholic who was governor of New York, supported adopting a law protecting abortions. See, e.g., Mario M. Cuomo, Religious Belief and Public Morality: A Catholic Governor's Perspective, No*tre Dame Journal of Law, Ethics, and Public Policy* 1: 13 (1989). Not all Roman Catholics, of course, agree with that position. For an explanation of why when cultural views are in sharp conflict, protecting the liberty on both sides is highly important, see Douglas Laycock, Religious Liberty and the Culture Wars, 2014 University of Illinois Law Review 839. A competing perspective offered by Douglas Nejaime and Reva B. Siegel, Conscience Wars: Complicity-Based Conscience Claims in Religion and Politics, 124 Yale Law Journal 2516 (2015), is that accommodating complicity-based claims of conscience outside the faith community may actually undermine, rather than advance, pluralistic values. Id. at 2591.

40. See Manian, note 36 supra.
41. See ibid.
42. Of course, the main proponents of such arguments turn out to be Roman Catholics, such as Thomas Aquinas and Robert George, and it is hard for outsiders to judge how far their religious convictions underlie what they see as convincing on nonreligious rational grounds. See Greenawalt, note 37 supra.
43. See Robin Fretwell Wilson, The Calculus of Accommodation: Contraception, Abortion, Same-Sex Marriage, and Other Clashes Between Religion and the State, *Boston College Law Review* 53: 1417, 1446–47 (2012).
44. Rachel Benson Gold, *Advocates Work to Preserve Reproductive Health Care Access When Hospitals Merge* (April 2000), http://www.guttmacher.org/pubs/tgr/03/2/gr030203.html.
45. Valley Hospital Assoc. v. Mat-Su Coalition for Choice, 948 P. 2d 963 (Alaska 1997).
46. See Wilson, note 2 supra.
47. Interesting regarding concerns about inequality are the respective views of men and women about abortion. Although different studies divide on whether more women or men believe abortion is wrongful, none of them indicate a large difference in relevant percentages. See Daniel Allott, Do Men and Women View Abortion Differently? *The American Spectator* (Aug. 22, 2012), http://spectator.org/blog/30346/do-men-and-women-view-abortion-differently:

> A 2002 Public Agenda poll found that men were two percentage points more likely to believe that "abortion should be generally available" to those who want it (44% to 42%), and that women were slightly more likely to think "abortion should not be permitted" (22% to 21%). A 2003 ABC/Washington Post poll found 58% of women and 54% of men felt abortion should be legal in all or most circumstances. More recently, a 2009 CBS News/New York Times poll found that 40% of men and 37% of women felt "abortion should be generally available" while 20% of men and 24% of women felt "abortion should be not permitted."

See Lydia Saad, *U.S. Still Split on Abortion: 47% Pro-Choice, 46% Pro-Life* (May 22, 2014), http://www.gallup.com/poll/170249/split-abortion-pro-choice-pro-life.aspx (finding 44 percent of men identifying as "pro-choice," compared to 50 percent of women, and 51 percent of men identifying as "pro-life," compared to 41 percent of women.).
48. Pub. L. 88–352, title VII, § 703, July 2, 1964, 78 Stat. 255, codified at 42 U.S.C. § 2000e et seq.
49. Id. at § 701(j), codified at 42 U.S.C. § 2000e (j).
50. Trans World Airlines v. Hardison, 432 U.S. 63, 84 (1971).
51. 42 U.S.C. §300a-7(b)(1).
52. Receipt of federal funding is what brings an entity under the provisions of the Church Amendment. Section (b) seems to be only partially preemptive, since the language states that the receipt of federal funding *does not authorize* a court or public official to require an individual to perform an abortion, meaning that relying on federal funding does not impose additional requirements. However, section (c), the discrimination prohibition, seems to preempt any state law that conflicts, since it bars any entity that receives federal funding from discriminating against an employee for performing or refusing to perform an abortion.
53. La. Rev. Stat. Ann. § 40: 1299-35-9 (2009).

54. In Mexico, apparently only a doctor can be a successful objector. See *Procedural Guidelines for the Legal Interpretation of Pregnancy in the Medical Units* (Feb. 1, 2008); Luisa Cabal, Monica Arango Olaya, and Valentina Montoya Robledo, Striking a Balance: Conscientious Objection and Reproductive Health Care from the Colombian Perspective, *Health and Human Rights Journal* 1612: 73, 80 (2014). In Colombia, the Constitutional Court held that only those directly involved in an abortion could object to participation. See T-388/2009 *Conscientious Objection and Abortion, A Global Perspective on the Colombian Experience,* O'Neil Institute for National & Global Health Law et al. Georgetown University Law Center, at 42 (2014). In Uruguay, only doctors or technicians directly involved in abortions can refuse. Cubal, supra, at 79. In the United Kingdom, the Supreme Court ruled that under Scotland's Abortion Act two Catholic midwives could not refuse to supervise or support other hospital staff providing abortions. Doogan v. Greater Glasgow and Clyde Health Bd. (2014) UK SC68, 2014 WL 6862756.
55. However, federal health care conscience clauses do have language covering any service. Robin Wilson, note 43 supra, at 1464.
56. Id. at 1462–68.
57. If a form of treatment were necessary to save the life of a woman but could also be seen as a form of abortion, one doubts that a hospital could decline to provide it if time did not allow its performance elsewhere.
58. See Robin Fretwell Wilson, The Erupting Clash Between Religion and the State over Contraception, Sterilization, and Abortion, in Allen D. Hertzke, ed., *Religious Freedom in America: Constitutional Roots and Contemporary Challenges* 135, 144 (University of Oklahoma Press, Norman, Okla 2015).
59. For an account of state cases, see Wilson, note 2 supra, at 57–60.
60. Wilson, note 58 supra, at 144.
61. In Colombia, one can decline to participate only if there is a feasible alternative for a timely procedure. See Cabal, note 54 supra. Regulations in Argentina require that institutions ensure that individuals can receive reproductive health care services. Law No. 25673/03, May 25, 2003, B. O. Decree 1282/03, May 26, 2003, B. O. Law No. 26130, Aug. 28, 2006. Despite language adopted by the Council of Europe that did not include a specified qualification, the European Court of Human Rights ruled that conscientious opposition cannot have the effect of limiting a woman's right to obtain a procedure. See R. R. v. Poland, no. 27617/04 Eur. Ct. H. R. (2011). In Ontario, Canada, the Ontario Human Rights Commission reviewing the guidelines of the College of Physicians and Surgeons of Ontario emphasized that a privilege for physicians not to perform is available only if it has no significant impact on a patient's health care, given established principles of clashes between equality rights and freedom of religion. A key feature of a new policy is that it "requires physicians to provide their patients with an effective referral to another health-care provider for those services the physician chooses not to provide for reasons of conscience or religion. An effective referral means a referral that is made in good faith with a view to supporting, not frustrating or impeding, access to care." The College of Physicians and Surgeons of Ontario, *College Council Approves New Policy That Safeguards Human Rights and Puts Patients First* (March 6, 2015), http://www.cpso.on.ca/Whatsnew/News-Releases/2015/College-Council-approves-new-policy; College of Physicians and Surgeons of Ontario, Policy Statement #2–15,

Professional Obligations and Human Rights (2015), http://www.cpso.on.ca/CPSO/media/documents/Policies/Policy-Items/Human-Rights.pdf?ext=.pdf.

62. See Elizabeth Sepper, Taking Conscience Seriously, 98 Virginia Law Review 1501 (2012).

6 ▪ CONTRACEPTIVES AND THE *HOBBY LOBBY* CASE

1. Burwell v. Hobby Lobby Stores, 134 S. Ct. 2751 (2014).
2. See generally Kent Greenawalt, How Persuasive Is Natural Law Theory? *Notre Dame Law Review* 75: 1647 (2000).
3. The updated link for the 2006 statement is http://usccb.org/about/doctrine/publications/upload/statement-happy-are-those-who-are-called-to-his-supper-2006-11-14.pdf.
4. See Robin Fretwell Wilson, The Erupting Clash Between Religion and the State over Contraception, Sterilization and Abortion, in Allen D. Hertzke, ed., *Religious Freedom in America* 135, 149–54 (University of Oklahoma Press, Norman, Oklahoma, 2015).
5. For an account of how these devices work, see Association of Reproductive Health Professionals, *Choosing a Birth Control Method: Intrauterine Contraception* (June 2014), https://www.arhp.org/Publications-and-Resources/Quick-Reference-Guide-for-Clinicians/choosing/IUC.
6. For an account of different uses, see Rachel Benson Gold, *The Implications of Defining When a Woman Is Pregnant* (May 2005), http://www.guttmacher.org/pubs/tgr/08/2/gr080207.html.
7. For an account of statutory protections, see Guttmacher Institute, *State Policies in Brief: Refusing to Provide Health Services* (Sept. 1, 2015), http://www.guttmacher.org/statecenter/spibs/spib_RPHS.pdf.

    As of 2015, thirteen states allow some health care providers to refuse to provide services related to contraception. Ten states allow individual health care providers to refuse to provide services related to contraception (Arizona, Arkansas, Colorado, Florida, Idaho, Illinois, Maine, Mississippi, Tennessee, and Washington). Kansas also has a broadly worded refusal clause that may apply. Kansas's law permits refusal if the provider "reasonably believes" the drug or device "may result" in abortion.

    Seven states explicitly permit pharmacists to refuse to dispense contraceptives (Arizona, Arkansas, Georgia, Idaho, Mississippi, South Dakota, and Washington). Six additional states have broad refusal clauses that do not specifically include pharmacists but may apply to them (Colorado, Florida, Illinois, Kansas, Maine, and Tennessee).

    Eight states allow health care institutions to refuse to provide services related to contraception (Arizona, Arkansas, Colorado, Illinois, Maine, Massachusetts, Mississippi, and Tennessee). Five states limit that exemption to private entities (Arkansas, Colorado, Maine, Massachusetts, and Tennessee).
8. For an account of laws and proposals in 2002, see Bryan A. Dykes, Proposed Rights of Conscience Legislation: Expanding to Include Pharmacists and Other Health Care Providers, *Georgia Law Review* 36: 565 (2002).
9. In urging a specific and very broad protection of pharmacists, Bryan Dykes has written that legislators should "subject any conduct or level of participation to a provider's conscience-based right to refuse." Id. at 593. As developed in the next section, I believe

issues about assessing convictions stand in the way of exemptions for those involved only very indirectly.

10. 494 U.S. 872 (1990).
11. 455 U.S. 252 (1982).
12. 406 U.S. 205 (1972).
13. 42 U.S.C. §§ 2000 bb-1–2000 bb-4 (1993).
14. For a comprehensive account of state RFRAs and their judicial application, see Christopher C. Lund, Religious Liberty After Gonzales: A Look at State RFRAs, 55 South Dakota Law Review 466 (2010).
15. 42 U.S.C.A. § 2000cc-5 (7) (A), §2000cc-3(g).
16. Public L. No. 111–152, 124 Stat. 1029.
17. 45 C.F.R. § 147.131 (b) (1)–(4) (2013) (amended 2014).
18. 134 Sup. Ct. 2806 (2014).
19. Coverage of Certain Preventive Services Under the Affordable Care Act, 79 Fed. Reg. 51, 092 (Aug. 27, 2014).
20. As of now, seven courts of appeal have rejected the claims of non-profit institutions challenging the accommodation: Catholic Archdiocese of New York v. Burwell, No. 14-427, 2015 WL 4665049 (2d Cir. Aug. 7, 2015), Geneva Coll. v. Sec'y U.S. Dep't of Health & Human Servs., 778 F. 3d 422 (3d Cir. 2015), East Texas Baptist Univ. v. Burwell, 793 F.3d 449 (5th Cir. 2015), Mich. Catholic Conf. & Catholic Family Servs. V. Burwell, No. 13-2723, 2015 WL 4979692 (6th Cir. Aug. 21, 2015), Univ. of Notre Dame v. Burwell, 786 F.3d 606 (7th Cir. 2015), Wheaton Coll. v. Burwell, 791 F.3d 792 (7th Cir. 2015), Grace Schools v. Burwell, No. 14-1430, 2015 WL 5167841 (7th Cir. Sept. 4, 2015), Little Sisters of the Poor Home for the Aged v. Burwell, 794 F.3d 1151 (10th Cir. 2015), Priests for Life v. U.S. Dep't of Health & Human Servs., 772 F.3d 229 (D.C. Cir. 2014).
21. Ave Maria v. Burwell, 63 F. Supp. 3d 1363 (M.D. Fla. 2014).
22. 134 S. Ct. at 2762-63
23. Braunfeld v. Brown, 366 U.S. 599 (1961).
24. See 134 S. Ct. at 2768.
25. For competing views about this coverage see James M. Oleske, Jr., Obamacare, RFRA, and the Perils of Legislative History, 67 Vanderbilt L. Rev. En Banc 77 (2014), and The Public Meaning of RFRA versus Legislators' Understanding of RLPA: A Response to Professor Laycock, 67 Vanderbilt L. Rev. En Banc, 125 (2014) (denying clear coverage), versus Douglas Laycock, Imaginary Contradictions: A Reply to Professor Oleske, 67 Vanderbilt L. Rev. En Banc 89 (2014).
26. On the general importance of liberty for religious organizations, see Thomas C. Berg, Progressive Arguments for Religious Organizational Freedom: Reflections on the HHS Mandate, 21 Journal of Contemporary Legal Issues 279 (2013).
27. Robert K. Vischer has urged that for profit corporations should be seen as having free exercise rights, although legislators need to be careful about how far these should extend, Do For-Profit Businesses Have Free Exercise Rights? 21 Journal of Contemporary Legal Issues 369 (2013).
28. For one suggestion about how to use manageable and sensible criteria to draw such a line, see Bartlett, Robert P. and Buxbaum, Richard M. and Gadinis, Stavros and McCrary, Justin and Talley, Eric L. and Davidoff Solomon, Steven, Comment on the

Definition of 'Eligible Organization' for Purposes of Coverage of Certain Preventive Services under the Affordable Care Act (October 8, 2014), http://webapps.dcl.gov/FederalRegister/HtmlDisplay.aspx?DocId=27756&Month=8&Year=2014

29. 134 S. Ct. at 2775–79.
30. Id. at 2797–99.
31. United States v. Lee, 455 U.S. 252 (1982).
32. 134 S. Ct. at 2784.
33. Id. at 2799–801.
34. Id. at 2779. The case cited is Gonzales v. O Centra Espirita Beneficente Uniao do Vegetal, 546 U.S. 418 (2006), referred to in Chapter 4, supra.
35. Id. at 2780.
36. Id. at 2785–86.
37. 134 S. Ct. at 2780.
38. Cutter v. Wilkinson, 544 U.S. 709 (2005).
39. 134 S. Ct. at 2780–81.
40. Id. at 2781–82.
41. The independent insurance company can recoup its costs through a direct reduction in the Federally Facilitated Exchange User Fee, which is a tax that the health plan must pay in order to participate in a federally facilitated exchange. The tax will be reduced by the amount of money the health plan paid during the previous year for contraceptive services. The tax will also be reduced by an "allowance" to cover the health plan's administrative costs for providing free contraceptives. For 2014, HHS proposed that the "allowance" equal 15% of the total dollar amount that the company paid for contraceptive services. But the companies will not receive reimbursement until the next year (i.e., tax credits will be granted in 2015 for services provided in 2014). See Susan W. Berson, Tara E. Swenson, and Bridgette A. Wiley, *Notice to Plans and PBMs: Pay for Contraceptive Services and Maybe We Will Pay You Back* (Feb. 18, 2014), http://www.healthlawpolicymatters.com/2014/02/18/notice-to-plans-and-pbms-pay-for-contraceptive-services-and-maybe-we-will-pay-you-back/. See also 45 C.F.R. § 156.50(d) (Adjustment of Federally Facilitated Exchange User Fee).
42. Since enactment of the PPACA, it is estimated that 57 percent of all health plans in the United States are self-funded. (Interest in this arrangement has grown since ERISA exempts these plans from state insurance laws.) Self-Insurance Institute of American, Inc.: *Understanding Self-Insured Group Health Plans,* http://www.hcc.com/portals/0/subsites/hcclife/downloads/HealthCareSuccessPublicationl.pdf.
43. Paul Horwitz has defended the decision as called for by the basic criteria of the statute. The Hobby Lobby Moment, 128 Harvard Law Review 154 (2014). Frederick Mark Gedicks and Andrew Koppelman have urged that the accommodation of religion in a for-profit workplace that burdens others should actually be seen as a violation of the Establishment Clause. They also believe that in the end the decision will be negative for religious liberty by generating intense opposition to exemptions that have negative consequences on others. Is Hobby Lobby Worse for Religious Liberty than Smith? St. Thomas Journal of Law & Public Policy 7 (2015). See also Leslie C. Griffin, Hobby Lobby: The Crafty Case That Threatens Woman's Rights and Religious Freedom, 42 Hastings Constitutional Law Quarterly 641 (2015). Toni M Massaro has proposed ways

in which the harm to others can be reduced. Nuts and Seeds: Mitigating Third-Party Harms of Religious Exemptions, Post Hobby-Lobby, 92 Denver University Law Review 325 (2015).

44. For a strong critique of vague standards like RFRA leading to decisions such as Hobby Lobby, see Ira C. Lupu, Hobby Lobby and the Dubious Enterprise of Religious Exemptions 38 Harvard Journal of Law and Gender 35 (2015).
45. See Wilson, note 4 supra, at 155–56.
46. Id. at 157.

7 ▪ PRISONS AND LAND USE

1. 42 U.S.C. §§ 2000cc to 2000cc-5 (2006).
2. See, e.g., Robert A. Ferguson, *Inferno: An Anatomy of American Punishment* (Harvard University Press, Cambridge, Mass., 2014).
3. Holt v. Hobbs, 135 S. Ct. 853 (2015).
4. O'Lone v. Estate of Shabazz, 482 U.S. 342 (1987).
5. Id. at 349.
6. Ibid.
7. Goldman v. Weinberger, 475 U.S. 503 (1986). A more extensive examination of the case is in Greenawalt, *Religion and the Constitution*, vol. I, Free Exercise and Fairness, 158–65.
8. The background of the case and basis for the officials' decision complicated the central issue in certain ways. Very likely, the fact that officials applied this rule strictly to the rabbi was a response to contentions over his related use outside the hospital since he had previously been allowed to wear the yarmulke within the building. One asserted concern about the need for consistent application was that allowing an exemption here could create a problem in respect to other possible religious personnel, such as Sikhs, whose required headgear is much more striking in appearance.
9. 475 U.S. at 507.
10. 10 U.S.C. § 774.
11. See Ira C. Lupu, The Failure of RFRA, 20 *University of Arkansas Little Rock Law Journal* 20: 575, 607–17 (1998).
12. 42 U.S.C. § 2000 cc-1(a)(2006).
13. 42 U.S.C. § 2000 cc-5 (7)(A) (2006).
14. Cutter v. Wilkinson, 544 U.S. 709, 716 (2005).
15. See S. Rep. No. 103–111, p. 10 (1993), referred to in Cutter v. Wilkinson, 544 U.S. at 717.
16. See, e.g., Todd R. Clear and Melvina T. Sumter, Prisoners, Prisons, and Religion: Religion and Adjustment to Prison, in Thomas P. O'Connor and Nathaniel J. Pallone, eds., *Religion, the Community, and the Rehabilitation of Criminal Offenders* 127–59 (Haworth Press, Binghamton, 2002).
17. Ira C. Lupu, Why the Congress Was Wrong and the Court Was Right—Reflections on City of Boerne v. Flores, *William & Mary Law Review* 39: 793, 802–03 (1998).
18. See Greenawalt, note 7 supra, at 169.
19. See Derek L. Gaubatz, RLUIPA at Four: Evaluating the Success and Constitutionality of RLUIPA's Prisoner Provisions, *Harvard Journal of Law and Public Policy* 28: 501, 557 (2005).

20. Holt v. Hobbs, 135 S. Ct. 853 (2015).
21. 912 F.2d 328 (9th Cir. 1990).
22. Id. at 331.
23. 774 F.2d 338, 348 (8th Cir. 1985).
24. 544 U.S. at 722–23.
25. See, e.g., Warsoldier v. Woodford, 418 F.3d 989 (9th Cir. 2005).
26. Mayweathers v. Terhune, 328 F. Supp. 2d 1086 (E.D. Cal. 2004).
27. Hoevenaar v. Lazaroff, 276 F. Supp. 2d 811 (S.D. Ohio 2003).
28. Note 3 supra.
29. See Dawinder S. Sidhu, Religious Freedom and Inmate Grooming Standards, *University of Miami Law Review* 66: 923 (2012).
30. 135 S. Ct. at 860.
31. Id. at 862.
32. During the first three and a half years of RLUIPA, only seven of forty-six prisoner cases had been dismissed for failing to establish a substantial burden, a striking change from 75 percent of prisoner RFRA cases. See Derek L. Gaubatz, RLUIPA at Four: Evaluating the Success and Constitutionality of RLUIPA's Prisoner Provisions, *Harvard Journal of Law and Public Policy* 28: 501, 569 (2005).
33. Id. at 863–64.
34. Id. at 864.
35. Id. at 865–66.
36. Id. at 866.
37. Id. at 867–68
38. Sasnett v. Sullivan, 908 F. Supp. 1429 (W.D. Wisc. 1995), aff'd, 91 F.3d 1018 (7th Cir. 1996), vacated and remanded, 521 U.S. 1114 (1997).
39. Lemay v. Dubois, No. CIV.A. 95-11912-PBS, 1996 WL 463680 (D. Mass. July 29, 1996).
40. Boles v. Neet, 333 F.Supp. 2d 1005 (D. Colo. 2004). See also Benning v. Georgia, 864 F. Supp. 2d 1358 (M.D.Ga. 2012), sustaining a Jewish prisoner's claim to grow earlocks.
41. See Aviva Orenstein, Once We Were Slaves, Now We Are Free: Legal, Administrative, and Social Issues Raised by Passover Celebrations in Prison, *Pepperdine Law Review* 41: 61, 90 (2013). Twenty-six of thirty-four states responding to a survey indicated that they do provide kosher food. Id. at 91.
42. Id. at 97–99.
43. Id. at 91. See, e.g. Bonnell v. Burnett, No. 07-CV-15444, 2011 WL 4533830 (E.D. Mich., Sept. 29, 2011). The Fifth Circuit did find a compelling interest in costs and order in Baranowski v. Hart, 486 F.3d 112–125 (5th Cir. 2007), cert. denied, 552 U.S. 1062 (2007).
44. Orenstein, note 41 supra, at 93.
45. According to one estimate, only about one-sixth of those receiving kosher meals are traditionally Jewish. Id. at 92.
46. It has been suggested that some cases here have been prompted by anti-Muslim bias and the imposition of religious orthodoxy. Id. at 115.
47. Id. at 108–11.
48. Developments in the Law, IV. In the Belly of the Whale: Religious Practice in Prison, *Harvard Law Review* 115: 1891, 1904–14 (2002).

49. Vigil v. Jones, No. 09-cv-01676-PAB-KLM 2010 U.S. Dist. LEXIS 95104 (D. Colo. Mar. 15, 2011); 2011 WL 1480679.
50. Sayed v. Profitt, 743 F. Supp. 2d. 1217 (D. Colo. 2010), aff'd 415 Fed App'x 946 (10th Cir. 2011).
51. McFaul v. Valenzuela, 684 F.3d 564 (5th Cir. 2012).
52. See First Amendment—Free Exercise in Prisons—Fifth Circuit Holds that Prison's Prohibition on All Objects Over Twenty-Five Dollars Did Not Violate Prisoner's First Amendment Rights or Substantially Burden His Religion Under RLUIPA—McFaul v. Valenzuela, 684 F.3d 564 (5th Cir. 2012), *Harvard Law Review* 126: 1158-59 (2013).
53. Williams v. Secretary Pennsylvania Department of Corrections, 450 F. App'x 191 (3d Cir. 2011).
54. 42 U.S.C. § 2000 cc-5(7)(A), 42 U.S.C. § 2000 cc-3(g).
55. Mack v. O'Leary, 80 F.3d 1175 (7th Cir. 1996), vacated and remanded 522 U.S. 801 (1997).
56. Bryant v. Gomez, 46 F.3d 948, 949 (9th Cir. 1995), cert. denied sub nom. Thomas v. McCotter, 515 U.S. 1166 (1995).
57. Texas Monthly, Inc. v. Bullock, 489 U.S. 1 (1989).
58. In *Matter of Diocese of Rochester v. Planning Bd. of Town of Brighton,* 1 N.Y.2d 508 (1956), the New York Court of Appeals held that a total exclusion of religious institutions from a residential district was beyond the scope of the local zoning authority. In *Cornell University v. Bagnardi,* 68 N.Y.2d 583 (1986), the Court of Appeals permitted religious entities to expand into neighborhoods where nonconforming uses would otherwise not have been allowed. More modernly, courts have required local governments and zoning boards to use a balancing test when considering variances or special permits for religious institutions. For example, in *Pine Knolls Alliance Church v. Zoning Board of Appeals of the Town of Moreau,* 5 N.Y.3d 407 (2005), the Court of Appeals used the balancing test to hold that a zoning board could grant a church's application for a special-use permit to expand but deny its request to build an additional access road. In another example, a village denied a church's request for a special-use permit allowing a structure in an area zoned as an industrial park to be used as a place of worship because the continuing industrial use outweighed the proposed benefit to the public welfare of the church, and the Erie County Supreme Court upheld the zoning board's decision. 2007 N.Y. Misc. Lexis 6126 (Sup. Ct. Erie Co. Aug. 28, 2007). It interpreted *Cornell University* to grant zoning boards authority to consider the "over-all impact on the public welfare." In short, New York municipalities conduct a balancing test to determine the impact on public welfare when reviewing zoning exemptions requested by religious institutions; it's therefore difficult for a municipality to exclude a use but reasonable conditions on use are acceptable.
59. See Roman P. Storzer and Anthony R. Picarello, Jr., The Religious Land Use and Institutionalized Persons Act of 2000: A Constitutional Response to Unconstitutional Zoning Practices, *George Mason Law Review* 9: 929, 932–33 (2001).
60. Id. at 933.
61. Id.; Free Exercise volume, note 7 supra, at 233.
62. Storzer and Picarello, note 59 supra, at 931.
63. Christopher Serkin and Nelson Tebbe, Condemning Religion: RLUIPA and the Politics of Eminent Domain, *Notre Dame Law Review* 85: 1, 4–5 (2009).

64. Ashira Perlman Ostrow, Judicial Review of Land Use Decisions: Lessons from RLUIPA, *Harvard Journal of Law and Public Policy* 31: 727-731 (2008).
65. See Marci A. Hamilton, Federalism and the Public Good: The True Story Behind the Religious Land Use and Institutionalized Persons Act, *Indiana Law Journal* 78: 311, 320–39 (2003).
66. Storzer and Picarello, note 59 supra, at 984.
67. Id. at 984–85.
68. 42 U.S.C. § 2000cc (b)(3)B. As Ira C. Lupu and Robert W. Tuttle explain in The Form and Limits of Religious Accommodation: The Case of RLUIPA, *Cardozo Law Review* 32: 1907, 1923–26 (2011), of these specific criteria, only the fourth will require estimations about sincerity, degree of burden, and strength of government interest.
69. Religious Land Use in the Federal Courts under RLUIPA, *Harvard Law Review* 120: 2178 (2007).
70. James E. Ryan, Note, *Smith* and the Religious Freedom Restoration Act: An Iconoclastic Assessment, *Virginia Law Review* 78: 1407, 1429–34 (1992).
71. Ira C. Lupu, The Failure of RFRA, *University of Arkansas Little Rock Law Journal* 20: 575, 591 (1998).
72. For an extensive and persuasive account of the need for RLUIPA, how it has been construed in different land use settings, and why one may conceive it as under-enforced in important respects, see Douglas Laycock and Luke W. Goodrich, RLUIPA Necessary, Modest, and Under-Enforced, XXXIX Fordham Urban L. Journal 1021 (2012).
73. Islamic Center of Mississippi, Inc. v. City of Starkville, 840 F.2d 293 (5th Cir. 1988). This was apparently the only free exercise land use case decided in favor of a plaintiff by a federal court of appeals prior to *Smith.* See Religious Land Use, note 69 supra, at 2183.
74. Civil Liberties for Urban Believers v. City of Chicago, 342 F.3d 752, 770 (7th Cir. 2003) (Posner, J., dissenting).
75. Id. at 761.
76. See Free Exercise volume, note 7 supra, at 235.
77. U.S. Dept. of Justice Report on the Tenth Anniversary of the Religious Land Use and Institutionalized Persons Act 6 (2010).
78. I put aside here claims that a particular site has a special sacred status.
79. Lakewood, Ohio Congregation of Jehovah's Witnesses, Inc. v. City of Lakewood, 699 F.2d 303 (6th Cir. 1983).
80. Messiah Baptist Church v. County of Jefferson, 859 F.2d 820 (10th Cir. 1988).
81. 456 F.3d 978 (9th Circ. 2006).
82. Rector of St. Bartholomew's Church v. City of New York, 914 F.2d 348 (2d. Cir. 1990).
83. Keeler v. Mayor and City Council of Cumberland, 940 F. Supp. 885-887 (D. Md. 1996).
84. See, e.g., Roman Catholic Bishop of Springfield v. City of Springfield, 724 F.3d 78 (1st Cir. 2013) (writing that the appellant "has presented a serious set of challenges" and that "the question of religious burdens is necessarily individualized and context-specific," citing *Gonzalez v. O Centro Espirita Beneficente Uniao do Vegetal,* 546 U.S. 418, 436 (2006), and therefore stating that it had "written narrowly today . . . grounded in the present facts of this case").
85. Grosz v. City of Miami Beach, 721 F.2d 729 (11th Cir. 1983).
86. Murphy v. Zoning Comm'n of New Milford, 148 F. Supp. 2d 173 (D. Conn. 2001).

87. See, e.g., Daytona Rescue Mission, Inc. v. City of Daytona Beach, 885 F. Supp. 1554 (M.D. Fla. 1995).
88. Storzer and Picarello, note 59 supra.
89. Jeffrey H. Goldfien, Thou Shalt Love Thy Neighbor: RLUIPA and the Mediation of Religious Land Use Disputes, *Journal of Dispute Resolution* 2: 435 (2006).
90. Serkin and Tebbe, note 63 supra.
91. Nonestablishment arguments can also be made, but most concessions to free exercise of religion do not amount to forbidden establishments, as developed at length in my two volumes on the religion clauses, Free Exercise, note 7 supra, and Religion and the Constitution, Vol. 2, Establishment and Fairness.
92. Lupu and Tuttle, note 68 supra, present a developed analysis of the problems with special treatment of religious claims, as connected to RLUIPA.

8 • SAME-SEX MARRIAGE AND SEXUAL RELATIONS

1. Obergefell v. Hodges, 135 S. Ct. 2584 (2015).
2. See, e.g. Laurie Goodstein, *Utah Passes Antidiscrimination Bill Backed by Mormon Leaders* (March 12, 2015), http://www.nytimes.com/2015/03/12/us/politics/utah-passes-antidiscrimination-bill-backed-by-mormon-leaders.html.
3. Robin Fretwell Wilson, The Calculus of Accommodation: Contraception, Abortion, Same-Sex Marriage, and Other Clashes Between Religion and the State, *Boston College Law Review* 53: 1417, 1433–45 (2012).
4. Douglas NeJaime, Marriage Inequality: Same-Sex Relationships, Religious Exemptions, and the Production of Sexual Orientation Discrimination, *California Law Review* 100: 1168-69 (2012).
5. See William N. Eskridge, Jr., A History of Same-Sex Marriage, *Virginia Law Review* 79: 1419, 1422 (1993): "Thus, the exclusion of same-sex couples from marriage in America is an expression of our society's persecution of sexual orientation minorities."
6. See generally Eskridge, note 5 supra.
7. Lawrence v. Texas, 539 U.S. 558 (2003). See Phong Duong, A Survey of Gay Rights Culminating in *Lawrence v. Texas*, *Gonzaga Law Review* 39: 539, 554–55 (2004).
8. William J. Jenkins, Can Anyone Tell Me Why I'm Gay? What Research Suggests Regarding the Origins of Sexual Orientation, *North American Journal of Psychology* 12: 279 (2010).
9. I explore this question of terminology in respect to "stop and frisk" and the race of those stopped in Kent Greenawalt, Probabilities, Perceptions, Consequences and "Discrimination": One Puzzle about Controversial "Stop and Frisk," *Ohio State Journal of Criminal Law* 12: 181 (2014).
10. Douglas Laycock, *Civil Unions: Making Religious Exemptions Work* (May 10, 2009) http://uchicagolaw.typepad.com/faculty/2009/05/civil-unions-making-religious-exemptions-work.html.
11. According to one account, the percentage of Americans who believed homosexual sex was not morally acceptable declined from 60 percent in 2001 to 41 percent in 2013. Frank Newport & Igor Himelfarb, *In U.S. Record-High Say Gay, Lesbian Relations*

Morally OK (May 20, 2013), http://www.gallup.com/poll/162689/record-high-say-gay-lesbian-relations-morally.aspx.

12. It does not follow that they would regard gay marriage as worse than gay sexual relations outside of marriage since they might favor the commitment involved in marriage to other sexual involvement.
13. Andrew Koppelman, Gay Rights, Religious Accommodations, and the Purposes of Antidiscrimination Law, *Southern California Law Review* 88: 619, 640 (2015). See Nan D. Hunter, Accommodating the Public Sphere: Beyond the Model Market, *Minnesota Law Review* 85: 1591, 1617–18 (2001). Preexisting common law may have been somewhat more limiting.
14. Exactly what is reached or not reached can vary significantly.
15. 42 U.S.C. § 3603(b) (2).
16. NeJaime, note 4 supra, at 1196–99. See also Chai R. Feldblum, Moral Conflict and Conflicting Liberties, in Douglas M. Laycock, Anthony R. Picarello, Jr., and Robin Fretwell Wilson, eds., *Same-Sex Marriage and Religious Liberty. Emerging Conflicts* 123–24 (Rowman & Littlefield, Lanham, Md., 2008).
17. See note 2, supra.
18. Loving v. Virginia, 388 U.S. 1 (1967). That such a decision would be forthcoming was clearly evident after *Brown v. Board of Education of Topeka,* 347 U.S. 483 (1954), although the opinion in that case was cast in more limited terms, almost certainly to minimize the intense opposition it was undoubtedly going to cause.
19. Michael Kent Curtis, A Unique Religious Exemptions from Anti-discrimination Laws in the Case of Gays: Putting the Call for Exemptions for Those Who Discriminate Against Married or Marrying Gays in Context, *Wake Forest Law Review* 47: 173–77 (2012).
20. See, e.g. William N. Eskridge, Jr., Noah's Curse: How Religion Often Conflates Status, Belief, and Conduct to Resist Antidiscrimination Norms, *Georgia Law Review* 45: 657 (2011). James M. Oleske, Jr. has suggested that the broader advocacy of exemptions for same-sex marriage is largely explicable by a radical variation in scholarly support. The Evolution of Accommodation: Comparing the Unequal Treatment of Religious Objections to Interracial and Same-Sex Marriages, 50 Harvard Civil Rights and Civil Liberties Law Review 99 (2015).
21. However, at some points, given negative views about sodomy, sexual relations between women were not viewed as negatively as those between men. See Eskridge, note 5 supra, at 1474–76.
22. In 1967, when *Loving v. Virginia* was decided, only sixteen states had such bans. Id. at 1508. Apparently in the 1950s, twenty-nine states maintained such a ban. Joe R. Feagin, *Systemic Racism: A Theory of Oppression* 126 (Routledge, New York, 2006).
23. See Rachel L. Swarns, *American Tapestry—The Story of the Black, White, and Multitracial Ancestors of Michelle Obama* (Harper Collins, New York 2012); F. James Davis, *Who Is Black? One Nation's Definition* 31–77 (Pennsylvania State University Press, University Park, Pennsylvania 2001); Paul Finkleman, The Crime of Color, *Tulane Law Review* 67: 2063, 2109–11 (1993).
24. As Charles L. Black, Jr., put it more generally, "the fact [is] that the social meaning of segregation is the putting of the Negro in a position of walled-off inferiority." The

Lawfulness of the Segregation Decision, *Yale Law Journal* 69: 421, 426–27 (1960). For one critique of my distinguishing of interracial marriage from same-sex marriage, see Nelson Tebbe, Religion and Marriage Equality Statutes, *Harvard Law and Policy Review* 9: 25, 41 (2015)

25. Jane Dailey, Sex, Segregation, and the Sacred After Brown, *Journal of American History* 91: 119, 121 (2004).
26. Eskridge, note 5 supra.
27. Id. at 1480.
28. See Gary J. Simson, Religion by Any Other Name? Prohibitions on Same-Sex Marriage and the Limits of the Establishment Clause, *Columbia Journal of Gender & Law* 23: 132, 151–58 (2012). He urges that statistics fail to support any such claims.
29. Koppelman, note 13 supra, at 655–56.
30. Id. at 656.
31. Eskridge, note 20- supra, at 681–714.
32. A person wishing not to give equal treatment to gays might, however, believe that doing so will broadly assist immoral sex; that basic view is much harder to separate cleanly from the conviction that one should disfavor already married same-sex couples.
33. See Charles J. Reid, Jr., Marriage and Its Relationship to Religion, Law, and the State, in Laycock, Picarello, and Wilson, eds., note 16 supra, at 157.
34. See U.S. Marriage Laws, American Marriage Ministries, https://theamm.org/marriage-laws/. Most states also include Quakers, who lack clerics.
35. See State Minister Licensing Requirements, American Marriage Ministries, https://theamm.org/minister-licensing/.
36. Hosanna-Tabor Evangelical Lutheran Church & School v. Equal Employment Opportunities Commission, 132 Sup. Ct. 694 (2012). Christopher C. Lund, in Free Exercise Reconceived: The Logic and Limits of Hosanna-Tabor, 108 Northwestern Law Review 1183 (2014), provides an account of how other courts have seen the basic principles relied on in the case and also offers a unifying theory to explain them.
37. See Ira C. Lupu and Robert W. Tuttle, Same-Sex Family Equality and Religious Freedom, *Northwestern Journal of Law and Social Policy* 5: 274, 282 (2010). Such a law might be challenged as unconstitutional, but a possible answer would be that governments could require all civil marriages to be performed by government officials, not clerics.
38. An intermediate position would be to allow refusals to marry based on some grounds, such as incompatibility or heretical beliefs, but not to do so on other grounds, such as race or sex, but even such a reform is not now at all probable.
39. See N.J. Stat. Ann. § 10:5–5(b) (now found in N.J. State Ann. 10:5-5(b) West 2015). For a brief account of this general development, see James M. Gottry, Just Shoot Me: Public Accommodation Anti-Discrimination Laws Take Aim at First Amendment Freedom of Speech, *Vanderbilt Law Review* 64: 961, 967–68 (2011).
40. See ACLU, *Non-Discrimination Laws: State by State Information,* https://www.aclu.org/map/non-discrimination-laws-state-state-information-map. The ACLU includes nineteen states and omits Utah, whose antidiscrimination laws prohibits discrimination based on sexual orientation or gender identity, but which exempts religious beliefs from the prohibition. For an account in 2012, see Sara A. Gelsinger, Right to Exclude or Forced to Include? Creating a Better Balancing Test for Sexual Orientation Discrimination Cases,

Penn State Law Review 116: 1155, 1161 (2012). For a classic account of when businesses open to the public may or may not refuse to serve people, see Joseph Singer, No Right to Exclude: Public Accommodations and Private Property, 90 Northwestern University Law Review 1258 (1996).

41. Lance Hernandez, Colorado Civil Rights Commission Rules That Masterpiece Cakeshop Discriminated Against Gay Couple, *ABC 7 Denver* (May 30, 2014). The baker lost before a state appeals court in August 2015, see Erik Eckholm, Baker Who Denied Cake to Gay Couple Loses Appeals, New York Times, Aug. 14, 2015, p. A15, col. 1.
42. Elane Photography, LLC v. Willock, 309 P. 3d 53 (N.M. 2013).
43. Bernstein v. Ocean Grove Camp Meeting Ass'n, No. PN 34XB-03008 (N.J. Dept. of Law and Public Safety, Dec. 29, 2008). See Lupu and Tuttle, note 37 supra, at 279–82, for an analysis of the case.
44. See Gottry, note 39 supra, at 979. For one analysis of this case, including the competing considerations and the difficult line drawing problems of protecting some involvements with same-sex weddings, see Richard A. Epstein, Public Accommodations Under the Civil Rights Act of 1964: Why Freedom of Association Counts as a Human Right, 66 Stanford Law Review 1241, 1277-86 (2014).
45. See, e.g., *Cakes Bake Tension Between Gay Rights, Religious Objections* (April 7, 2015), http://www.nytimes.com/aponline/2015/04/07/us/ap-us-anti-gay-cake-discrimination.html; Abby Ohlheiser, *This Colorado Baker Refused to Put an Anti-Gay Message on Cakes. Now She Is Facing a Civil Rights Complaint* (Jan. 28, 2015), http://www.washingtonpost.com/news/post-nation/wp/2015/01/22/this-colorado-baker-refused-to-put-an-anti-gay-message-on-cakes-now-she-is-facing-a-civil-rights-complaint/ (describing baker's refusal to make two cakes in the shape of Bibles declaring "God hates gays"); see also Michael McGough, *Opinion: Can a Baker Refuse to Make an Anti-Gay Cake?* (Jan. 23, 2015), http://www.latimes.com/opinion/opinion-la/la-ol-gays-weddingcake-marriage-20150123-story.html.

    For a position that is more restrictive than mine about appropriate exemptions, see Douglas NeJaime and Reva B. Siegel, Conscience Wars: Complicity-Based Conscience Claims in Religion and Politics, 124 Yale Law Journal 2516 (2015). They draw a sharp distinction between actions within a faith community and "complicity" that extends to other activities.
46. However, a model statute, which has been developed by a group of scholars who have been highly active in working out appropriate exemptions and who, like myself, stress the importance of perceiving the reasons both for antidiscrimination statutes and certain exemptions, provides that individuals and businesses not "be required to . . . provide goods or services that assist or promote the solemnization or celebration of any marriage . . ." if that would violate sincere religious beliefs. See Letter from Edward McGlynn Gaffney et al., to Rosalyn H. Baker, State Senator, Hawaii 4–5 (Oct. 17, 2013), http://mirrorofjustice.blogs.com/files/hawaii-special-session-letter-10-17-13-1.pdf. This language presumably would cover a baker since a cake is definitely part of a celebration.
47. See Lupu and Tuttle, note 37 supra, at 280. After the ruling against it, and the revocation of its tax exemption, the organization withdrew its treatment of the facility as open broadly to the public.

48. The common features on both sides are emphasized by Alan Brownstein, Gays, Jews, and Other Strangers in a Strange Land: The Case for Reciprocal Accommodation of Religious Liberty with the Right of Same-Sex Couples to Marry, *University of San Francisco Law Review* 45: 389 (2010). Richard W. Garnett, Religious Accommodations And—And Among—Civil Rights: Separation, Toleration, and Accommodation, 88 Southern California Law Review493, 500 (2015), characterizes tension as "among civil rights claims."
49. See, e.g., Robin Fretwell Wilson, Matters of Conscience: Lessons for Same-Sex Marriage from the Healthcare Context, in Laycock, Picarello, Wilson, eds., note 16 supra at 77, 81; and Douglas Laycock, Afterword, in id. at 189–92.
50. See NeJaime, note 4 supra, at 1207, 1234; Lupu and Tuttle, note 37 supra, at 281–82.
51. Koppelman, note 13 supra.
52. Id. at 627–28.
53. Id. at 644.
54. Id. at 639–44. He also recognizes cultural change as a goal.
55. Taylor Flynn, Clarion Call or False Alarm: Why Proposed Exemptions to Equal Marriage Statutes Return Us to a Religious Understanding of the Public Marketplace, *Northwestern Journal of Law & Social Policy* 5: 236 (2010).
56. A summary of many of these various positions within states is in Koppelman, note 13 supra, at 631–38.
57. Boy Scouts of America v. Dale, 530 U.S. 640 (2000). For one account of the importance of freedom of association in respect to public accommodations, see Epstein, note 44 supra.
58. See generally Brownstein, note 48 supra, at 428.
59. See, e.g., Ira C. Lupu and Robert W. Tuttle, note 37 supra, at 294.
60. This conclusion is strongly supported by Robin Fretwell Wilson, Insubstantial Burdens: The Case for Government Employee Exemptions to Same-Sex Marriage Laws, *Northwestern Journal of Law & Social Policy* 5: 318, who provides both a careful analysis and an account of relevant laws and cases.
61. See S.B. 296, 2015 Leg. Gen. Sess. (Utah 2015). The prior case was Kitchen v. Herbert, 961 F. Supp. 2d 1181 (D. Utah 2013), affirmed, 755 F. 3d 1193 (10th Cir. 2014).
62. I reflect here on the analogy to my wish as deputy solicitor general not to be involved in what I took to be a deeply troubling, even outrageous, position on one legal issue. Although as Chapter 1 explains, my sense did not really rise to a claim of conscience, did it indicate that I was ill-suited to hold the position at all? I do not believe so.
63. Wilson, note 60 supra, at 332, provides a formulation of such a balance. See also Wilson, note 49 supra, at 90–100; Laycock, note 49 supra, at 197–98.
64. See Arizona Supreme Court Judicial Ethics Advisory Committee, Judicial Obligation to Perform Same-Sex Marriages, Revised Advisory Opinion 15-01 (March 9, 2015) (determining that a judge may not distinguish between same-sex and opposite-sex couples when determining whether to perform a marriage ceremony, may not decline to perform the same-sex marriage, and that these answers do not change based on the judge's personal belief or sincerely held religious belief that marriage is the union between one man and one woman); see also Ariz. Code of Judicial Conduct Rule 2.3(b) (stating that a judge shall not, "in the performance of judicial duties," manifest bias or prejudice based on sexual orientation).

65. Wilson, note 60 supra, at 332–33.
66. See generally Greenawalt, *Religion and the Constitution,* vol. 2, Establishment and Fairness, 208–10 (Princeton University Press, New Jersey 2008). The complexities of military chaplaincy are explored in Ira C. Lupu and Robert W. Tuttle, Secular Government, Religious People 251-62 (2014).
67. NeJaime, note 4 supra.
68. Of course, it can still matter legally if a broader exemption is specifically afforded for marriage.
69. See Gottry, note 39 supra, at 981–82.
70. This does leave open whether those individuals and small enterprises that provide personal services should generally be free from antidiscrimination requirements.
71. Alan Brownstein has developed an argument that this comparison is more generally relevant than ones about unequal treatment based on other categorizations, note 48 supra.
72. Jonathan Turley, An Unholy Union: Same-Sex Marriage and the Use of Governmental Programs to Penalize Religious Groups with Unpopular Practices, in Laycock, Picarello, and Wilson, note 16 supra at 59, 74–75.
73. However, one *might* think it defensible for the organization not to count the gay married couple as married in its view.
74. Laycock, note 49 supra, at 200.
75. Most commonly equal benefits for domestic partners and spouses are provided via local ordinance. San Francisco passed the first such ordinance, S.F. Cal., Admin. Code ch. 12B.1 (1996), and other cities and municipalities have followed. See, e.g., Berkeley, Cal., Mun. Code ch. 13.29 (2005); Minneapolis, Minn. Code of Ordinances § 18.200(2002); New York City, N.Y., Admin. Code § 6–126 (2004); Seattle, Wash., Mun. Code ch. 20.45 (2005). California is the first, and currently only, state to enact a state-wide Equal Benefits Ordinance. See Cal. Pub. Cont. Code § 10295.3 (West Supp. 2005).
76. Hosanna-Tabor Evangelical Lutheran Church and School v. E.E.O.C., 132 S. Ct. 694 (2012).
77. Boy Scouts of America v. Dale, 530 U.S. 640 (2000). An in depth analysis of this case and related decisions, which sees the decision as somewhat obscure, is Andrew Koppelman with Tobias Barrington Wolff, A Right to Discriminate, (Yale Univ. Pr. 2009). The organization accepted openly gay youths in 2013 and in July 2015 decided to accept gay individuals in leadership positions, see Erik Eckholm, Mormons Assail Boy Scouts' Shift on Gay Leaders, New York Times, July 28, 2015, p. A1.
78. If the group regards all sexual relationships outside marriage as equally wrongful, it would not have a basis to prefer nonmarried couples involving men with women over same-sex couples.

9 • RELIGIOUS BODIES AND THE ROLE OF COMMON LAW

1. Elane Photography, LLC v. Willock, 309 P. 3d 53 (N.M. 2013); Tomic v. Catholic Diocese of Peoria, 442 F.3d 1036, 1042 (7th Cir. 2006); abrogated on other grounds by Hosanna-Tabor Evangelical Lutheran Church School v. E.E.O.C. 132 S. Ct. 694 (2012); Sutton v. Providence Medical Ctr. 192 F.3d 826, 834 (9th Cir. 1999).
2. 42 U.S.C. §§ 2000 bb-1(a)–(b) (1993).

3. 132 S. Ct. 694 (2012).
4. Id. at 710.
5. See Burwell v. Hobby Lobby Stores, Inc., 134 S. Ct. 2751 (2014). Of course, part of the basis for the Court's resolution in *Hobby Lobby,* discussed in Chapter 6, was that the employees would not actually suffer as a consequence. See 134 S. Ct. at 2759–60.

   A much more extensive account of existing cases and analysis of why the federal and state RFRAs should be understood to cover private suits is by Shruti Chaganti, Why the Religious Freedom Restoration Act Provides a Defense in Suits by Private Plaintiffs, Notes 99 Virginia Law Review 343 (2013). To be clear about what the government *can* do, given that RFRA is a statute, another statute dealing with a particular problem could explicitly override the application of RFRA so long as its doing so were not unconstitutional.
6. See, e.g. Sanders v. Shephard, 645 N.E. 2d 900 (Ill. S. Ct. 1994), upholding a seven-year incarceration for a man's refusal to provide information about a "civil" whereabouts. Whether and to what extent reporting requirements apply to clergy is an unresolved, state-specific question. See generally Thomas L. Gowen & Richard J. Kohlman, "Professional Liability for Failure to Report Child Abuse," 38 *American Jurisprudence Trials* 1, at § 38 (rev. ed. 2015).
7. "In 1974, Congress enacted the Child Abuse Protection and Treatment Act (CAPTA), requiring states to pass and comply with specific criteria in their reporting statutes in order to qualify for federal funding." Rachel Goldenberg, Unholy Clergy: Amending State Child Abuse Reporting Statutes to Include Clergy Members as Mandatory Reporters in Child Sexual Abuse Cases, *Family Court Review* 51: 289, 299 (2013).
8. For example, in Alaska, teachers, doctors, peace officers, child care workers, and others are explicitly required to report whenever they have "reasonable cause to suspect that a child has suffered harm as a result of child abuse or neglect." Alaska Stat. Ann. §47.17.020 (2012): See Mary Harter Mitchell, Must Clergy Tell? Child Abuse Reporting Requirements Versus the Clergy Privilege and Free Exercise of Religion, *Minnesota Law Review* 71: 723, 725 n. 10 (1987) (cataloguing laws in every state that contain reporting requirements for child abuse). Texas, for example, refers to "[a] person having cause to believe. . . ." Tex. Fam. Code Ann. §261.101(a)(2005).
9. See Goldenberg, note 7 supra, who urges that clergy should have to report sexual abuse. As far as what the law actually requires, if only other groups are specifically indicated, clerics would not need an exemption to remain uncovered, though many states do provide such exemptions. If the reporting requirement were cast more broadly, clergy would need a specific exemption unless it were assumed that a requirement not to testify would include not reporting. A specific indication that clergy did have to report would presumably qualify as a general testimonial privilege (since it would be incongruous to demand that someone report something but need not testify about it).
10. The Roman Catholic Seal of Confession has been established since at least the Fourth Council of the Lateran, in Canon 21. See *Medieval Sourcebook: Twelfth Ecumenical Council: Lateran IV 1215,* Internet History Sourcebooks Project, Fordham University (Paul Halsall, ed.), http://legacy.fordham.edu/halsall/basis/lateran4.asp. In a movie, *Full Confession,* one acquaintance of a priest confesses to a murder for which another

acquaintance has been convicted and sentenced to death. The priest does not reveal that confession to others, but he does strongly urge the confessor to do so.

11. These are explored in some depth with references to historical sources in Charles Alan Wright and Kenneth W. Graham Jr., 26 Federal Practice and Procedure, Federal Rules of Evidence Rejected Rules 506 to 509, § 5612, pp. 79–93 (St. Paul's West, 1992).
12. See, e.g., Trammel v. United States, 445 U.S. 40, 51 (1980).
13. See, e.g., Idaho R. Evidence 505(b) (1992) (adopting this language); Miss. Code. Ann. § 13–1–22 (2012) (same). See Wright and Graham, note 11 supra § 5611, at 8.
14. Ariz. Rev. Stat. Ann. § 12–2233 (2013). ("In a civil action a clergyman or priest shall not, without the consent of the person making a confession, be examined as to any confession made to him in his character as clergyman or priest in the course of discipline enjoined by the church to which he belongs."). Maine requires reporting of abuse by clergy, except "for information received during confidential communications," a much wider scope. Me. Rev. Stat. tit. 22, § 4011-A (2011). Maryland, in contrast, has a notably narrow definition, demanding church doctrine to require confidence before privilege attaches: "A minister of the gospel, clergyman, or priest of an established church of any denomination is not required to [report suspected abuse] if . . . : (i) the communication was made to the minister, clergyman, or priest in a professional character in the course of discipline enjoined by the church to which the minister, clergyman, or priest belongs; and (ii) the minister, clergyman, or priest is bound to maintain the confidentiality of that communication under canon law, church doctrine, or practice." Md. Code Ann., Fam. Law § 5-705(3) (2012).
15. See, e.g., State v. Glenn, 62 P. 3d 921, 925 (Wash. App. Ct. 2003) ("The courts usually strictly construe testimonial privileges, but they should not so construe the word 'confession' in the clergy/penitent privilege."). See also State v. MacKinnon, 957 P. 2d 23, 28 (Mont. 1998) (finding that a Utah court case persuasively argued that the Free Exercise Clause supported a capacious reading of penitent's privilege).
16. See generally David M. Greenwald, Robert B. Stauffer, & Erin R. Schrantz, *Testimonial Privileges* (3d ed. Thomas/West 2014).
17. See, e.g., Pritchard-Keang Nam Corp. v. Jaworski, 751 F.2d 277 (8th Cir. 1984)
18. Kristen Johnson, *Doctor Patient Privilege Lawyers,* http://www.legalmatch.com/law-library/article/doctor-patient-privilege.html.
19. See Greenwald et al., note 16 supra, at § 7:29.
20. The balance is often struck differently for different professions. In respect to child abuse, for example, only two states have explicitly abrogated the attorney–client privilege, and the piece urging elimination of a clerical privilege for child sexual abuse considers as stronger the argument that it should be maintained for lawyers revealed secrets by clients. Goldenberg, note 7 supra, at 305.
21. In considering the now-rejected but still influential proposed federal priest-penitent privilege rule, the advisory committee rejected a suggestion to make communications subject to privilege if "made privately and not intended for further disclosure." Wright and Graham, note 11 supra, § 5615, at 148. Instead, the committee required the communication to be "confidential," id. "A requirement of confidentiality has been read into most state statutes," id. at 151, and this includes "the intention that the communication will not go beyond the member of the clergy," id. at 151.

22. See, e.g., Hannah Roberts, *One in 50 Priests Is a Paedophile: Pope Francis Says Child Abuse Is "Leprosy" Infecting the Catholic Church* (July 15, 2014), http://www.dailymail.co.uk/news/article-2690575/Pope-Francis-admits-two-cent-Roman-Catholic-priests-paedophiles-interview-Italian-newspaper.html; *Report: Accused Priests Shuffled Worldwide* (June 19, 2004), http://usatoday30.usatoday.com/news/religion/2004-06-19-church-abuse_x.htm.
23. "Many states have age-gap provisions that legalize sexual relations among young people as long as they are within a certain age range. If the minor is above a certain age, a crime is committed only if the defendant is a specified number of years older. As of 2012, thirty-one U.S. states have an age-gap provision. Depending on the state, the age gap may be from two to six years older than the minor, but most often it is three or four years." Jana L. Kern, Trends in Teen Sex Are Changing, but Are Minnesota's Romeo and Juliet Laws? *William Mitchell Law Review* 39: 1607, 1611–12 (2013).
24. Depending on exactly how the authority was exercised, the sexual involvement might be seen as coercive and even rape. Since some professions may restrict this kind of sexual involvement, being disciplined or losing a license is another possibility.
25. As some readers will be aware, my wonderful late wife Sanja had been a master's student in a class of mine. She was three years younger, and we did not date until she had graduated and had undertaken work for the United Nations.
26. Nally v. Grace Community Church of the Valley, 240 Cal. Rptr. 215, 219 (Cal. Ct. App. 1987), rev'd on other grounds, 763 P. 2d 998 (Cal. 1988), cert. denied, 490 U.S. 1007 (1989).
27. See Kent Greenawalt, *Speech, Crime, and the Uses of Language* 266–76 (Oxford Univ. Pr., New York,1989).
28. Guinn v. Church of Christ of Collinsville, 775 P. 2d 766 (Okla. 1989).
29. Hadnot v. Shaw, 826 P. 2d 978 (1992).
30. In Islam, for example, the process of being excommunicated or leaving designates an individual as a "kafir." Many Islamic scholars, but not all, consider apostasy as a Hudud (or Hadd) crime, that is one of six "crimes against God" a Muslim can commit, one that deserves the fixed punishment of death as that is a "claim of God." See Rudolph Peters and Gert J. J. De Vries, Die Welt des Islams, *New Series* 17 (1/4): 1–25 (1976), http://www.jstor.org/discover/10.2307/1570336?uid=2&uid=4&sid=21106445374423.
31. See text accompanying note 28 supra.
32. 376 U.S. 234 (1964).
33. McNair v. Worldwide Church of God, 242 Cal. Rptr. 823 (Cal. App. 2d Dist. 1987).
34. As of 2003, forty-three states had abolished "alienation of affection" as a cause of action. David M. Cotter, The Well-Deserved Erosion of the Tort of Alienation of Affections and the Potential Liability of Nonresident Defendants, *Divorce Litigation* 15 (12): 204 (2003).
35. Bear v. Reformed Mennonite Church, 462 Pa. 330, 341 A.2d 105 (1975).
36. Paul v. Watchtower Bible and Tract Society of New York, 819 F.2d 875(9th Cir. 1987). See Sands v. Living World Fellowship, 34 P. 3d 955 (Alaska 2001).
37. For a similar approach, see Carl H. Estbeck, Tort Claims Against Churches and Ecclesiastical Officers: The First Amendment Considerations, *West Virginia Law Review* 89: 1, 102 (1986).

38. In light of the burdens shunning can entail, any right to encourage it should probably be limited to groups with settled convictions, not extended to any individual who becomes upset with another's behavior.
39. Wollersheim v. Church of Scientology, 66 Cal. Rptr. 2d 1, 11 (Ct. App. 2d Dist. 1989). For a more recent and detailed account, see Lawrence Wright, *Going Clear: Scientology, Hollywood, and the Prison of Belief* (Vintage Books, New York, 2013).
40. N.A.A.C.P. v. Claiborne Hardware Co., 458 U.S. 886 (1992).
41. See Murphy v. I.S.K. Con. of New England, Inc., 409 Mass. 842, 851–52 (1991).
42. Molko v. Holy Spirit Ass'n, 762 P. 2d 46 (Cal. 1988).

10 ▪ CONCLUSION

1. See, e.g., Gerald James Larson, ed., *Religion and Personal Law in Secular India* (Indiana University Press, Bloomington, 2001).
2. See, e.g., Cyra Akila Choudbury, (Mis)Appropriated Liberty: Identity, Gender Justice, and Muslim Personal Law Reform in India, *Columbia Journal of Gender and Law* 17: 45 (2008); Siobhan Mullally, Feminism and Multicultural Dilemma in India: Revisiting the *Shah Bano* Case, *Oxford Journal of Legal Studies* 24: 671 (2004).

Acknowledgments

SINCE SOME OF the chapters in this book build up research and writing I did on earlier in my career, a full account of what I owe to others would need to go back many decades and reach a great many colleagues and research assistants. Rather than attempting that, I limit my acknowledgments here to those who have contributed to the work directly involved in this effort.

Among those who have contributed are Vince Blasi, Thomas Berg, Jessica Bulman-Pozen, Kimberlé Crenshaw, Harold Edgar, Elizabeth Emens, Katherine Franke, Richard Garnett, Suzanne Goldberg, Jamal Greene, Philip Hamburger, Bernard Harcourt, Michael Heller, Jeremy Kessler, Andrew Koppelman, Thomas Merrill, Ira Lupu, Douglas Laycock, Gilliam Metzger, Henry Monaghan, David Pozen, Carol Sanger, Elizabeth Scott, Susan Sturm, Eric Talley, and Robin Fretwell Wilson. Paul Horwitz and Nelson Tebbe offered extensive and helpful comments both about the text as a draft and imporances sources. Especially on the chapter regarding same-sex marriage, I benefitted from discussions of the draft at a conference on Religion and the Law in June 2015 and at a law school lunch in August.

I have benefitted a great deal from the very helpful research assistance of Ryan Chabot, Courtney Chin, Jacqueline Ma, Gatsby Miller, Gautam Rao, Abigail Shaw, Nicole Taykhman, Vi Tran, Marco Wong, and Catherine Yoon.

As in other efforts of mine, given my handwriting, the efforts of Caroline Lukaszewski to see that I got help in putting all this into form has been vital. On this project, the overwhelming contribution has been by Michael Roig. Through many stages, despite a number of other responsibilities, he has responding to my drafts quickly, conscientiously, cheerfully, and accurately. Without his help, it might well have taken months longer for this book to be completed.

I would like to express my appreciation to both Thomas LeBien and John Shannon for supervising this manuscript through the editing process in a friendly, prompt, and careful way that has brought about publication sooner than would otherwise have been possible.

Index

Abortion: claims of conscience limiting, 1, 20, 213; equality in, 1, 7–8, 213–214; societal division on, 3, 98–100, 237n42; medical staff refusing, 5–6, 79–82, 109–110, 237n54, 238n61; exemption laws on, 9, 13–14, 77; contraceptives as, 16, 19–20, 112–113, 114; societal right of, 18–19, 97–98; medical staff required to do, 77–78, 109–110; federal funding of, 78, 107–108, 237n52; for mature teenagers, 91, 235n25; circumstances justifying, 98, 236n35; medical institutions favoring, 98, 236n35, 238n57; religious concerns on, 98, 102, 216, 237n42; *Roe v. Wade* on, 98, 99–100, 236n34; miscarriage contrasted with, 98–99, 236n38; morality debate of, 98–99, 100; medical procedure exemptions protected for, 100, 213, 214, 215, 216; individual autonomy issues with, 100–102, 213; Roman Catholic doctrine on, 102–103, 113–114, 216; medical institutions exemption on, 102–105, 214, 215; religious hospital exemptions for, 102–105, 214, 215; gender equity in, 105–106; medical procedure exemption messaging on, 105–106, 213, 214; as social progress measure, 105–106; legal standards on, 106–111, 236n36; undue religious burden claim in, 107, 216; Church and Hyde Amendments protecting, 107–108, 109–110, 237n52; perform or assist concept in, 108–111, 213, 214, 215, 216; dignity in, 213; minor children parental permission for, 235n25; religion supporting, 236n39; gender-based views of, 237n47

ACA. *See* Affordable Care Act

Administration: exemptions regulated through, 10, 20–21; assessment of, 15–16, 19; of exemption requests,

Administration *(continued)*
15–16, 19, 218–219; conviction threshold for, 15–17, 20–21, 35–38, 217, 230n47; of forbidden substances enforcement difficult, 66; of exemptions impractical, 219
Adoption, 180–182
Affordable Care Act (ACA), 116; contraceptive coverage under, 119, 120; Hobby Lobby contraceptive burden for, 123–125
Alcohol: as forbidden substance, 65–66; enforcement challenges with, 66
Alito, Samuel: on religious exemptions, 11; on *Hobby Lobby,* 121–127; on *Holt v. Hobbs,* 139–140
Alternative exemptions: categories of, 8, 10, 20–21, 30, 43–46, 219, 230n55; discretionary choices of, 10, 30, 43–46, 219, 230n55; burden of, 21, 33–35, 63, 139, 213, 214, 230n55, 243n32; during Vietnam War, 42, 43, 44
Amish: Free Exercise protections for, 27, 37, 84–85, 117, 133, 234n5; *Wisconsin v. Yoder* on, 84–85, 117, 133, 234n5; *United States v. Lee* on tax exemption for, 117–118
Asser, Seth M., 234nn14,16,19
Assessment: of administrability, 15–16, 19; of sincerity and conviction, 15–17, 20–21, 35–38, 217–218, 230n47

Bainton, Roland H., 24, 227n1, 229n37
Berg, Thomas C., 240n26
Berson, Susan W., 241n41
Bill of Rights, 25, 26–27
Bittker, Boris I., 53–55, 231n18
Black market, 66–67
Boardwalk Pavilion, 170, 171–172
Bob Jones University v. United States, 56
Boy Scouts, 183–184, 251n77
Brody, Evelyn, 232nn38,40
Brownstein, Alan, 249n48, 251n71
Burden: of alternative exemptions, 21, 33–35, 63, 139, 213, 214, 230n55, 243n32; as extra under legal duties, 21, 33–35, 230n55; of exemption on community, 63, 213; of law, 70–71; as undue under Title VII, 106–107; abortion as undue religious form of, 107, 216; exemption application as, 119–120; of ACA contraceptive rule for, 123–125; of Hobby Lobby, 123–125; religious land use claims of, 145, 146; of historic preservation, 150; of religious structure zoning, 151–152, 246n91

Charitable deductions: equality of, 60–62, 232n36; for individual taxes, 60–62, 232n36
Charitable organizations. *See* Nonprofit organizations
Child Abuse Prevention and Treatment Act (1974) (CAPTA): religious exemptions in, 234n15; mandatory reporting for, 252n6
Children. *See* Mature teenagers; Minor children
Choper, Jesse, 229n36
Christian Science, 81, 84, 86, 87, 89, 234n10
Church Amendment: federal abortion funding in, 107–108, 237n52; medical protection under, 107–108; nonparticipation exception lack in, 109–110, 213

Civility, 22, 212
Civil Rights Act (1964), Title VII, 106–107
Civil War Draft Act (1864), 25–26
Claims of conscience, 229n33, 230nn47,50; abortion limited through, 1, 20, 213; equality balanced with, 1, 31, 35; freedom and liberty balanced with, 1, 31; from moral convictions, 1; from religious convictions, 1; individual autonomy, dignity and, 4, 213; fraudulent claims of, 32, 36–37, 45
Closely held for-profit corporations: RFRA apply to, 9, 12–13, 19–20 118–119, 121–123, 126–127, 128–129; ACA exemption request under RFRA for, 120–121; as person under RFRA, 121–123
Cocaine, 66, 67
Colombo, John D., 232nn28,39
Common law: harm balanced with reasons under, 12; protecting children under, 86; tort issues in, 187, 197–198, 202–209, 213, 216, 254nn34,38; defamation tort recovery under, 203–204; exemptions in, 222–223
Community: religion benefiting, 57–58, 213; exemption burden on, 63, 213; children as members of, 83; as defining child welfare, 84; vaccination for immunity of, 95, 96, 97; tort recovery in issues of, 208–209; Unification Church and Molko case of, 208–209. *See also* Society
Compelling interest test: for *Hobby Lobby,* 125–126; *Hobby Lobby* contrasted with prison claims of, 130–131, 139, 243n32
Compliance, 13
Conception: life begins at, 3, 98–99, 114, 165, 236nn36,37; as contrasted with implantation and fertilization, 114
Confidential information: religious groups disclosing, 198–201, 216, 254n30; tort remedies to disclosure of, 202–203
Congress, U. S.: as federal exemption source, 8–9, 27, 117, 213, 222–223; Constitution *vs.* law language for, 26–27; Church and Hyde Amendments of, 107–108, 109–110, 237n52; RLUIPA reasoning of, 131–132; *Goldman v. Weinberger* response of, 134; CAPTA of, 234n15
Conscience. *See* Claims of conscience
Conscientious objectors, 230nn47,50; Continental Congress on, 25; Civil War Draft Act on, 25–26; WWI Draft Act on, 25–26; military exemption for, 25–43; Selective Service Act on, 26, 229n33; as religious and nonreligious, 27, 28–29, 35–36, 38–43, 228n19; during Vietnam War, 28–29, 30, 43; draft board review of, 30, 228n25; exemption considerations for, 31–32, 33–35, 214, 216; fraudulent claims of, 32, 36–37, 45
Conscription. *See* Military service draft
Constitution, U. S.: as exemption source, 8, 18; Free Exercise Clause of, 8, 11, 12, 27–28, 37, 58, 68, 69, 73–74, 84–85, 116, 117, 133–134, 168, 214, 227n10, 229n34, 234n5, 240n27, 242n8; Madison Bill of Rights draft for, 25, 26–27; law

Constitution, U. S. *(continued)* contrasted with requirements of, 26–27; Establishment Clause of, 27–28, 58, 229n34; First Amendment of, 58
Continental Congress, 25
Contraceptives: insurance for, 1, 5, 13–14, 20, 30, 112–113, 114, 115–116, 187, 214, 216, 251n5; societal division on, 3, 77; private enterprise denying coverage for, 5–6; exemptions for pharmacies on, 13, 16, 114–115; pharmacists exemptions on, 13, 16, 114–115; as abortion, 16, 19–20, 112–113, 114; exemptions on providing, 77, 112–113, 119, 120, 214, 215; private enterprise required coverage for, 77–78, 112–113; as after fertilization, 112–113, 114–115; RFRA exemptions for, 112–113, 214, 215; intrauterine devices as, 113, 114, 115–116, 119; Roman Catholic doctrine on, 113–114; ella as, 114, 115–116, 119; Plan B as, 114, 115–116, 119; dignity harm and, 115, 214; under RFRA, 115–116; ACA providing, 119, 120; government pays for exempting, 119, 127, 241n41; ACA burden for Hobby Lobby as, 123–125; insurance bears exemption cost for, 127–128; *Hobby Lobby* decision alternatives for, 128–129. *See also Hobby Lobby* case
Conviction, personal: claims of conscience as, 1; threshold of, 15–17, 20–21, 35–38, 217, 230n47; medical procedure exemptions for, 76–77
Courts: exemption determinations of, 9–10; legislative standards contrasted with, 78–79
Coverdale, John, 231nn4,7,8,18
Culture, 2
Cuomo, Mario M., 236n39
Curtis, Michael Kent, 247n19
Cutter v. Wilkinson, 135–136, 138

Dailey, Jane, 247n25
Davis, F. James, 247n23
Deception, 14, 158, 159, 178, 212
Defamation, 203–204
Dignity: claims of, 4, 213; harm to, 4, 15, 115, 173–174, 213, 214; interracial marriage with, 15, 105; for same-sex marriage, 15, 105–106, 154–155, 213–214; in abortion, 213
Discretionary choices, 10, 30, 43–46, 219, 230n55
Discrimination: on personal characteristics, 6; on status of others, 6; personal nonparticipation as, 6–7; by government, 11–12, 148–149, 245nn72,73,84; against same-sex couples, 49, 103, 154–155, 156, 167, 170–172, 248nn32,39,40, 249nn44,45,46,47; on sexual orientation, 49, 103, 154–155, 156, 167, 170–172, 248nn32,39,40, 249nn44,45,46,47; Bob Jones violating public values as, 56; exemptions denied for, 56; NeJaime on same-sex marriage and, 158, 160–161, 162, 177–179; same-sex history of, 159; Title VII treatment of, 161, 179; private right of, 169–174
Donations, 49
Draft. *See* Military service draft
Draft Act (1917), 25–26
Duties: civil, 2, 12–13, 24, 31, 32; employee, 13, 78, 214, 215

Duties, legal: culture influencing, 2; exemptions from, 2, 12–13; individual autonomy contrasted with, 2, 12–13, 24, 31, 32; objections to, 13; extra burden of, 21, 33–35, 230n55
Dykes, Bryan A., 239nn8,9

Educational institutions: as tax exempt, 56, 59–60; autonomy of, 59–60; vaccinations required by, 95. *See also* Private universities
Elane Photography, 170, 180, 249n44
ella, 114, 115–116, 119
Employment Division v. Smith (1990): on RFRA application to states, 8–9, 18, 70, 116, 118; Supreme Court, U.S, decision in, 8–9, 11, 17–18, 27, 69–70, 84, 116, 118; on Peyote, 69–70
End of life: life-support at, 77, 94–95, 233n1; medical procedure exemptions at, 77
Epstein, Richard A., 249n44
Equality: for abortion, 1, 7–8, 213–214; claims of conscience balanced with, 1, 31, 35; exemption inequity and, 6, 14, 15, 31, 78, 213, 214, 215; for sexual orientation, 6, 7–8, 213; of treatment, 6, 7–8, 56, 155–179, 183–84, 213, 214, 215; for same-sex marriage, 7–8, 154–155, 172–173, 182–184, 213–214; harm to, 15, 213; interracial marriage with, 15, 105; morality contrasted with, 19; exemptions contrasted with, 24, 31–35; exemption for sexual orientation in, 56, 155–177; tax exemption inequity in, 59, 61; of charitable deductions, 60–62, 232n36; of gender, 98, 105–106; same-sex marriage exemption against, 155–168, 177–179, 183–184, 214, 215
Eskridge, William, 164–165, 167
Establishment Clause: of Constitution, U. S., 27–28, 58, 229n34; Free Exercise Clause balanced with, 27–28, 58, 229n34; *Hobby Lobby* case against, 241n43
Estbeck, Carl H., 254n37
Executive branch determinations, 9–10
Exemption categories: no-harm, 5–6, 214, 215; possible harm, 5–6, 213, 214, 215; inequity of, 6, 14, 15, 31, 35, 214; alternatives, 8, 10, 20–21, 30, 43–46, 219, 230n55; justified, 8, 19–20, 33, 217; misguided, 8, 19–20, 32, 217; necessary, 8, 17–19, 217
Exemptions: from legal duties, 2, 12–13; as special treatment, 2; for treatment, 2, 78, 80–81, 82–83, 86, 89, 90–91, 92, 93, 94, 234n15; dignity harm from, 4, 15, 115, 173–174, 213, 214; as no-harm, 5–5, 214, 215; as possible harm, 5–6, 213, 214, 215; symbolic messages of, 6, 14, 15, 31, 78, 105–106, 174, 176, 183, 213, 214, 215; federal law sources of, 8–9, 18, 27, 117, 213, 222–223; in state law, 8–9, 25, 26–27, 222–223; court determination of, 9–10; administrative regulation of, 10, 20–21; range of, 12–13; compliance with, 13; for groups, 13; law objectives impaired by, 14, 15, 213, 214, 215; law purpose impaired by, 14, 15; administrating requests for, 15–16, 19, 218–219; equality contrasted with, 24, 31–35; for forbidden substances, 70–75, 216;

Exemptions *(continued)*
for providing contraceptives, 77, 112–113, 119, 120, 214, 215; for same-sex marriage noninvolvement, 77, 157–158, 167–177, 214, 215; harm contrasted with symbolic message of, 78, 213; for prisoners, 130–145, 214; prison security weighed against, 136; same-sex marriage arguments against, 156–167, 214, 215; impracticality of, 219; evaluating religious claims of, 219–222; for individuals or groups, 222. *See also* specific topics

Fairness. *See* Equality
Feagin, Joe R., 247n22
Federal funding: of abortion, 78, 107–108, 237n52; CAPTA on, 234n15
Federal law: exemption source in, 8–9, 18, 27, 117, 213, 222–223; Constitution *vs.* law language in, 26–27
Feldblum, Chai R., 247n16
Ferguson, Robert A., 242n2
Fertilization: contraceptives after, 112–113, 114–115; as contrasted with implantation and conception, 114
First Amendment, 58
Flynn, Taylor, 250n55
Forbidden substances: prohibition of, 64, 67; in religion, 64, 71–73; RFRA on, 64, 70–71, 73, 75; heroin as, 65, 66–67; risks from, 65, 66, 67; alcohol as, 65–66; harm from, 65–67; cocaine as, 66, 67; enforcement challenges of, 66; marijuana as, 66, 67; methamphetamine as, 66; peyote as, 66, 67; prison for, 66, 232n3; tobacco contrasted with, 66, 232n1; black market in, 66–67; medical need for, 67, 233n6; individual or group religious use of, 68–69, 71–73, 216; exemptions allowing, 70–75, 216
For-profit corporations: as closely held in RFRA and *Hobby Lobby* case, 9, 12–13, 19–20, 118–119, 120–123, 126–127, 128–129; taxation for, 47, 51–52, 54, 57; Free Exercise rights of, 240n27
Franz, Raymond, 228n28
Fraudulent claims: for medical exemption, 16, 19, 67, 75, 90, 94–95, 117; of conscientious objectors, 32, 36–37, 45; risks of, 67; for peyote use, 73–74
Freedom: of conscience, 1, 31; of religion, 31, 32
Free Exercise Clause: for religion, 8, 11, 12, 58, 116, 168, 227n10; on military service, 27; protections for Amish, 27, 37, 84–85, 117, 133, 234n5; Supreme Court, U. S., on, 27, 116; Establishment Clause balanced with, 27–28, 58, 229n34; on peyote, 68, 69, 73–74, 214; *Wisconsin v. Yoder* on, 84–85, 117, 133, 234n5; *Sherbert v. Verner* on, 133, 134; *Goldman v. Weinberger* on, 133–134, 242n8; on for-profit corporations, 240n27
Friedman v. Arizona, 137–138

Garnett, Richard W., 231nn7,24, 250n48
Gaubatz, Derek L., 242n19, 243n32

Gelsinger, Sara A., 248n40
Gender: equality of, 98, 105–106; abortion viewpoints by, 237n47
Gibson, Matthew, 233n16
Gillette v. United States, 29–30, 228n25
Ginsburg, Ruth Bader, 123, 125–126
Goldenberg, Rachel, 252nn7,9, 253n20
Goldfien, Jeffrey H., 245n89
Goldman v. Weinberger: as Free Exercise case, 133–134, 242n8; Congress response to, 134
Goodrich, Luke W., 245n72
Goodstein, Laurie, 246n2
Gottry, James M., 248n39, 249n44, 251n69
Government: discrimination by, 11–12, 148–149, 245nn72,73,84; nonprofits save money of, 51, 53, 213; nonprofits more effective and efficient than, 51–52, 53, 213; as encouraging caring, 52; independence and diversity from, 52; abortion funded by, 78, 107–108; contraceptives exemptions paid by, 119, 127, 241n41; same-sex marriage exemptions for workers of, 174–177
Gowen, Thomas L., 252n6
Griffin, Leslie C., 241n43
Groups: exemptions applying to, 13; peyote use by religious individuals or, 68–69, 71–73, 216; exemptions for individuals or, 222

Hamilton, Marci A., 244n65
Hansmann, Henry, 55
Harm considerations: dignity in, 4, 15, 115, 173, 213, 214; no-harm exemptions in, 5–6, 214, 215; possible harm exemptions in, 5–6, 213, 214, 215; inequality of exemptions in, 6, 214; common law balancing, 12; to equality, 15, 213; of forbidden substances, 65–67; unproductive prison time in, 66; of medical procedure exemptions, 78, 213, 214, 215; message of medical exemptions contrasted with, 78, 213; of child medical exemptions, 82–83, 86–91, 95–97, 214; balancing benefits with, 82–84; from avoiding vaccination, 95–97, 214, 235n28; from shunning, 206–207, 214
Heroin, 65, 66–67
Hill v. Blackwell, 138
Himelfarb, Igor, 246n11
Historic preservation, 150
Hobby Lobby case: Supreme Court, U.S, decision in, 8–9, 12–13, 14, 19–20, 112–113, 115–116, 119, 120–121, 222; as closely held for-profit corporation, 9. 12–13, 19–20, 118–119, 120–123, 126–127, 128–129; financing treatment exemptions from, 76–77, 112–113; ACA exemption request under RFRA for, 120–121; Alito on, 121–127; Ginsburg dissent in, 123, 125–126; *Lee* contrasted with, 124–125; compelling interest test in, 125–126, 130–131, 139, 243n32; less restrictive means test in, 126–128, 130–131; on contraceptive alternatives, 128–129; decision alternatives to, 128–129; prison claims contrasted with, 130–131; Supreme Court, U.S, mistake in, 224; Koppelman reaction to, 241n43; reaction to, 241n43

Hobby Lobby company: financing treatment exemptions for, 76–77, 112–113; ACA contraceptive burden for, 123–125. *See also Hobby Lobby* case
Holt v. Hobbs: on religious exemptions in prison, 138–141; Alito on, 139–140
Horwitz, Paul, 227n13, 229n34, 231n7, 232n29, 241n43
Hosanna-Tabor Evangelical Lutheran Church and School v. Equal Employment Opportunity Commission: ministerial, coverage and purpose exceptions from, 11; Supreme Court, U.S, decision in, 11, 168, 183, 186, 248nn36,37,38
Howell, Shirley Darby, 234nn10,12,22
Hunter, Nan D., 246n13
Hyde Amendment, 107–108

Implantation: life begins at, 98–99, 114; as contrasted with fertilization and conception, 114
Individual autonomy: civil and legal duties contrasted with, 2, 12–13, 24, 31, 32; claims of conscience and dignity in, 4, 213; peyote use in, 68–69, 71–72; refusing medical treatment in, 79–82, 214, 215; abortion issues in, 100–102, 213; exemptions for groups or, 222
Institutional liability, 209–210
Insurance, 241n42; for contraceptives, 1, 5, 13–14, 20, 30, 112–113, 114, 115–116, 187, 214, 216, 251n5; paying tax contrasted with, 124–125, 126, 216; contraceptive exemption cost borne by, 127–128; coverage of same-sex marriage by, 182–183
Internal Revenue Service (IRS): nonprofit exemption justifications of, 49–51, 213, 216; Code §501(c)(3) of, 50
Interracial marriage: dignity and equality in, 15, 105; religion on, 15; same-sex marriage and, 15, 156, 163–164, 247nn20,24; Supreme Court, U.S, legalizing, 163, 247n18
Intrauterine devices, 113, 114, 115–116, 119
IRS. *See* Internal Revenue Service

Jail. *See* Prison
Justified exemptions, 8, 19–20, 33, 217

Kern, Jana L., 254n23
Kessler, Jeremy, 228nn8,25, 230n50
Kohlman, Richard J., 252n6
Koppelman, Andrew, 230n47, 246n13, 251n77; sexual orientation solidarity of, 166; same-sex marriage exception views of, 172–173; *Hobby Lobby* case reaction of, 241n43

Land use: RLUIPA on, 10, 48, 130, 131–132, 145, 146–147, 152; religious burden claims in, 145, 146; religious tax exemptions in, 145–146; religious zoning exemptions in, 145–146, 244n58; burden of religious zoning in, 151–152, 246n91; RLUIPA guidance standards on, 223–224
Language, legal, 9–10 12–13, 26–27
Larson, Gerald James, 255n1
Law: duties under, 2, 12–13, 24, 31, 32; exemption defined in, 2; limited

capacity of, 3–4; exemption source in, 8–9, 18, 27, 117, 213, 222–223; of abortion exemption, 9, 13–14, 77; military draft exemptions in, 9, 13, 14, 23–43, 31–32, 213; on tax exemptions, 9, 13, 14; RFRA as general exemption in, 9–10, 70, 93, 103–104, 118, 223–224; language of, 9–10 12–13, 26–27; range of exemptions from, 12–13; objections to, 13; exemptions impairing object of, 14, 15, 213, 214, 215; exemptions impair objectives of, 14, 15, 213, 214, 215; impaired purpose of, 14, 15; extra burden under, 21, 33–35, 230n55; Locke on religion and, 25, 33; contrasted with requirements of Constitution, 26–27; burden of, 70–71; allowing general marijuana use under, 72, 232n2; RFRA vague and inadequate as, 90, 103–104; medical procedure exemptions protected by, 100, 213, 214, 215, 216; Church and Hyde Amendments in, 107–108, 109–110, 237n52; perform or assist concept of, 108–111, 213, 214, 215, 216

Laycock, Douglas, 160, 236n39, 240n25, 245n72, 246n10, 250nn49,63, 251n74

Lee. See United States v. Lee

Legal liability: of parents, 82, 87–91, 234n21, 235n24; wrongful actions of institutions as, 209–210

Legal standards: contrasted with court provisions, 78–79; on abortion, 106–111, 236n36; perform or assist concept in, 108–111, 213, 214, 215, 216

Legal test: compelling interest as, 125–126, 130–131, 139, 243n32; less restrictive means as, 125–128, 130–131

Less restrictive means test: in *Hobby Lobby* case, 126–128; *Hobby Lobby* contrasted with prison claims of, 130–131

Lewis, Paul, 233n6

Liberty: claims of conscience balanced with, 1; of conscience, 31; of religion, 31, 32

Life: conception as beginning of, 3, 98–99, 114, 165, 236nn36,37; end of, 77, 94–95, 233n1; implantation as beginning of, 98–99, 114; fertilization as beginning of, 114; science on beginning of, 236n37

Limits of legal capacity, 3–4

Local municipalities: property tax exemptions in, 49; federal deduction for taxes of, 61–62

Locke, John, 25, 33

Loue, Sana, 234nn21,23

Lund, Christopher C., 240n14, 248n36

Lupu, Ira C., 242nn11,17, 245nn68,71, 246n92, 248n37, 249n47, 250nn50,59,66

Madison, James, 25, 26–27

Malani, Anup, 57

Manian, Maya, 236n36

Marijuana: as forbidden substance, 66, 67; allowing general use of, 72, 232n2

Marriage rights, 1, 18–19, 154, 161

Mature teenagers, 235nn31,32; harm of medical exemptions for, 82–83, 86–91, 95–97, 214; as community members, 83; community defines welfare of, 84; common law

Mature teenagers *(continued)* protecting, 86; treatment exemption standards for, 90, 92, 93, 94; abortion for, 91, 235n25; medical procedure exemptions for, 91–94; RFRA medical treatment exemption guidance for, 93; vaccination exemption for, 95; religion-motivated death of, 234n14; CAPTA for, 252n6
Medical exemption: fraudulent claims for, 16, 19, 67, 75, 90, 94–95, 117; for forbidden substances, 67, 233n6; for vaccination, 95–97, 235nn31,32; burden of applying for, 119–120
Medical institutions: abortion favored by, 98, 236n35, 238n57; abortion exemptions for, 102–105, 214, 215; states protect objectors in, 115–116, 239n7
Medical procedure exemptions: as right to refuse, 5–6, 79–82, 109–110, 214, 215, 237n54, 238n61; as financing treatment, 76–77; to giving treatment, 76–77; for personal convictions, 76–77; at end of life, 77; end of life life-support as, 77, 94–95, 233n1; harm contrasted with symbolic message of, 78, 213; harm of, 78, 213, 214, 215; risks from, 78, 80–81, 83, 86, 89, 93; standards of reasonableness for, 80, 82–83, 90, 92, 93, 94; for Christian Science, 81, 84, 86, 87, 89, 234n10; parental liability from, 82, 87–91, 234n21, 235n24; state protecting minors from, 84–91; RFRA guidance for, 90–91, 93; for mature teenagers, 91–94; non-essential treatment contrasted with, 94; law protecting, 100, 213, 214, 215, 216; Church and Hyde Amendments protecting, 107–108, 237n52; perform or assist concept in, 108–111, 213, 214, 215, 216
Medical staff: abortions refused by, 5–6, 79–82, 109–110, 237n54, 238n61; as required to perform abortions, 77–78, 109–110; individual autonomy concerns with, 100–102, 213; Church and Hyde Amendments protecting, 107–108, 237n52; nonparticipation exception for, 109–110, 213; states protect objectors in, 115–116, 239n7
Messaging: of exemption inequity, 6, 14, 15, 31, 78, 213, 214, 215; of medical exemptions contrasted with harm, 78, 213; of symbolism of medical procedure exemptions, 78, 105–106, 213, 214; of abortion exemptions, 105–106, 213, 214; in same-sex marriage exemptions, 174, 176, 183, 213
Methamphetamine, 66
Military service draft: exemption laws on, 9, 13, 14, 23–43, 31–32, 213; pacifists exemption from, 23–39, 40–46, 213, 216, 228n28; Madison Bill of Rights draft on, 25, 26–27; Civil War Draft Act on, 25–26; WWI Draft Act on, 25–26; exemption for conscientious objectors to, 25–43; Selective Service Act on, 26, 229n33; Free Exercise Clause and, 27; *United States v. Seeger* on, 28; *Welsh v. United States* on, 28–29, 228nn19,25; *Gillette v. United States* on, 29–30, 228n25; registration for, 30; exemption considerations for, 31–32, 33–35, 214, 216;

Vietnam War exemptions for, 35, 229n29, 230n52; tax exemptions contrasted with those for, 48
Minor children: harm of medical exemptions for, 82–83, 86–91, 95–97, 214; parents health decisions for, 82–91; as community members, 83; community defines welfare of, 84; common law protecting, 86; RFRA medical treatment exemption guidance for, 90–91; state making health decisions for, 90–91; vaccination exemption for, 95; priest sex with, 188, 194; religion-motivated death of, 234n14; parental abortion permission for, 235n25; CAPTA for, 252n6
Minorities, 149
Miscarriage, 98–99, 236n38
Misguided exemptions, 8, 19–20, 32, 217
Molko, David, 208–209
Morality: claims of conscience in, 1; equality contrasted with, 19; abortion debate in, 98–99, 100; right to and not to perform from, 111

Native American Church, 67–68, 73–74, 214, 216
Necessary exemptions, 8, 17–19, 217
NeJaime, Douglas, 158, 160–161, 162, 177–179, 236n39, 249n45
Newport, Frank, 246n11
Nonprofit organizations: tax exemption justifications for, 49–51, 213, 216; IRS Code §501(c)(3) for, 50; as saving government money, 51, 53, 213; as effective and efficient, 51–52, 53, 213; caring encouraged by, 52; independence and diversity of, 52; Bittker and Rahdert on income of, 53–55, 231n18; Hansmann on capital limits of, 55; Malani and Posner profit incentive for, 57; member and community benefit of, 57–58, 213; wealthy favored in exemptions for, 58–59; RFRA protecting, 119–120, 240n20. *See also* Closely held for-profit corporations

Oleske, James M., Jr., 240n25, 247n20
Orenstein, Aviva, 243nn41,44,45,46,47
Organizational autonomy: tax exemptions promoting, 52, 57–60, 213; of religious institutions, 57–58; of universities, 59–60
Oversimplification, 3, 22, 212

Pacifism: imprisonment for, 20, 21, 30, 31–32, 34, 39, 45; military exemption for, 23–39, 40–46, 213, 215, 228n28; in religion, 23–39, 40–46, 228n28; of Quakers, 25, 33, 37, 48; as religious and nonreligious, 27, 28–29, 35–36 38–43, 228n19; Welsh as nonreligious in, 28–29, 228nn19,25; draft board review of, 30, 228n25. *See also* Conscientious objectors
Parents: religious treatment choices of, 81–82; criminal liability of, 82, 86–91; medical procedure exemptions liability of, 82–83, 86–91, 214, 234n21, 235n24; minors health decisions of, 82–91; society overriding, 83–84; abortion for

Parents *(continued)*
mature teenagers of, 91, 235n25; vaccination decisions of, 95–97; religion-motivated child death from, 234n14; minor children abortion permission from, 235n25
Patient Protection and Affordable Care Act (2010) (ACA or PPACA), 116, 119, 120–121, 123–125, 241n42. *See also* Affordable Care Act
Perform or assist concept, 108–111, 213, 214, 215, 216
Person, corporation as, 121–123
Personal characteristics, 6
Personal nonparticipation: same-sex marriage exemptions for, 3, 6–7, 8, 155, 157, 162, 163, 167–168, 170–171, 177–178, 180, 214, 215, 216, 250n62; as discrimination, 6–7
Peyote: as forbidden substance, 66, 67; sacrament of, 67–68, 73–74, 214, 216; as contrasted with communion wine in religion, 68; Supreme Court, CA, on, 68, 69; individual or group religious use of, 68–69, 71–73, 216; *Employment Division v. Smith* on, 69–70; fraudulent use claims for, 73–74
Pharmacies: exemptions for, 13, 16, 114–115; states protect objectors in, 115–116, 239nn7,9
Pharmacists: exemptions for, 13, 16, 114–115; states protect objections of, 115–116, 239nn7,9
Picarello, Anthony R., Jr., 244nn59,60,62, 245nn66,67,88
Plan B, 114, 115–116, 119
Political rhetoric: oversimplification of, 3, 212; as deceptive, 14, 158, 159, 178, 212; civility contrasted with, 22, 212
Posner, Eric A., 57
PPACA. *See* Patient Protection and Affordable Care Act
Priest-penitent privilege: social interest contrasted with religious exercise in, 188–189, 192–194 252nn6,7,8,9,10,11, 216; as contrasted with professional privileges, 190–192, 195–197, 253nn14,15,20,21; improper adult activity and, 194–195, 254nn23,24; inadequate advice in, 195–197
Prison: for pacifists, 20, 21, 30, 31–32, 34, 39, 45; for forbidden substances, 66, 232n3; unproductive time in, 66; *Hobby Lobby* contrasted with claims in, 130–131, 139, 243n32; prisoner exemptions in, 130–145, 214; RLUIPA for, 130–145; exemptions weighed against security in, 136; religion in, 136; *Friedman v. Arizona* on religious exceptions in, 137–138; religious grooming cases in, 137–139, 214, 243n32; *Hill v. Blackwell* on religious exceptions in, 138; *Holt v. Hobbs* on religious exemptions in, 138–141; religious food exemptions in, 141–142; RLUIPA guidance standards on, 223–224
Private enterprise: contraceptive coverage denied by, 5–6; employee duty exemptions from, 13, 78, 214, 215; contraceptives as abortion to, 19–20; financing treatment exemptions for, 76–77, 112–113; contraceptive coverage required for, 77–78, 112–113. *See also* Closely held for-profit corporations
Private lawsuits, 170, 185–187, 251n5

Private universities: tax exemptions for, 60–61; property tax exemptions for, 62–63
Professional privileges: priest-penitent privilege contrasted with, 190–192, 195–197, 253nn14,15,20,21; improper activity and, 194–195, 254nn23,24; inadequate advice in, 195–197
Prohibition, 64, 67
Property taxes: tax exemptions from, 49; private university exemptions for, 62–63
Public. *See* Society

Quakers, 25, 33, 37, 48

Race. *See* Interracial marriage
Rahdert, George K., 53–55, 231n18
Reasonableness. *See* Standards of reasonableness
Registration for draft, 30
Reid, Charles J., Jr., 248n33
Religion: claims of conscience in, 1; beginning of life in, 3, 98–99, 114, 236nn36,37; on same-sex marriage, 3, 4, 5, 6, 216; Free Exercise Clause for, 8, 11, 12, 58, 116, 168, 227n10; Alito on exceptions for, 11; *Hosanna-Tabor Evangelical Lutheran Church and School v. Equal Employment Opportunity Commission* for, 11, 168, 183, 186, 248nn36,37,38; ministerial, coverage and purpose exceptions for, 11; interracial marriage in, 15; Locke on law and, 25, 33; Amish Free Exercise protections for, 27, 37, 84–85, 117, 133, 234n5; freedom of, 31, 32; tax exemptions for, 49; autonomy of institutions of, 57–58; member and community benefit of, 57–58, 213; property tax exemptions for, 62–63; peyote sacrament of, 67–68, 73–74, 214, 216; peyote contrasted with communion wine in, 68; individual or group use of peyote in, 68–69, 71–73, 216; end of life life-support in, 77, 94–95, 233n1; Christian Science as, 81, 84, 86, 87, 89, 234n10; parental treatment choices in, 81–82; *Wisconsin v. Yoder* on, 84–85, 117, 133, 234n5; vaccination exemptions for, 96–97, 235nn31,32; vaccination opposed by, 96–97; abortion concerns of, 98, 102, 216, 237n42; Roman Catholic abortion doctrine in, 102–103, 113–114, 216; hospital abortion exemptions for, 102–105, 214, 215; undue burden under Title VII for, 106–107; undue burden claim in abortion, 107, 216; right to and not to perform from, 111; Roman Catholic contraceptives doctrine in, 113–114; *United States v. Lee* in, 117–118; ACA contraceptive exemptions for, 119, 120; exemption application as burden for, 119–120; prisoner exemptions for, 130–145, 214; *Sherbert v. Verner* on, 133, 134; *Goldman v. Weinberger* on, 133–134, 242n8; belief contrasted with exercise of, 135, 139; in prison, 136; *Friedman v. Arizona* on prison exceptions for, 137–138; prison grooming cases in, 137–139, 214, 243n32; *Hill v. Blackwell* on prison exceptions for, 138; *Holt v. Hobbs* on prison

Religion *(continued)*
exemptions for, 138–141; prison food exemptions for, 141–142; prison practice and meeting exemptions in, 142–145; land use burden claims in, 145, 146; zoning exemptions for, 145–146, 244n58; historic preservation burden for, 150; burden of zoning for, 151–152, 246n91; same-sex marriage opposed by, 160, 165–166, 216; historical same-sex acceptance of, 167; same-sex marriage refusal right of, 168, 171–172, 183–184, 251n78; Elane Photography discrimination for, 170, 180, 249n44; same-sex marriage discrimination through, 170–172, 216, 249nn44,45,46,47; of public employees under Title VII, 174; on same-sex marriage adoption, 180–182; social interest contrasted with priest-penitent privilege in, 188–189, 192–194 252nn6,7,8,9,10,11, 216; as disclosing confidential information, 198–201, 216, 254n30; shunning in, 204–208, 213, 216, 254nn34,38; evaluating exemption claims of, 219–222; child death from, 234n14; CAPTA on, 234n15; abortion support in, 236n39; *Hobby Lobby* case negative for, 241n43

Religious Freedom Restoration Act (RFRA): *Employment Division v. Smith* (1990) on, 8–9, 18, 70, 116, 118; *Hobby Lobby* decision for, 8–9, 12–13, 14, 19–20, 112–113, 115–116, 119, 120–121; for closely held for-profit corporations, 9, 12–13, 19–20, 118–119, 120–123, 126–127, 128–129; as invalid for states, 9, 70, 118, 130, 131; as general exemption law, 9–10, 70, 93, 103–104, 118, 223–224; RLUIPA similar to, 10, 49, 130, 135, 147; forbidden substances under, 64, 70–71, 73, 75; as vague and inadequate law, 90, 103–104; medical treatment exemption guidance from, 90–91, 93, 214; contraceptives exemption under, 112–113, 214, 215; contraceptives under, 115–116; as protecting nonprofits, 119–120, 240n20; RLUIPA clarifying or extending, 121, 130, 147; corporation as person under, 121–123; *Hobby Lobby* decision alternatives to, 128–129; belief contrasted with religious exercise in, 135, 139; *Cutter v. Wilkinson as,* 135–136, 138; private lawsuits not covered by, 170, 185–187, 251n5; common law tort applicability of, 187, 197–198

Religious Land Use and Institutionalized Persons Act (RLUIPA): on land use, 10, 48, 130, 131–132, 145, 146–147, 152; RFRA similar to, 10, 49, 130, 135, 147; RFRA clarified or extended by, 121, 130, 147; for prisoner exemptions, 130–145; Congress reasoning in, 131–132; belief contrasted with religious exercise in, 135, 139; *Cutter v. Wilkinson* upholding, 135–136, 138; zoning issues under, 145–146, 151–152, 244n58; *Sherbert v. Verner* similar to, 147; minorities supported by, 149; guidance standards of, 223–224

RFRA. *See* Religious Freedom Restoration Act

Right to refuse, 5–6, 79–82, 109–110, 214, 215, 237n54, 238n61
Risks: from forbidden substances, 65, 66, 67; of fraudulent claims, 67; from medical treatment exemptions, 78, 80–81, 83, 86, 89, 93; of vaccination, 95–96; vaccination avoidance as, 235n28
RLUIPA. *See* Religious Land Use and Institutionalized Persons Act
Roe v. Wade, 98, 99–100, 236n34
Roman Catholic Church: abortion doctrine of, 102–103, 113–114, 216; contraceptives doctrine of, 113–114; on same-sex adoption, 180–181; sex with minors by priests of, 188, 194; social interest contrasted with priest-penitent privilege in, 188–189, 192–194 252nn6,7,8,9,10,11 216

Sabet, Kevin, 232nn1,3
Same-sex marriage: established right of, 1, 18–19, 154, 161; social right of, 1, 18–19, 154, 161; direct participation exemptions in, 3, 6–7, 8, 155, 157, 162, 163, 167–168, 170–171, 177–178, 180, 214, 215, 216, 250n62; religion on, 3, 4, 5, 6, 216; societal division on, 3, 4, 5, 6, 159–162; equality for, 7–8, 154–155, 172–173, 182–184, 213–214; dignity and equality in, 15, 105–106, 154–155, 213–214; interracial marriage and, 15, 156, 163–164, 247nn20,24; discrimination against, 49, 103, 154–155, 156, 167, 170–172, 248nn32,39,40, 249nn44,45,46,47; involvement exemptions for, 77, 157–158, 167–177, 214, 215; as social progress measure, 105–106; exemption from equal treatment for, 155–168, 177–179, 183–184, 214, 215; arguments for no exemptions in, 156–167, 214, 215; exemptions promote acceptance of, 157–158; states action on, 157–158, 179–180, 250n64, 251n75; NeJaime on discrimination against, 158, 160–161, 162, 177–179; historical discrimination against, 159; religion against, 160, 165–166, 216; Eskridge on historical acceptance of, 164–165, 167; refusal right of religion in, 168, 171–172, 183–184, 251n78; private right to discriminate against, 169–174; Boardwalk Pavilion discrimination on, 170, 171–172; Elane Photography discrimination for, 170, 180, 249n44; religious discrimination on, 170–172, 216, 249nn44,45,46,47; Koppelman on exceptions to, 172–173; exemption messaging in, 174, 176, 183, 213; government worker involvement exemptions for. 174–177; sexual orientation issues in, 177–179, 246nn11,12, 247n21; adoption in, 180–182; insurance coverage for, 182–183
Science, on life, 236n37
Selective objection: nonreligious pacifism as, 28–29, 38–43, 215–216, 228N19; to unjust wars, 38–43
Selective Service Act (1940): on conscientious objectors, 26, 229n33; Supreme Being language in, 26, 27, 28
Sepper, Elizabeth, 111, 238n62
Serkin, Christopher, 244n63, 246n90

Sexual orientation: equal treatment for, 6, 7–8, 213; discrimination based on, 49, 103, 154–155, 156, 167, 170–172, 248nn32,39,40, 249nn44,45,46,47; exemption from equal treatment for, 56, 155–177; discrimination history for, 159; Eskridge on historical acceptance of, 164–165, 167; Koppelman solidarity on, 166; same-sex marriage issues of, 177–182, 246nn11,12, 247n21; Boy Scouts exemption for, 183–184, 251n77
Seymore, Malinda L., 235n25
Sherbert v. Verner: on Free Exercise Clause, 133, 134; RLUIPA similar to, 147
Shunning: tort recovery for, 204–208, 213, 216, 254nn34,38; harm from, 206–207, 214
Sidhu, Dawinder S., 243n29
Siegel, Reva B., 236n39, 249n45
Sincerity: assessment of, 15–17, 20–21, 35–38, 217–218, 230n47; unjust wars and, 38–43
Society: same-sex marriage as right in, 1, 18–19, 154, 161; abortion dividing, 3, 98–99, 100, 237n42; contraception dividing, 3, 77; same-sex marriage dividing, 3, 4, 5, 6, 159–162; abortion as right in, 18–19, 97–98; tax exemption reasons for, 48, 213, 214; Bob Jones violating public values of, 56; parents overridden by, 83–84; as defining child welfare, 84; circumstances justifying abortion for, 98, 236n35; abortion as progress of, 105–106; priest-penitent privilege contrasted with interests of, 188–189, 192–194 252nn6,7,8,9,10,11, 216
Society of Friends. *See* Quakers
Special treatment: exemptions as, 2; non-essential medical treatment as, 94
Standards of reasonableness: for medical treatment exemptions, 80, 82–83, 90, 92, 93, 94; in balancing harms and benefits, 82–84
States: exemptions of, 8–9, 25, 26–27, 222–223; RFRA invalid for, 9, 70, 118, 130, 131; federal deduction for taxes of, 61–62; minors protected by, 84–91; minor children health decision by, 90–91; *Roe v. Wade* for, 98, 99–100, 236n34; medical institutions protected by, 115–116, 239n7; protecting health-care objectors, 115–116, 239nn7,9; same-sex marriage actions of, 157–158, 179–180, 250n64, 251n75; same-sex marriage promoted by, 157–158; abortion support in, 236n39
Status, 6
Statutes. *See* Law
Storzer, Roman P., 244nn59,60,62, 245nn66,67,88
Substance abuse. *See* Forbidden substances
Suicide, 80–81
Supreme Being, 26, 27, 28
Supreme Court, California: on peyote and Free Exercise Clause, 68, 69; *Wisconsin v. Yoder* of, 84–85, 117, 133, 234n5
Supreme Court, U. S., 227n10, 228nn19,25; *Employment Division v. Smith* decision of, 8–9, 11, 17–18, 27, 69–70, 84, 116, 118; *Hobby Lobby* decision of, 8–9, 12–13, 14, 19–20, 112–113, 115–116, 119, 120–121, 222; *Hosanna-Tabor Evangelical*

Lutheran Church and School v. Equal Employment Opportunity Commission decision of, 11, 168, 183, 186, 248nn36,37,38; on Free Exercise Clause, 27, 116; *United States v. Seeger* decision of, 28; *Welsh v. United States* of, 28–29, 228n19; on Vietnam War, 28–30; *Gillette v. United States* of, 29–30, 228n25; *Bob Jones University v. United States* of, 56; *Roe v. Wade* of, 98, 99–100, 236n34; *United States v. Lee* of, 117–118; Ginsburg *Hobby Lobby* dissenting, 123, 125–126; *Sherbert v. Verner* of, 133, 134; *Goldman v. Weinberger* of, 133–134, 242n8; *Cutter v. Wilkinson* of, 135–136, 138; interracial marriage legalized by, 163, 247n18; Boy Scouts sexual orientation exemption of, 183–184, 251n77; *Hobby Lobby* as mistake by, 224; reaction to *Hobby Lobby* decision of, 241n43

Swan, Rita, 234nn14,16,19

Swarns, Rachel L., 247n23

Swenson, Tara E., 241n41

Taxation: of for-profit corporations, 47, 51–52, 54, 57; providing insurance contrasted with, 124–125, 126, 216

Tax exemptions: laws on, 9, 13, 14; draft exemptions contrasted with, 48; reasons for, 48, 213, 214; for donations, 49; local property tax exemptions as, 49, 62–63; for religion, 49; nonprofit justification of, 49–51, 213, 216; organizational autonomy promoted by, 52, 57–60, 213; *Bob Jones University v. United States* on, 56; for educational institutions, 56, 59–60; inequity of, 59, 61; charitable deductions as, 60–62, 232n36; for local and state taxes, 61–62; for private universities, 62–63; *United States v. Lee* on, 117–118; religious land use exemptions for, 145–146

Tebbe, Nelson, 244n63, 246n90, 247n24

Teenagers. *See* Mature teenagers

Title VII: of Civil Rights Act, 106–107; discrimination treatment under, 161, 179; on religion of public employees, 174

Tobacco, 66, 232n1

Tolerance, of viewpoints, 4–5

Tort. *See* Common law

Treatment: exemptions for, 2, 78, 80–81, 82–83, 86, 89, 90–91, 92, 93, 94, 234n15; equality of, 6, 7–8, 56, 155–179, 183–84, 213, 214, 215; financing of, 76–77, 112–113; giving, 76–77; suicide as refusing, 80–81; as non-essential, 94; Title VII on, 161, 179

Turley, Jonathan, 251n72

Tuttle, Robert W., 245n68, 246n92, 248n37, 249n47, 250nn50,59,66

Unification Church, 208–209

United States v. Lee: for Amish tax exemption, 117–118; *Hobby Lobby* contrasted with, 124–125

United States v. Seeger, 28

Vaccination: children exempted from, 95; community immunity through, 95, 96, 97; educational institutions

Vaccination *(continued)*
requiring, 95; risks of, 95–96; harm from avoidance of, 95–97, 214, 235n28; medical exemptions to, 95–97, 235nn31,32; religious exemption from, 96–97, 235nn31,32; religious opposition to, 96–97; risks of avoiding, 235n28
Vietnam War: conscientious objectors during, 28–29, 30, 43; Supreme Court, U.S, on, 28–30; exemptions during, 35, 229n29, 230n52; alternate service during, 42, 43, 44
Viewpoints, tolerance of, 4–5
Vischer, Robert K., 240n27

War: Civil War as, 25–26; WWI as, 25–26; Vietnam as, 28–30, 35, 42, 43, 44, 229n29, 230n52; WWII as, 38, 40, 43, 230n52; as just or unjust, 38–43
Wealthy, 58–59
Welsh, Elliot, 28–29, 228nn19,25
Welsh v. United States, 28–29, 228nn19,25
Wiley, Bridgette A., 241n41
Williams, Rebecca, 234n7
Wilson, Robin Fretwell, 227n12, 233n2, 237nn43,46, 238nn55,58,60, 239n4, 242nn45,46, 246n3, 250nn49,60,63,65
Wisconsin v. Yoder, 84–85, 117, 133, 234n5
Wolff, Tobias Barrington, 251n77
World War I (WWI), 25–26
World War II (WWII), 38, 40, 43, 230n52
Wright, Lawrence, 255n39